Andrew Murray Four Book Treasury

Humility

Absolute Surrender

Lord, Teach Us to Pray

and Waiting on God

~ ※ ~

By *Andrew Murray*

I am crucified with Christ: nevertheless I live; yet not I, but Christ liveth in me: and the life which I now live in the flesh I live by the faith of the Son of God, who loved me, and gave himself for me. Gal. 2:20

TABLE OF CONTENTS

Humility

~ ※ ~

By *Andrew Murray*

Lord Jesus! may our Holiness be perfect Humility!
Let Thy perfect Humility be our Holiness!

Preface

There are three great motives that urge us to humility. It becomes me as a creature, as a sinner, as a saint. The first we see in the heavenly hosts, in unfallen man, in Jesus as Son of Man. The second appeals to us in our fallen state, and points out the only way through which we can return to our right place as creatures. In the third we have the mystery of grace, which teaches us that, as we lose ourselves in the overwhelming greatness of redeeming love, humility becomes to us the consummation of everlasting blessedness and adoration.

In our ordinary religious teaching, the second aspect has been too exclusively put in the foreground, so that some have even gone to the extreme of saying that we must keep sinning if we are indeed to keep humble. Others again have thought that the strength of self-condemnation is the secret of humility. And the Christian life has suffered loss, where believers have not been distinctly guided to see that, even in our relation as creatures, nothing is more natural and beautiful and blessed than to be nothing, that God may be all; or where it has not been made clear that it is not sin that humbles most, but grace, and that it is the soul, led through its sinfulness to be occupied with God in His wonderful glory as God, as Creator and Redeemer, that will truly take the lowest place before Him.

In these meditations I have, for more than one reason, almost exclusively directed attention to the humility that becomes us as creatures. It is not only that the connection between humility and sin is so abundantly set forth in all our religious teaching, but because I believe that for the fullness of the Christian life it is indispensable that prominence be given to the other aspect. If Jesus is indeed to be our example in His lowliness, we need to understand the principles in which it was rooted, and in which we find the common ground on which we stand with Him, and in which our likeness to Him is to be attained. If we are indeed to be humble, not only before God but towards men, if humility is to be our joy, we must see that it is not only the mark of shame, because of sin, but, apart from all sin, a being clothed upon with the very beauty and blessedness of heaven and of Jesus. We shall see that just as Jesus found His glory in taking the form of a servant, so when He said to us, 'Whosoever would be first among you, shall be your servant,' He simply taught us the blessed truth that there is nothing so divine and heavenly as being the servant and helper of all. The faithful servant, who recognizes his position, finds a real pleasure in supplying the wants of the master or his guests. When we see that humility is something infinitely deeper than contrition, and accept it as our participation in the life of Jesus, we shall begin to learn that it is our true nobility, and that to prove it in being servants of all is the highest fulfilment of our destiny, as men created in the image of God.

When I look back upon my own religious experience, or round upon the Church of Christ in the world, I stand amazed at the thought of how little humility is sought after as the distinguishing feature of the discipleship of Jesus. In preaching and living, in the daily intercourse of the home and social life, in the more special fellowship with Christians, in the direction and performance of work for Christ, —alas! how much proof there is that humility is not esteemed the cardinal virtue, the only root from which the graces can grow, the one indispensable condition of true fellowship with Jesus. That it should have been possible for men to say of those who claim to be seeking the higher holiness, that the profession has not been accompanied with increasing humility, is a loud call to all earnest Christians, however much or little truth there be in the charge, to prove that meekness and lowliness of heart are the chief mark by which they who follow the meek and lowly Lamb of God are to be known.

Humility: The Beauty of Holiness

Humility: The Glory of the Creature

*'They shall cast their crowns before the throne, saying: Worthy art Thou, our Lord
and our God, to receive the glory, and the honor and the power: for Thou
didst create all things, and because of Thy will they were, and were created.'
—REV. iv. 11.*

WHEN God created the universe, it was with the one object of making the creature partaker of His perfection and blessedness, and so showing forth in it the glory of His love and wisdom and power. God wished to reveal Himself in and through created beings by communicating to them as much of His own goodness and glory as they were capable of receiving. But this communication was not a giving to the creature something which it could possess in itself, a certain life or goodness, of which it had the charge and disposal. By no means. But as God is the ever-living, ever-present, ever-acting One, who upholdeth all things by the word of His power, and in whom all things exist, the relation of the creature to God could only be one of unceasing, absolute, universal dependence. As truly as God by His power once created, so truly by that same power must God every moment maintain. The creature has not only to look back to the origin and first beginning of existence, and acknowledge that it there owes everything to God; its chief care, its highest virtue, its only happiness, now and through all eternity, is to present itself an empty vessel, in which God can dwell and manifest His power and goodness.

The life God bestows is imparted not once for all, but each moment continuously, by the unceasing operation of His mighty power. Humility, the place of entire dependence on God, is, from the very nature of things, the first duty and the highest virtue of the creature, and the root of every virtue.

And so pride, or the loss of this humility, is the root of every sin and evil. It was when the now fallen angels began to look upon themselves with self-complacency that they were led to disobedience, and were cast down from the light of heaven into outer darkness. Even so it was, when the serpent breathed the poison of his pride, the desire to be as God, into the hearts of our first parents, that they too fell from their high estate into all the wretchedness in which man is now sunk. In heaven and earth, pride, self-exaltation, is the gate and the birth, and the curse, of hell.[1]

---

[1] 'All this is to make it known the region of eternity that pride can degrade the highest angels into devils, and humility raise fallen flesh and blood to the thrones of angels. Thus, this is the great end of God raising a new creation out of a fallen kingdom of angels: for this end it stands in its state of war betwixt the fire and pride of fallen angels, and the humility of the Lamb of God, that the last trumpet may sound the great truth through the depths of eternity, that evil can have no beginning but from pride, and no end but from humility. The truth is this: Pride may die in you, or nothing of heaven can live in you. Under the banner of the truth, give yourself up to the meek and humble spirit of the holy Jesus. Humility must sow seed, or there can be no reaping in Heaven. Look not at pride only as an unbecoming temper, nor at humility only as a decent virtue: for the one is death, and the other is life; the one is all hell, the other is all heaven. So much as you have of pride within you, you have of the fallen angels alive in you; so much as you have of true humility, so much you have of the Lamb of God within you. Could you see what every stirring of pride does to your soul, you would beg of everything you meet to tear the viper from you, though with the loss of a hand or an eye. Could you see what a sweet, divine, transforming power there is in humility, how it expels the poison of your nature, and makes room for the Spirit of God to live in you, you would rather

Hence it follows that nothing can be our redemption, but the restoration of the lost humility, the original and only true relation of the creature to its God. And so Jesus came to bring humility back to earth, to make us partakers of it, and by it to save us. In heaven He humbled Himself to become man. The humility we see in Him possessed Him in heaven; it brought Him, He brought it, from there. Here on earth 'He humbled Himself, and became obedient unto death'; His humility gave His death its value, and so became our redemption. And now the salvation He imparts is nothing less and nothing else than a communication of His own life and death, His own disposition and spirit, His own humility, as the ground and root of His relation to God and His redeeming work. Jesus Christ took the place and fulfilled the destiny of man, as a creature, by His life of perfect humility. His humility is our salvation. His salvation is our humility.

And so the life of the saved ones, of the saints, must needs bear this stamp of deliverance from sin, and full restoration to their original state; their whole relation to God and man marked by an all-pervading humility. Without this there can be no true abiding in God's presence, or experience of His favor and the power of His Spirit; without this no abiding faith, or love or joy or strength. Humility is the only soil in which the graces root; the lack of humility is the sufficient explanation of every defect and failure. Humility is not so much a grace or virtue along with others; it is the root of all, because it alone takes the right attitude before God, and allows Him as God to do all.

God has so constituted us as reasonable beings, that the truer the insight into the real nature or the absolute need of a command, the readier and fuller will be our obedience to it. The call to humility has been too little regarded in the Church because its true nature and importance has been too little apprehended. It is not a something which we bring to God, or He bestows; it is simply *the sense of entire nothingness, which comes when we see how truly God is all, and in which we make way for God to be all.* When the creature realizes that this is the true nobility, and consents to be with his will, his mind, and his affections, the form, the vessel in which the life and glory of God are to work and manifest themselves, he sees that humility is simply acknowledging the truth of his position as creature, and yielding to God His place.

In the life of earnest Christians, of those who pursue and profess holiness, humility ought to be the chief mark of their uprightness. It is often said that it is not so. May not one reason be that in the teaching and example of the Church, it has never had that place of supreme importance which belongs to it? And that this, again, is owing to the neglect of this truth, that strong as sin is as a motive to humility, there is one of still wider and mightier influence, that which makes the angels, that which made Jesus, that which makes the holiest of saints in heaven, so humble; that the first and chief mark of the relation of the creature, the secret of his blessedness, is the humility and nothingness which leaves God free to be all?

I am sure there are many Christians who will confess that their experience has been very much like my own in this, that we had long known the Lord without realizing that meekness and lowliness of heart are to be the distinguishing feature of the disciple as they were of the Master. And further, that this humility is not a thing that will come of itself, but that it must be made the object of special desire and prayer and faith and practice. As we study the word, we shall see what very distinct and oft-repeated instructions Jesus gave His disciples on this point, and how slow they were in understanding Him. Let us, at the very commencement of our meditations, admit that there is nothing so natural to man, nothing so insidious and hidden from our sight, nothing so difficult and dangerous, as pride. Let us feel that nothing but a very determined and persevering waiting on God and Christ will discover how lacking we are in the grace of humility, and how impotent to obtain what we seek. Let us study the character of Christ until our souls are filled with the love and admiration of His lowliness. And let us believe that, when we are broken down under a sense of our pride, and our impotence to cast it out, Jesus Christ Himself will come in to impart this grace too, as a part of His wondrous life within us.

---

wish to be the footstool of all the world than want the smallest degree of it.' —Spirit of Prayer, Pt. II. p. 73, Edition of Moreton, Canterbury, 1893.

Humility: The Secret of Redemption

'Have this mind in you which was also in Christ Jesus: who emptied Himself;
taking the form of a servant; and humbled Himself; becoming obedient even
unto death. Wherefore God also highly exalted Him.' —PHIL. ii. 5-7.

NO tree can grow except on the root from which it sprang. Through all its existence it can only live with the life that was in the seed that gave it being. The full apprehension of this truth in its application to the first and the Second Adam cannot but help us greatly to understand both the need and the nature of the redemption there is in Jesus.

The Need. — When the Old Serpent, he who had been cast out from heaven for his pride, whose whole nature as devil was pride, spoke his words of temptation into the ear of Eve, these words carried with them the very poison of hell. And when she listened, and yielded her desire and her will to the prospect of being as God, knowing good and evil, the poison entered into her soul and blood and life, destroying forever that blessed humility and dependence upon God which would have been our everlasting happiness. And instead of this, her life and the life of the race that sprang from her became corrupted to its very root with that most terrible of all sins and all curses, the poison of Satan's own pride. All the wretchedness of which this world has been the scene, all its wars and bloodshed among the nations, all its selfishness and suffering, all its ambitions and jealousies, all its broken hearts and embittered lives, with all its daily unhappiness, have their origin in what this cursed, hellish pride, either our own, or that of others, has brought us. It is pride that made redemption needful; it is from our pride we need above everything to be redeemed. And our insight into the need of redemption will largely depend upon our knowledge of the terrible nature of the power that has entered our being.

No tree can grow except on the root from which it sprang. The power that Satan brought from hell, and cast into man's life, is working daily, hourly, with mighty power throughout the world. Men suffer from it; they fear and fight and flee it; and yet they know not whence it comes, whence it has its terrible supremacy. No wonder they do not know where or how it is to be overcome. Pride has its root and strength in a terrible spiritual power, outside of us as well as within us; as needful as it is that we confess and deplore it as our very own, is to know it in its Satanic origin. If this leads us to utter despair of ever conquering or casting it out, it will lead us all the sooner to that supernatural power in which alone our deliverance is to be found—the redemption of the Lamb of God. The hopeless struggle against the workings of self and pride within us may indeed become still more hopeless as we think of the power of darkness behind it all; the utter despair will fit us the better for realizing and accepting a power and a life outside of ourselves too, even the humility of heaven as brought down and brought nigh by the Lamb of God, to cast out Satan and his pride.

No tree can grow except on the root from which it sprang. Even as we need to look to the first Adam and his fall to know the power of the sin within us, we need to know well the Second Adam and His power to give within us a life of humility as real and abiding and overmastering as has been that of pride. We have our life from and in Christ, as truly, yea more truly, than from and in Adam. We are to walk 'rooted in Him,' 'holding fast the Head from whom the whole body increaseth with the increase of God.' The life of God which in the incarnation entered human nature, is the root in which we are to stand and grow; it is the same almighty power that worked there, and thence onward to the resurrection, which works daily in us. Our one need is to study and know and trust the life that has been revealed in Christ as the life that is now ours, and waits for our consent to gain possession and mastery of our whole being.

In this view it is of inconceivable importance that we should have right thoughts of what Christ is, of what really constitutes Him the Christ, and specially of what may be counted His chief characteristic, the root and essence of all His character as our Redeemer. There can be but one answer: it is His humility. What is the incarnation but His heavenly humility, His emptying Himself and becoming man? What is His life on earth but humility; His taking the form of a servant? And what is His atonement but humility? 'He humbled Himself and became obedient unto death.' And what is His ascension and His glory, but humility exalted to the throne and crowned with glory? 'He humbled Himself, therefore God highly exalted Him.' In heaven, where He was with the Father, in His birth, in His life, in His death, in His sitting on the throne, it is all, it is nothing but humility. Christ is the humility of God embodied in human nature; the Eternal Love humbling itself, clothing itself in the garb of meekness and gentleness, to win and serve and save us. As the love and condescension of God makes Him the benefactor and helper and servant of all, so Jesus of necessity was the Incarnate Humility. And so He is still in the midst of the throne, the meek and lowly Lamb of God.

If this be the root of the tree, its nature must be seen in every branch and leaf and fruit. If humility be the first, the all-including grace of the life of Jesus, —if humility be the secret of His atonement, —then the health and strength of our spiritual life will entirely depend upon our putting this grace first too, and making humility the chief thing we admire in Him, the chief thing we ask of Him, the one thing for which we sacrifice all else.[2]

Is it any wonder that the Christian life is so often feeble and fruitless, when the very root of the Christ life is neglected, is unknown? Is it any wonder that the joy of salvation is so little felt, when that in which Christ found it and brings it, is so little sought? Until a humility which will rest in nothing less than the end and death of self; which gives up all the honor of men as Jesus did, to seek the honor that comes from God alone; which absolutely makes and counts itself nothing, that God may be all, that the Lord alone may be exalted, —until such a humility be what we seek in Christ above our chief joy, and welcome at any price, there is very little hope of a religion that will conquer the world.

I cannot too earnestly plead with my reader, if possibly his attention has never yet been specially directed to the want there is of humility within him or around him, to pause and ask whether he sees much of the spirit of the meek and lowly Lamb of God in those who are called by His name. Let him consider how all want of love, all indifference to the needs, the feelings, the weakness of others; all sharp and hasty judgments and utterances, so often excused under the plea of being outright and honest; all manifestations of temper and touchiness and irritation; all feelings of bitterness and estrangement, have their root in nothing but pride, that ever seeks itself, and his eyes will be opened to see how a dark, shall I not say a devilish pride, creeps in almost everywhere, the assemblies of the saints not excepted. Let him begin to ask what would be the effect, if in himself and around him, if towards fellow-saints and the world, believers were really permanently guided by the humility of Jesus; and let him say if the cry of our whole heart, night and day, ought not to be, Oh for the humility of Jesus in myself and all around me! Let him honestly fix his heart on his own lack of the humility which has been revealed in the likeness of Christ's life, and in the whole character of His redemption, and he will begin to feel as if he had never yet really known what Christ and His salvation is.

Believer! *study the humility of Jesus*. This is the secret, the hidden root of thy redemption. Sink down into it deeper day by day. Believe with thy whole heart that this Christ, whom God has given thee, even as His divine humility wrought the work for thee, will enter in to dwell and work within thee too, and make thee what the Father would have thee be.

---

[2] 'We need to know two things: 1. That our salvation consists wholly in being saved from ourselves, or that which we are by nature; 2. That in the whole nature of things nothing could be this salvation or savior to us but such a humility of God as is beyond all expression. Hence the first unalterable term of the Savior to fallen man: Except a man denies himself, he cannot be My disciple. Self is the whole evil of fallen nature; self-denial is our capacity of being saved; humility is our savior.... Self is the root, the branches, the tree, of all the evil of our fallen state. All the evils of fallen angels and men have their birth in the pride of self. On the other hand, all the virtues of the heavenly life are the virtues of humility. It is humility alone that makes the unpassable gulf between heaven and hell. What is then, or in what lies, the great struggle for eternal life? It all lies in the strife between pride and humility: pride and humility are the two master powers, the two kingdoms in strife for the eternal possession of man. There never was, nor ever will be, but one humility, and that is the one humility of Christ. Pride and self have the all of man, till man has his all from Christ. He therefore only fights the good fight whose strife is that the self-idolatrous nature which he hath from Adam may be brought to death by the supernatural humility of Christ brought to life in him.' —W. Law, Address to the Clergy, p. 52.

Humility in the Life of Jesus

'I am in the midst of you as he that serveth.' —LUKE xxii. 26.

IN the Gospel of John we have the inner life of our Lord laid open to us. Jesus speaks frequently of His relation to the Father, of the motives by which He is guided, of His consciousness of the power and spirit in which He acts. Though the word humble does not occur, we shall nowhere in Scripture see so clearly wherein His humility consisted. We have already said that this grace is in truth nothing but that simple consent of the creature to let God be all, in virtue of which it surrenders itself to His working alone. In Jesus we shall see how both as the Son of God in heaven, and as man upon earth, He took the place of entire subordination, and gave God the honor and the glory which is due to Him. And what He taught so often was made true to Himself: 'He that humbleth him: shall be exalted.' As it is written, 'He humbled Himself, therefore God highly exalted Him.'

Listen to the words in which our Lord speaks of His relation to the Father, and how unceasingly He uses the words *not*, and *nothing*, of Himself. The *not I*, in which Paul expresses his relation to Christ, is the very spirit of what Christ says of His relation the Father.

'The Son can do *nothing* of Himself' (John v. 19).

'I can of My own self do *nothing*; My judgment is just, because I seek *not* Mine own will' (John v 30).

'I receive *not* glory from men' (John v. 41).

'I am come *not* to do Mine own will' (John vi. 38).

'My teaching is *not* Mine' (John vii. 16).

'I am *not* come of Myself' (John vii. 28).

'I do *nothing* of Myself' (John vii. 28).

'I have *not* come of Myself, but He sent Me' (John viii. 42).

'I seek *not* Mine own glory' (John viii. 50).

'The words that I say, I speak *not* from Myself' (John xiv. 10).

'The word which ye hear is *not* Mine' (John xiv. 24).

These words open to us the deepest roots of Christ's life and work. They tell us how it was that the Almighty God was able to work His mighty redemptive work through Him. They show what Christ counted the state of heart which became Him as the Son of the Father. They teach us what the essential nature and life is of that redemption which Christ accomplished and now communicates. It is this: He was nothing, that God might be all. He resigned Himself with His will and His powers entirely for the Father to work in Him. Of His own power, His own will, and His own glory, of His whole mission with all His works and His teaching, —of all this He said, It is not I; I am nothing; I have given Myself to the Father to work; I am nothing, the Father is all.

This life of entire self-abnegation, of absolute submission and dependence upon the Father's will, Christ found to be one of perfect peace and joy. He lost nothing by giving all to God. God honored His trust, and did all for Him, and then exalted Him to His own right hand in glory. And because Christ had thus humbled Himself before God, and God was ever before Him, He found it possible to humble Himself before men too, and to be the Servant of all. His humility was simply the surrender of Himself to God, to allow Him to do in Him what He pleased, whatever men around might say of Him, or do to Him.

It is in this state of mind, in this spirit and disposition, that the redemption of Christ has its virtue and efficacy. It is to bring us to this disposition that we are made partakers of Christ. This is the true self-denial to which our Savior calls us, the acknowledgment that self has nothing good in it, except as an empty vessel which God must fill, and that its claim to be or do anything may not for a moment be allowed. It is in this, above and before everything, in which the conformity to Jesus consists, the being and doing nothing of ourselves, that God may be all.

Here we have the root and nature of true humility. It is because this is not understood or sought after, that our humility is so superficial and so feeble. We must learn of Jesus, how He is meek and lowly of heart. He teaches us where true humility takes its rise and finds its strength—in the knowledge that it is God who worketh all in all, that our place is to yield to Him in perfect resignation and dependence, in full consent to be and to do nothing of ourselves. This is the life Christ came to reveal and to impart—a life to God that came through death to sin and self. If we feel that this life is too high for us and beyond our reach, it must but the more urge us to seek it in Him; it is the indwelling Christ who will live in us this life, meek and lowly. If we long for this, let us, meantime, above everything, seek the holy secret of the knowledge of the nature of God, as He every moment works all in all; the secret, of which all nature and every creature, and above all, every child of God, is to be the witness, —that it is nothing but a vessel, a channel, through which the living God can manifest the riches of His wisdom, power, and goodness. The root of all virtue and grace, of all faith and acceptable worship, is that we know that we have nothing but what we receive, and bow in deepest humility to wait upon God for it.

It was because this humility was not only a temporary sentiment, wakened up and brought into exercise when He thought of God, but the very spirit of His whole life, that Jesus was just as humble in His intercourse with men as with God. He felt Himself the Servant of God for the men whom God made and loved; as a natural consequence, He counted Himself the Servant of men, that through Him God might do His work of love. He never for a moment thought of seeking His honor, or asserting His power to vindicate Himself. His whole spirit was that of a life yielded to God to work in. It is not until Christians study the humility of Jesus as the very essence of His redemption, as the very blessedness of the life of the Son of God, as the only true relation to the Father, and therefore as that which Jesus must give us if we are to have any part with Him, that the terrible lack of actual, heavenly, manifest humility will become a burden and a sorrow, and our ordinary religion be set aside to secure this, the first and the chief of the marks of the Christ within us.

Brother, are you clothed with humility? Ask your daily life. Ask Jesus. Ask your friends. Ask the world. And begin to praise God that there is opened up to you in Jesus a heavenly humility of which you have hardly known, and through which a heavenly blessedness you possibly have never yet tasted can come in to you.

Humility in the Teaching of Jesus

'Learn of Me, for I am meek and lowly of heart.' —MATT. xi. 29. 'Whosoever will be chief among you, let him be your servant, even as the Son of Man came to serve.' —MATT. xx. 27.

WE have seen humility in the life of Christ, as He laid open His heart to us: let us listen to His teaching. There we shall hear how He speaks of it, and how far He expects men, and specially His disciples, to be humble as He was. Let us carefully study the passages, which I can scarce do more than quote, to receive the full impression of how often and how earnestly He taught it: it may help us to realize what He asks of us.

1. Look at the commencement of His ministry. In the Beatitudes with which the Sermon on the Mount opens, He speaks: *'Blessed are the poor in spirit; for theirs is the kingdom of heaven. Blessed are the meek; for they shall inherit the earth.'* The very first words of His proclamation of the kingdom of heaven reveal the open gate through which alone we enter. The poor, who have nothing in themselves, to them the kingdom comes. The meek, who seek nothing in themselves, theirs the earth shall be. The blessings of heaven and earth are for the lowly. For the heavenly and the earthly life, humility is the secret of blessing.

2. *'Learn of Me; for I am meek and lowly of heart, and ye shall find rest for your souls.'* Jesus offers Himself as Teacher. He tells what the spirit both is, which we shall find Him as Teacher, and which we can learn and receive from Him. Meekness and lowliness the one thing He offers us; in it we shall find perfect rest of soul. Humility is to be a salvation.

3. The disciples had been disputing who would be the greatest in the kingdom, and had agreed to ask the Master (Luke 9:46; Matt. 18:3). He set a child in their midst and said, *'Whosoever shall humble himself as this little child, shall be exalted.'* 'Who the greatest in the kingdom of heaven?' The question is indeed a far-reaching one. What will be the chief distinction in the heavenly kingdom? The answer, none but Jesus would have given. The chief glory of heaven, the true heavenly-mindedness, the chief of the graces, is humility. *'He that is least among you, the same shall be great.'*

4. The sons of Zebedee had asked Jesus to sit on His right and left, the highest place in the kingdom. Jesus said it was not His to give, but the Father's, who would give it to those for whom it was prepared. They must not look or ask for it. Their thought must be of the cup and the baptism of

humiliation. And then He added, *'Whosoever will be chief among you, let him be your servant. Even as the Son of Man came to serve.'* Humility, as it is the mark of Christ the heavenly, will be the one standard of glory in heaven: the lowliest is the nearest to God. The primacy in the Church is promised to the humblest.

5. Speaking to the multitude and the disciples, of the Pharisees and their love of the chief seats, Christ said once again (Matt. xxxiii. 11), *'He that is greatest among you shall be your servant.'* Humiliation is the only ladder to honor in God's kingdom.

6. On another occasion, in the house of a Pharisee, He spoke the parable of the guest who would be invited to come up higher (Luke xiv. 1-11), and added, *'For whosoever exalteth himself shall be abased; and he that humbleth himself shall be exalted.'* The demand is inexorable; there is no other way. Self-abasement alone will be exalted.

7. After the parable of the Pharisee and the Publican, Christ spake again (Luke xviii. 14), *'Everyone that exalteth himself shall be abased; and he that humbleth himself shall be exalted.'* In the temple and presence and worship of God, everything is worthless that is not pervaded by deep, true humility towards God and men.

8. After washing the disciples' feet, Jesus said (John xiii. 14), *'If I then, the Lord and Master, have washed your feet, ye also ought to wash one another's feet.'* The authority of command, and example, every thought, either of obedience or conformity, make humility the first and most essential element of discipleship.

9. At the Holy Supper table, the disciples still disputed who should be greatest (Luke xxii. 26). Jesus said, *'He that is greatest among you, let him be as the younger; and he that is chief, as he that doth serve. I am among you as he that serveth.'* The path in which Jesus walked, and which He opened up for us, the power and spirit in which He wrought out salvation, and to which He saves us, is ever the humility that makes me the servant of all.

How little this is preached. How little it is practiced. How little the lack of it is felt or confessed. I do not say, how few attain to it, some recognizable measure of likeness to Jesus in His humility. But how few ever think, of making it a distinct object of continual desire or prayer. How little the world has seen it. How little has it been seen even in the inner circle of the Church.

'Whosoever will be chief among you, let him be your servant.' Would God that it might be given us to believe that Jesus means this! We all know what the character of a faithful servant or slave implies. Devotion to the master's interests, thoughtful study and care to please him, delight in his prosperity and honor and happiness. There are servants on earth in whom these dispositions have been seen, and to whom the name of servant has never been anything but a glory. To how many of us has it not been a new joy in the Christian life to know that we may yield ourselves as servants, as slaves to God, and to find that His service is our highest liberty, —the liberty from sin and self? We need now to learn another lesson, —that Jesus calls us to be servants of one another, and that, as we accept it heartily, this service too will be a most blessed one, a new and fuller liberty too from sin and self. At first it may appear hard; this is only because of the pride which still counts itself something. If once we learn that to be nothing before God is the glory of the creature, the spirit of Jesus, the joy of heaven, we shall welcome with our whole heart the discipline we may have in serving even those who try to vex us. When our own heart is set upon this, the true sanctification, we shall study each word of Jesus on self-abasement with new zest, and no place will be too low, and no stooping too deep, and no service too mean or too long continued, if we may but share and prove the fellowship with Him who spake, 'I am among you as he that serveth.'

Brethren, here is the path to the higher life. Down, lower down! This was what Jesus ever said to the disciples who were thinking of being great in the kingdom, and of sitting on His right hand and His left. Seek not, ask not for exaltation; that is God's work. Look to it that you abase and humble yourselves, and take no place before God or man but that of servant; that is your work; let that be your one purpose and prayer. God is faithful. Just as water ever seeks and fills the lowest place, so the moment God finds the creature abased and empty, His glory and power flow in to exalt and to bless. He that humbleth himself—that must be our one care—shall be exalted; that is God's care; by His mighty power and in His great love He will do it.

Men sometimes speak as if humility and meekness would rob us of what is noble and bold and manlike. Oh that all would believe that this is the nobility of the kingdom of heaven, that this is the royal spirit that the King of heaven displayed, that this is Godlike, to humble oneself, to become the servant of all! This is the path to the gladness and the glory of Christ's presence ever in us, His power ever resting on us.

Jesus, the meek and lowly One, calls us to learn of Him the path to God. Let us study the words we have been reading, until our heart is filled with the thought: My one need is humility. And let us believe that what He shows, He gives; what He is, He imparts. As the meek and lowly One, He will come in and dwell in the longing heart.

Humility in the Disciples of Jesus

'Let him that is chief among you be as he that doth serve.' —LUKE xxii. 26

WE have studied humility in the person and teaching of Jesus; let us now look for it in the circle of His chosen companions—the twelve apostles. If, in the lack of it we find in them, the contrast between Christ and men is brought out more clearly, it will help us to appreciate the mighty change which Pentecost wrought in them, and prove how real our participation can be in the perfect triumph of Christ's humility over the pride Satan had breathed into man.

In the texts quoted from the teaching of Jesus, we have already seen what the occasions were on which the disciples had proved how entirely wanting they were in the grace of humility. Once, they had been disputing the way which of them should be the greatest Another time, the sons of Zebedee with their mother had asked for the first places—the seat on the right hand and the left. And, later on, at the Supper table on the last night, there was again a contention which should be accounted the greatest. Not that there were not moments when they indeed humbled themselves before their Lord. So it was with Peter when he cried out, 'Depart from me, Lord, for I am a sinful man.' So, too, with the disciples when they fell down and worshipped Him who had stilled the storm. But such occasional expressions of humility only bring out into stronger relief what was the habitual tone of their mind, as shown in the natural and spontaneous revelation given at other times of the place and the power of self. The study of the meaning of all this will teach us most important lessons.

First, *How much there may be of earnest and active, religion while humility is still sadly wanting.* —See it in the disciples. There was in them fervent attachment to Jesus. They had forsaken all for Him. The Father had revealed to them that He was the Christ of God. They believed in Him, they loved Him, they obeyed His commandments. They had forsaken all to follow Him. When others went back, they clave to Him. They were ready to die with Him. But deeper down than all this there was a dark power, of the existence and the hideousness of which they were hardly conscious, which had to be slain and cast out, ere they could be the witnesses of the power of Jesus to save. It is even so still. We may find professors and ministers, evangelists and workers, missionaries and teachers, in whom the gifts of the Spirit are many and manifest, and who are the channels of blessing to multitudes, but of whom, when the testing time comes, or closer intercourse gives fuller knowledge, it is only too painfully manifest that the grace of humility, as an abiding characteristic, is scarce to be seen. All tends to confirm the lesson that humility is one of the chief and the highest graces; one of the most difficult of attainment; one to which our first and chiefest efforts ought to be directed; one that only comes in power, when the fullness of the Spirit makes us partakers of the indwelling Christ, and He lives within us.

Second, *How impotent all external teaching and all personal effort is, to conquer pride or give the meek and lowly heart.* —For three years the disciples had been in the training school of Jesus. He had told them what the chief lesson was He wished to teach them: 'Learn of Me, for I am meek and lowly in heart.' Time after time He had spoken to them, to the Pharisees, to the multitude, of humility as the only path to the glory of God. He had not only lived before them as the Lamb of God in His divine humility, He had more than once unfolded to them the inmost secret of His life: 'The Son of Man came not to be served, but to serve'; 'I am among you as one that serveth.' He had washed their feet, and told them they were to follow His example. And yet all had availed but little. At the Holy Supper there was still the contention as to who should be greatest. They had doubtless often tried to learn His lessons, and firmly resolved not again to grieve Him. But all in vain. To teach them and us the much needed lesson, that no outward instruction, not even of Christ Himself; no argument however convincing; no sense of the beauty of humility, however deep; no personal resolve or effort, however sincere and earnest, —can cast out the devil of pride. When Satan casts out Satan, it is only to enter afresh in a mightier, though more hidden power. Nothing can avail but this, that the new nature in its divine humility be revealed in power to take the place of the old, to become as truly our very nature as that ever was.

Third, *It is only by the indwelling of Christ in His divine humility that we become truly humble.* —We have our pride from another, from Adam; we must have our humility from Another too. Pride is ours, and rules in us with such terrible power, because it is ourself, our very nature. Humility must be ours in the same way; it must be our very self, our very nature. As natural and easy as it has been to be proud, it must be, it will be, to be humble. The promise is, 'Where,' even in the heart, 'sin abounded, grace did abound more exceedingly.' All Christ's teaching of His disciples, and all their vain efforts, were the needful preparation for His entering into them in divine power, to give and be in them what He had taught them to desire. In His death He destroyed the power of the devil, He put away sin, and effected an everlasting redemption. In His resurrection He received from the Father an entirely new life, the life of man in the power of God, capable of being communicated to men, and entering and renewing and filling their lives with His divine power. In His ascension He received the Spirit of the Father, through whom He might do what He could not do while upon earth, make Himself one with those He loved, actually live their life for them, so that they could live before the Father in a humility like His, because it was Himself who lived and breathed in them. And on Pentecost He came and took possession. The work of preparation and conviction, the awakening of desire and hope which His teaching had effected, was perfected by the mighty change that Pentecost wrought. And the lives and the epistles of James and Peter and John bear witness that all was changed, and that the spirit of the meek and suffering Jesus had indeed possession of them.

What shall we say to these things? Among my readers I am sure there is more than one class. There may be some who have never yet thought very specially of the matter, and cannot at once realize its immense importance as a life question for the Church and its every member. There are others who have felt condemned for their shortcomings, and have put forth very earnest efforts, only to fail and be discouraged. Others, again, may be able to give joyful testimony of spiritual blessing and power, and yet there has never been the needed conviction of what those around them still see as wanting. And still others may be able to witness that in regard to this grace too the Lord has given deliverance and victory, while He has taught them how much they still need and may expect out of the fullness of Jesus. To whichever class we belong, may I urge the pressing need there is for our all seeking a still deeper conviction of the unique place that humility holds in the religion of Christ, and the utter impossibility of the Church or the believer being what Christ would have them be, as long as *His humility is not recognized as His chief glory, His first command, and our highest blessedness.* Let us consider deeply how far the disciples were advanced while this grace was still so terribly lacking, and let us pray to God that other gifts may not so satisfy us, that we never grasp the fact that the absence of this grace is the secret cause why the power of God cannot do its mighty work. It is only where we, like the Son, truly know and show that we can do nothing of ourselves, that God will do all.

It is when the truth of an indwelling Christ takes the place it claims in the experience of believers, that the Church will put on her beautiful garments and humility be seen in her teachers and members as the beauty of holiness.

Humility in Daily Life

'He that loveth not his brother whom he hath seen, how can he love God whom he hath not seen?' —1 JOHN iv. 20.

WHAT a solemn thought, that our love to God will be measured by our everyday intercourse with men and the love it displays; and that our love to God will be found to be a delusion, except was its truth is proved in standing the test of daily life with our fellowmen. It is even so with our humility. It is easy to think we humble ourselves before God: humility towards men will be the only sufficient proof that our humility before God is real; that humility has taken up its abode in us; and become our very nature; that we actually, like Christ, have made ourselves of no reputation. When in the presence of God lowliness of heart has become, not a posture we pray to Him, but the very spirit of our life, it will manifest itself in all our bearing towards our brethren. The lesson is one of deep import: the only humility that is really ours is not that which we try to show before God in prayer, but that which we carry with us, and carry out, in our ordinary conduct; the insignificances of daily life are the importances and the tests of eternity, because they prove what really is the spirit that possesses us. It is in our most unguarded moments that we really show and see what we are. To know the humble man, to know how the humble man behaves, you must follow him in the common course of daily life.

Is not this what Jesus taught? It was when the disciples disputed who should be greatest; when He saw how the Pharisees loved the chief place at feasts and the chief seats in the synagogues; when He had given them the example of washing their feet, —that He taught His lessons of humility. Humility before God is nothing if not proved in humility before men.

It is even so in the teaching of Paul. To the Romans He writes: 'In honor preferring one *another*'; 'Set not your mind on high things, but condescend to *those that are lowly.*' 'Be not wise in your own conceit.' To the Corinthians: 'Love,' and there is no love without humility as its root, 'vaunteth not itself, is not puffed up, seeketh not its own, is not provoked.' To the Galatians: 'Through love be servants *one of another.* Let us not be desirous of vainglory, provoking *one another,* envying *one another.*' To the Ephesians, immediately after the three wonderful chapters on the heavenly life: 'Therefore, walk with all lowliness and meekness, with long-suffering, forbearing *one another* in love'; 'Giving thanks always, subjecting yourselves *one to another* in the fear of Christ.' To the Philippians: 'Doing nothing through faction or vainglory, but in lowliness of mind, each counting *other* better than himself. Have the mind in you which was also in Christ Jesus, who emptied Himself, taking the form of a servant, and humbled Himself.' And to the Colossians: 'Put on a heart of compassion, kindness, humility, meekness, long-suffering, forbearing *one another*, and forgiving *each other*, even as the Lord forgave you.' It is in our relation to one another, in our treatment of one another, that the true lowliness of mind and the heart of humility are to be seen. Our humility before God has no value, but as it prepares us to reveal the humility of Jesus to our fellow-men. Let us study humility in daily life in the light of these words.

The humble man seeks at all times to act up to the rule, *'In honor preferring one another; Servants one of another; Each counting others better than himself; Subjecting yourselves one to another.'* The question is often asked, how we can count others better than ourselves, when we see that they are far below us in wisdom and in holiness, in natural gifts, or in grace received. The question proves at once how little we understand what real lowliness of mind is. True humility comes when, in the light of God, we have seen ourselves to be nothing, have consented to part with and cast away self, to let God be all. The soul that has done this, and can say, So have I lost myself in finding Thee, no longer compares itself with others. It has given up forever every thought of self in God's presence; it meets its fellow-men as one who is nothing, and seeks nothing for itself; who is a servant of God, and for His sake a servant of all. A faithful servant may be wiser than the master, and yet retain the true spirit and posture of the servant. The humble man looks upon every, the feeblest and unworthiest, child of God, and honors him and prefers him in honor as the son of a King. The spirit of Him who washed the disciples' feet, makes it a joy to us to be indeed the least, to be servants one of another.

The humble man feels no jealousy or envy. He can praise God when others are preferred and blessed before him. He can bear to hear others praised and himself forgotten, because in God's presence he has learnt to say with Paul, 'I am nothing.' He has received the spirit of Jesus, who pleased not Himself, and sought not His own honor, as the spirit of his life.

Amid what are considered the temptations to impatience and touchiness, to hard thoughts and sharp words, which come from the failings and sins of fellow-Christians, the humble man carries the oft-repeated injunction in his heart, and shows it in his life, *'Forbearing one another, and forgiving one another, even as the Lord forgave you.'* He has learnt that in putting on the Lord Jesus he *has put on the heart of compassion, kindness, humility, meekness, and long-suffering.* Jesus has taken the place of self, and it is not an impossibility to forgive as Jesus forgave. His humility does not consist merely in thoughts or words of self-depreciation, but, as Paul puts it, in 'a heart of humility,' encompassed by compassion and kindness, meekness and long-suffering, —the sweet and lowly gentleness recognized as the mark of the Lamb of God.

In striving after the higher experiences of the Christian life, the believer is often in danger of aiming at and rejoicing in what one might call the more human, the manly, virtues, such as boldness, joy, contempt of the world, zeal, self-sacrifice, —even the old Stoics taught and practiced these, — while the deeper and gentler, the diviner and more heavenly graces, those which Jesus first taught upon earth, because He brought them from heaven; those which are more distinctly connected with

His cross and the death of self, —poverty of spirit, meekness, humility, lowliness, —are scarcely thought of or valued. Therefore, let us put on a heart of compassion, kindness, humility, meekness, long-suffering; and let us prove our Christlikeness, not only in our zeal for saving the lost, but before all in our intercourse with the brethren, forbearing and forgiving one another, *even as the Lord forgave us.*

Fellow-Christians, do let us study the Bible portrait of the humble man. And let us ask our brethren, and ask the world, whether they recognize in us the likeness to the original. Let us be content with nothing less than taking each of these texts as the promise of what God will work in us, as the revelation in words of what the Spirit of Jesus will give as a birth within us. And let each failure and shortcoming simply urge us to turn humbly and meekly to the meek and lowly Lamb of God, in the assurance that where He is enthroned in the heart, His humility and gentleness will be one of the streams of living water that flow from within us.[3]

Once again I repeat what I have said before. I feel deeply that we have very little conception of what the Church suffers from the lack of this divine humility, —the nothingness that makes room for God to prove His power. It is not long since a Christian, of an humble, loving spirit, acquainted with not a few mission stations of various societies, expressed his deep sorrow that in some cases the spirit of love and forbearance was sadly lacking. Men and women, who in Europe could each choose their own circle of friends, brought close together with others of uncongenial minds, find it hard to bear, and to love, and to keep the unity of the Spirit in the bond of peace. And those who should have been fellow-helpers of each other's joy, became a hindrance and a weariness. And all for the one reason, the lack of the humility which counts itself nothing, which rejoices in becoming and being counted the least, and only seeks, like Jesus, to be the servant, the helper and comforter of others, even the lowest and unworthiest.

And whence comes it that men who have joyfully given up themselves for Christ, find it so hard to give up themselves for their brethren? Is not the blame with the Church? It has so little taught its sons that the humility of Christ is the first of the virtues, the best of all the graces and powers of the Spirit. It has so little proved that a Christlike humility is what it, like Christ, places and preaches first, as what is in very deed needed, and possible too. But let us not be discouraged. Let the discovery of the lack of this grace stir us to larger expectation from God. Let us look upon every brother who tries or vexes us, as God's means of grace, God's instrument for our purification, for our exercise of the humility Jesus our Life breathes within us. And let us have such faith in the All of God, and the nothing of self, that, as nothing in our own eyes, we may, in God's power, only seek to serve one another in love.

Humility and Holiness

'Which say, Stand by thyself; for I am holier than thou.' —ISAIAH lxv. 5.

WE speak of the Holiness movement in our times, and praise God for it. We hear a great deal of seekers after holiness and professors of holiness, of holiness teaching and holiness meetings. The blessed truths of holiness in Christ, and holiness by faith, are being emphasized as never before. The great test of whether the holiness we profess to seek or to attain, is truth and life, will be *whether it be manifest in the increasing humility it produces.* In the creature, humility is the one thing needed to allow God's holiness to dwell in him and shine through him. In Jesus, the Holy One of God who makes us holy, a divine humility was the secret of His life and His death and His exaltation; the one infallible test of our holiness will be the humility before God and men which marks us. Humility is the bloom and the beauty of holiness.

The chief mark of counterfeit holiness is its lack of humility. Every seeker after holiness needs to be on his guard, lest unconsciously what was begun in the spirit be perfected in the flesh, and pride creep in where its presence is least expected. Two men went up into the temple to pray: the one a Pharisee, the other a publican. There is no place or position so sacred but the Pharisee can enter there. Pride can lift its head in the very temple of God, and make His worship the scene of its

---

[3] 'I knew Jesus, and He was very precious to my soul: but I found something in me that would not keep sweet and patient and kind. I did what I could to keep it down, but it was there. I besought Jesus to do something for me, and when I gave Him my will, He came to my heart, and took out all that would not be sweet, all that would not be kind, all that would not be patient, and then He shut the door.' —George Foxe

self exaltation. Since the time Christ so exposed his pride, the Pharisee has put on the garb of the publican, and the confessor of deep sinfulness equally with the professor of the highest holiness, must be on the watch. Just when We are most anxious to have our heart the temple of God, we shall find the two men coming up to pray. And the publican will find that his danger is not from the Pharisee beside him, who despises him, but the Pharisee within who commends and exalts. In God's temple, when we think we are in the holiest of all, in the presence of His holiness, let us beware of pride. 'Now there was a day when the sons of God came to present themselves before the Lord, and Satan came also among them.'

'God, I thank thee, I am not as the rest of men, or even as this publican.' It is in that which is just cause for thanksgiving, it is in the very thanksgiving which we render to God, it may be in the very confession that God has done it all, that self finds its cause of complacency. Yes, even when in the temple the language of penitence and trust in God's mercy alone is heard, the Pharisee may take up the note of praise, and in thanking God be congratulating himself. Pride can clothe itself in the garments of praise or of penitence. Even though the words, 'I am not as the rest of men' are rejected and condemned, their spirit may too often be found in our feelings and language towards our fellow-worshippers and fellow-men. Would you know if this really is so, just listen to the way in which Churches and Christians often speak of one another. How little of the meekness and gentleness of Jesus is to be seen. It is so little remembered that deep humility must be the keynote of what the servants of Jesus say of themselves or each other. Is there not many a Church or assembly of the saints, many a mission or convention, many a society or committee, even many a mission away in heathendom, where the harmony has been disturbed and the work of God hindered, because men who are counted saints have proved in touchiness and haste and impatience, in self-defense and self-assertion, in sharp judgments and unkind words, that they did not each reckon others better than themselves, and that their holiness has but little in it of the meekness of the saints?[4] In their spiritual history men may have had times of great humbling and brokenness, but what a different thing this is from being clothed with humility, from having an humble spirit, from having that lowliness of mind in which each counts himself the servant of others, and so shows forth the very mind which was also in Jesus Christ.

'Stand by; for I am holier than thou!' What a parody on holiness! Jesus the Holy One is the humble One: the holiest will ever be the humblest. There is none holy but God: we have as much of holiness as we have of God. And according to what we have of God will be our real humility, because humility is nothing but the disappearance of self in the vision that God is all. The holiest will be the humblest. Alas! though the barefaced boasting Jew of the days of Isaiah is not often to be found, —even our manners have taught us not to speak thus, how often his spirit is still seen, whether in the treatment of fellow-saints or of the children of the world. In the spirit in which opinions are given, and work is undertaken, and faults are exposed, how often, though the garb be that of the publican, the voice is still that of the Pharisee: 'Oh God, I thank Thee that I am not as other men.'

And is there, then, such humility to be found, that men shall indeed still count themselves 'less than the least of all saints,' the servants of all? There is. 'Love vaunteth not itself, is not puffed up, seeketh not its own.' Where the spirit of love is shed abroad in the heart, where the divine nature comes to a full birth where Christ the meek and lowly Lamb of God is truly formed within, there is given the power of a perfect love that forgets itself and finds its blessedness in blessing others, in bearing with them and honoring them, however feeble they be. Where this love enters, there God enters. And where God has entered in His power, and reveals Himself as All, there the creature becomes nothing. And where the creature becomes nothing before God; it cannot be anything but humble towards the fellow-creature. The presence of God becomes not a thing of times and seasons, but the covering under which the soul ever dwells, and its deep abasement before God becomes the holy place of His presence whence all its words and works proceed.

---

[4] ME is a most exacting personage, requiring the best seat and the highest place for itself, and feeling grievously wounded if its claim is not recognized. Most of the quarrels among Christian workers arise from the clamoring of this gigantic ME. How few of us understand the true secret of taking our seats in the lowest rooms. —Mrs. Smith, Everyday Religion.

May God teach us that our thoughts and words and feelings concerning our fellowmen are His test of our humility towards Him, and that our humility before Him is the only power that can enable us to be always humble with our fellow-men. Our humility must be the life of Christ, the Lamb of God, within us.

Let all teachers of holiness, whether in the pulpit or on the platform, and all seekers after holiness, whether in the closet or the convention, take warning. There is no pride so dangerous, because none so subtle and insidious, as the pride of holiness. It is not that a man ever says, or even thinks, 'Stand by; I am holier than thou.' No, indeed, the thought would be regarded with abhorrence. But there grows up, all unconsciously, a hidden habit of soul, which feels complacency its attainments, and cannot help seeing how far it is in advance of others. It can be recognized, not always in any special self-assertion or self-laudation, but simply in the absence of that deep self-abasement which cannot but be the mark of the soul that has seen the glory of God (Job xlii. 5, 6; Isa. vi. 5). It reveals itself, not only in words or thoughts, but in a tone, a way of speaking of others, in which those who have the gift of spiritual discernment cannot but recognize the power of self. Even the world with its keen eyes notices it, and points to it as a proof that the profession of a heavenly life does not bear any specially heavenly fruits. O brethren! let us beware. Unless we make, with each advance in what we think holiness, the increase of humility our study, we may find that we have been delighting in beautiful thoughts and feelings, in solemn acts of consecration and faith, while the only sure mark of the presence of God, the disappearance of self, was all the time wanting. Come and let us flee to Jesus, and hide ourselves in Him until we be clothed upon with His humility. That alone is our holiness.

Humility and Sin

'Sinners, of whom I am chief.' —1 TIM. i. 15

HUMILITY is often identified with penitence and contrition. As a consequence, there appears to be no way of fostering humility but by keeping the soul occupied with its sin. We have learned, I think, that humility is something else and something more. We have seen in the teaching of our Lord Jesus and the Epistles how often the virtue is inculcated without any reference to sin. In the very nature of things, in the whole relation of the creature to the Creator, in the life of Jesus as He lived it and imparts it to us, humility is the very essence of holiness as of blessedness. It is the displacement of self by the enthronement of God. Where God is all, self is nothing.

But though it is this aspect of the truth I have felt it specially needful to press, I need scarce say what new depth and intensity man's sin and God's grace give to the humility of the saints. We have only to look at a man like the Apostle Paul, to see how, through his life as a ransomed and a holy man, the deep consciousness of having been a sinner lives inextinguishably. We all know the passages in which he refers to his life as a persecutor and blasphemer. 'I am *the least of the apostles*, that am *not worthy to be called an apostle*, because I persecuted the Church of God…. I labored more abundantly than they all; yet not I, but the grace of God which was with me' (1 Cor. xv. 9,10). 'Unto me, who am *less than the least of all saints,* was this grace given, to preach to the heathen' (Eph. iii. 8). 'I was before a *blasphemer, and a persecutor, and injurious;* howbeit I obtained mercy, because I did it ignorantly in unbelief…. Christ Jesus came into the world to save *sinners, of whom I am chief'* (1 Tim. i. 13, 15). God's grace had saved him; God remembered his sins no more for ever; but never, never could he forget how terribly he had sinned. The more he rejoiced in God's salvation, and the more his experience of God's grace filled him with joy unspeakable, the clearer was his consciousness that he was a saved sinner, and that salvation had no meaning or sweetness except as the sense of his being a sinner made it precious and real to him. Never for a moment could he forget that it was a sinner God had taken up in His arms and crowned with His love.

The texts we have just quoted are often appealed to as Paul's confession of daily sinning. One has only to read them carefully in their connection, to see how little this is the case. They have a far deeper meaning, they refer to that which lasts throughout eternity, and which will give its deep undertone of amazement and adoration to the humility with which the ransomed bow before the throne, as those who have been washed from their sins in the blood of the Lamb. Never, never, even in, glory, can they be other than ransomed sinners; never for a moment in this life can God's child live in the full light of His love, but as he feels that the sin, out of which he has been saved, is his one only right and title to all that grace has promised to do. The humility with which first he came as a sinner, acquires a new meaning when he learns how it becomes him as a creature. And then ever again, the humility, in which he was born as a creature, has its deepest, richest tones of adoration, in the memory of what it is to be a monument of God's wondrous redeeming love.

The true import of what these expressions of St. Paul teach us comes out all the more strongly when we notice the remarkable fact that, through his whole Christian course, we never find from his pen, even in those epistles in which we have the most intensely personal unbosomings, anything like confession of sin. Nowhere is there any mention of shortcoming or defect, nowhere any suggestion to his readers that he has failed in duty, or sinned against the law of perfect love. On the contrary, there are passages not a few in which he vindicates himself in language that means nothing if it does not appeal to a faultless life before God and men. 'Ye are witnesses, and God also, how holily, and righteously, and unblameably we behaved ourselves toward you' (1 Thess. ii. 10). 'Our glorying is this, the testimony of our conscience, that in holiness and sincerity of God we behaved ourselves in the world, and more abundantly to you ward' (2 Cor. i. 12). This is not an ideal or an aspiration; it is an appeal to what his actual life had been. However we may account for this absence of confession of sin, all will admit that it must point to a life in the power of the Holy Ghost, such as is but seldom realized or expected in these our days.

The point which I wish to emphasize is this—that the very fact of the absence of such confession of sinning only gives the more force to the truth that it is not in daily sinning that the secret of the deeper humility will be found, but in the habitual, never for a moment to be forgotten position, which just the more abundant grace will keep more distinctly alive, that our only place, the only place of blessing, our one abiding position before God, must be that of those whose highest joy it is to confess that they are sinners saved by grace.

With Paul's deep remembrance of having sinned so terribly in the past, ere grace had met him, and the consciousness of being kept from present sinning, there was ever coupled the abiding remembrance of the dark hidden power of sin ever ready to come in, and only kept out by the presence and power of the indwelling Christ. 'In me, that is, in my flesh, dwelleth no good thing;' —these words of Rom. vii. describe the flesh as it is to the end. The glorious deliverance of Rom. viii. —'The law of the Spirit of life in Christ Jesus hath now made me free from the law of sin, which once led me captive' —is neither the annihilation nor the sanctification of the flesh, but a continuous victory given by the Spirit as He mortifies the deeds of the body. As health expels disease, and light swallows up darkness, and life conquers death, the indwelling of Christ through the Spirit is the health and light and life of the soul. But with this, the conviction of helplessness and danger ever tempers the faith in the momentary and unbroken action of the Holy Spirit into that chastened sense of dependence which makes the highest faith and joy the handmaids of a humility that only lives by the grace of God.

The three passages above quoted all show that it was the wonderful grace bestowed upon Paul, and of which he felt the need every moment, that humbled him so deeply. The grace of God that was with him, and enabled him to labor more abundantly than they all; the grace to preach to the heathen the unsearchable riches of Christ; the grace that was exceeding abundant with faith and love which is in Christ Jesus, —it was this grace of which it is the very nature and glory that it is for sinners, that kept the consciousness of his having once sinned, and being liable to sin, so intensely alive. 'Where sin abounded, grace did abound more exceedingly.' This reveals how the very essence of grace is to deal with and take away sin, and how it must ever be the more abundant the experience of grace, the more intense the consciousness of being a sinner. It is not sin, but God's grace showing a man and ever reminding him what a sinner he was, that, will keep him truly humble. It is not sin, but grace, that will make me indeed know myself a sinner, and make the sinner's place of deepest self-abasement the place I never leave.

I fear that there are not a few who, by strong expressions of self-condemnation and self-denunciation, have sought to humble themselves, and have to confess with sorrow that a humble spirit, a 'heart of humility,' with its accompaniments of kindness and compassion, of meekness and forbearance, is still as far off as ever. Being occupied with self, even amid the deepest self-abhorrence, can never free us from self. It is the revelation of God, not only by the law condemning sin but by His grace delivering from it, that will make us humble. The law may break the heart with fear; it is only grace that works that sweet humility which becomes a joy to the soul as its second nature. It was the revelation of God in His holiness, drawing nigh to make Himself known in His grace, that made Abraham and Jacob, Job and Isaiah, bow so low. It is the soul in which God the Creator, as the All of the creature in its nothingness, God the Redeemer in His grace, as the All of the sinner in his sinfulness, is waited for and trusted and worshipped, that will find itself so filled with His presence, that there will be no place for self. So alone can the promise be fulfilled: 'The haughtiness of man shall be brought low, and the Lord alone be exalted in that day.'

It is the sinner dwelling in the full light of God's holy, redeeming love, in the experience of that full indwelling of divine love, which comes through Christ and the Holy Spirit, who cannot but be humble. Not to be occupied with thy sin, but to be occupied with God, brings deliverance from self.

Humility and Faith

'How can ye believe, which receive glory from one another, and the glory that cometh from the only God ye seek not?' JOHN v. 44.

In an address I lately heard, the speaker said that the blessings of the higher Christian life were often like the objects exposed in a shop window, —one could see them clearly and yet could not reach them. If told to stretch out his hand and take, a man would answer, I cannot; there is a thick pane of plate-glass between me and them. And even so Christians may see clearly the blessed promises of perfect peace and rest, of overflowing love and joy, of abiding communion and fruitfulness, and yet feel that there was something between hindering the true possession. And what might that be? *Nothing but pride.* The promises made to faith are so free and sure; the invitations and encouragements so strong; the mighty power of God on which it may count is so near and free, —that it can only be something that hinders faith that hinders the blessing being ours. In our text Jesus discovers to us that it is indeed pride that makes faith impossible. 'How can ye believe, which receive glory from one another?' As we see how in their very nature pride and faith are irreconcilably at variance, we shall learn that faith and humility are at root one, and that we never can have more of true faith than we have of true humility; we shall see that we may indeed have strong intellectual conviction and assurance of the truth while pride is kept in the heart, but that it makes the living faith, which has power with God, an impossibility.

We need only think for a moment what faith is. Is it not the confession of nothingness and helplessness, the surrender and the waiting to let God work? Is it not in itself the most humbling thing there can be, —the acceptance of our place as dependents, who can claim or get or do nothing but what grace bestows? Humility is 'simply the disposition which prepares the soul for living on trust. And every, even the most secret breathing of pride, in self-seeking, self-will, self-confidence, or self-exaltation, is just the strengthening of that self which cannot enter the kingdom, or possess the things of the kingdom, because it refuses to allow God to be what He is and must be there—the All in All.

Faith is the organ or sense for the perception and apprehension of the heavenly world and its blessings. Faith seeks the glory that comes from God, that only comes where God is All. As long as we take glory from one another, as long as ever we seek and love and jealously guard the glory of this life, the honor and reputation that comes from men, we do not seek, and cannot receive the glory that comes from God. Pride renders faith impossible. Salvation comes through a cross and a crucified Christ. Salvation is the fellowship with the crucified Christ in the Spirit of His cross. Salvation is union with and delight in, salvation is participation in, the humility of Jesus. Is it wonder that our faith is so feeble when pride still reigns so much, and we have scarce learnt even to long or pray for humility as the most needful and blessed part of salvation?

Humility and faith are more nearly allied in Scripture than many know. See it in the life of Christ. There are two cases in which He spoke of a great faith. Had not the centurion, at whose faith He marveled, saying, 'I have not found so great faith, no, not in Israel!' spoken, *'I am not worthy* that Thou shouldst come under my roof'? And had not the mother to whom He spoke, 'O woman, great is thy faith!' accepted the name of dog, and said, *'Yea, Lord, yet the dogs eat of the crumbs'?* It is the humility that brings a soul to be nothing before God, that also removes every hindrance to faith, and makes it only fear lest it should dishonor Him by not trusting Him wholly.

Brother, have we not here the cause of failure in the pursuit of holiness? Is it not this, though we knew it not, that made our consecration and our faith so superficial and so short-lived? We had no idea to what an extent pride and self were still secretly working within us, and how alone God by His incoming and His mighty power could cast them out. We understood not how nothing but the new and divine nature, taking entirely the place of the old self, could make us really humble. We knew not that absolute, unceasing, universal humility must be the root-disposition of every prayer and every approach to God as well as of every dealing with man; and that we might as well attempt to see without eyes, or live without breath, as believe or draw nigh to God or dwell in His love, without an all-pervading humility and lowliness of heart.

Brother, have we not been making a mistake in taking so much trouble to believe, while all the time there was the old self in its pride seeking to possess itself of God's blessing and riches? No wonder we could not believe. Let us change our course. Let us seek first of all to humble ourselves under the mighty hand of God: *He will exalt us.* The cross, and the death, and the grave, into which Jesus humbled Himself, were His path to the glory of God. And they are our path. Let our one desire and our fervent prayer be, to be humbled with Him and like Him; let us accept gladly whatever can humble us before God or men; —this alone is the path to the glory of God.

You perhaps feel inclined to ask a question. I have spoken of some who have blessed experiences, or are the means of bringing blessing to others, and yet are lacking in humility. You ask whether these do not prove that they have true, even strong faith, though they show too clearly that they still seek too much the honor that cometh from men. There is more than one answer can be given. But the principal answer in our present connection is this: They indeed have a measure of faith, in proportion to which, with the special gifts bestowed upon them, is the blessing they bring to others. But in that very blessing the work of their faith is hindered, through the lack of humility. The blessing is often superficial or transitory, just because they are not the nothing that opens the way for God to be all. A deeper humility would without doubt bring a deeper and fuller blessing. The Holy Spirit not only working in them as a Spirit of power, but dwelling in them in the fullness of His grace, and specially that of humility, would through them communicate Himself to these converts for a life of power and holiness and steadfastness now all too little seen.

'How can ye believe, which receive glory from one another?' Brother! nothing can cure you of the desire of receiving glory from men, or of the sensitiveness and pain and anger which come when it is not given, but giving yourself to seek only the glory that comes from God. Let the glory of the All-glorious God be everything to you. You will be freed from the glory of men and of self, and be content and glad to be nothing. Out of this nothingness you will grow strong in faith, giving glory to God, and you will find that the deeper you sink in humility before Him, the nearer He is to fulfil the every desire of your faith.

Humility and Death to Self

'He humbled Himself and became obedient unto death.' —PHIL. ii. 8.

HUMILITY is the path to death, because in death it gives the highest proof of its perfection. Humility is the blossom of which death to self is the perfect fruit. Jesus humbled Himself unto death, and opened the path in which we too must walk. As there was no way for Him to prove His surrender to God to the very uttermost, or to give up and rise out of our human nature to the glory of the Father but through death, so with us too. Humility must lead us to die to self: so we prove how wholly we have given ourselves up to it and to God; so alone we are freed from fallen nature, and find the path that leads to life in God, to that full birth of the new nature, of which humility is the breath and the joy.

We have spoken of what Jesus did for His disciples when He communicated His resurrection life to them, when in the descent of the Holy Spirit He, the glorified and enthroned Meekness, actually came from heaven Himself to dwell in them. He won the power to do this through death: in its inmost nature the life He imparted was a life out of death, a life that had been surrendered to death, and been won through death. He who came to dwell in them was Himself One who had been dead and now lives for evermore. His life, His person, His presence, bears the marks of death, of being a life begotten out of death. That life in His disciples ever bears the death-marks too; it is only as the Spirit of the death, of the dying One, dwells and works in the soul, that the power of His life can be known. The first and chief of the marks of the dying of the Lord Jesus, of the death-marks that show the true follower of Jesus, is humility. For these two reasons: Only humility leads to perfect death; Only death perfects humility. Humility and death are in their very nature one: humility is the bud; in death the fruit is ripened to perfection.

Humility leads to perfect death. —Humility means the giving up of self and the taking of the place of perfect nothingness before God. Jesus humbled Himself, and became obedient unto death. In death He gave the highest, the perfect proof of having given up His will to the will of God. In death He gave up His self, with its natural reluctance to drink the cup; He gave up the life He had in union with our human nature; He died to self, and the sin that tempted Him; so, as man, He entered into the perfect life of God. If it had not been for His boundless humility, counting Himself as nothing except as a servant to do and suffer the will of God, He never would have died.

This gives us the answer to the question so often asked, and of which the meaning is so seldom clearly apprehended: How can I die to self? The death to self is not your work, it is God's work. In Christ *you are dead* to sin the life there is in you has gone through the process of death and resurrection; you may be sure you are indeed dead to sin. But the full manifestation of the power of this death in your disposition and conduct, depends upon the measure in which the Holy Spirit imparts the power of the death of Christ And here it is that the teaching is needed: if you would enter into full fellowship with Christ in His death, and know the full deliverance from self, humble yourself. This is your one duty. Place yourself before God in your utter helplessness; consent heartily to the fact of your impotence to slay or make alive yourself; sink down into your own nothingness, in the spirit of meek and patient and trustful surrender to God. Accept every humiliation, look upon every fellow-man who tries or vexes you, as a means of grace to humble you. Use every opportunity of humbling yourself before your fellow-men as a help to abide humble before God. God will accept such humbling of yourself as the proof that your whole heart desires it, as the very best prayer for it, as your preparation for His mighty work of grace, when, by the mighty strengthening of His Holy Spirit, He reveals Christ fully in you, so that He, in His form of a servant, is truly formed in you, and dwells in your heart. It is the path of humility which leads to perfect death, the full and perfect experience that we are dead in Christ.

Then follows: *Only this death leads to perfect humility.* Oh, beware of the mistake so many make, who would fain be humble, but are afraid to be too humble. They have so many qualifications and limitations, so many reasonings and questionings, as to what true humility is to be and to do, that they never unreservedly yield themselves to it. Beware of this. Humble yourself unto the death. It is in the death to self that humility is perfected. Be sure that at the root of all real experience of more grace, of all true advance in consecration, of all actually increasing conformity to the likeness of Jesus, there must be a deadness to self that proves itself to God and men in our dispositions and habits. It is sadly possible to speak of the death-life and the Spirit-walk, while even the tenderest love cannot but see how much there is of self. The death to self has no surer death-mark than a humility which makes itself of no reputation, which empties out itself, and takes the form of a servant. It is possible to speak much and honestly of fellowship with a despised and rejected Jesus, and of bearing His cross, while the meek and lowly, the kind and gentle humility of the Lamb of God is not seen, is scarcely sought. The Lamb of God means to two things—meekness and death. Let us seek to receive Him in both forms. In Him they are inseparable: they must be in us too.

What a hopeless task if we had to do the work! Nature never can overcome nature, not even with the help of grace. Self can never cast out self, even in the regenerate man. Praise God! the work has been done, and finished and perfected for ever. The death of Jesus, once and forever, is our death to self. And the ascension of Jesus, His entering once and for ever into the Holiest, has given us the Holy Spirit to communicate to us in power, and make our very own, the power of the death-life. As the soul, in the pursuit and practice of humility, follows in the steps of Jesus, its consciousness of the need of something more is awakened, its desire and hope is quickened, its faith is strengthened, and it learns to look up and claim and receive that true fullness of the Spirit of Jesus, which can daily maintain His death to self and sin in its full power, and make humility the all pervading spirit of our life.[5]

---

[5] 'To die to self, or come from under its power, is not, cannot be done, by any active resistance we can make to it by the powers of nature. The one true way of dying to self is the way of patience, meekness, humility, and resignation to God. This is the truth and perfection of dying to self…. For if I ask you what the Lamb of God means, must you not tell me that it is and means the perfection of patience, meekness, humility, and resignation to God? Must you not therefore say that a desire and faith of these virtues is an application to Christ, is a giving up yourself to Him and the perfection of faith in Him? And then, because

'Are ye ignorant that all we who were baptized into Jesus Christ were *baptized into His death?* Reckon yourselves to be *dead unto sin,* but alive unto God in Christ Jesus. Present yourself unto God, as *alive from the dead.'* The whole self consciousness of the Christian is to be imbued and characterized by the spirit that animated the death of Christ. He has ever to present himself to God as one who has died in Christ, and in Christ is alive from the dead, bearing about in his body the dying of the Lord Jesus. His life ever bears the two-fold mark: its roots striking in true humility deep into the grave of Jesus, the death to sin and self; its head lifted up in resurrection power to the heaven where Jesus is.

Believer, claim in faith the death and the life of Jesus as thine. Enter in His grave into the rest from self and its work—the rest of God. With Christ, who committed His spirit into the Father's hands, humble thyself and descend each day into that perfect, helpless dependence upon God. God will raise thee up and exalt thee. Sink every morning in deep, deep nothingness into the grave of Jesus; every day the life of Jesus will be manifest in thee, Let a willing, loving, restful, happy humility be the mark that thou hast indeed claimed thy birthright—the baptism into the death of Christ. 'By one offering He has perfected for ever them that are sanctified.' The souls that enter into *His* humiliation will find *in Him* the power to see and count self dead, and, as those who have learned and received of Him, to walk with all lowliness and meekness, forbearing one another in love. The death-life is seen in a meekness and lowliness like that of Christ.

Humility and Happiness

'Most gladly therefore will I rather glory in my weaknesses, that the strength of Christ may rest upon me. Wherefore I take pleasure in weakness: for when I am weak then am I strong.' —2 COR. xii. 9. 10.

LEST Paul should exalt himself, by reason of the exceeding greatness of the revelations, a thorn in the flesh was sent him to keep him humble. Paul's first desire was to have it removed, and he besought the Lord thrice that it might depart. The answer came that the trial was a blessing; that, in the weakness and humiliation it brought, the grace and strength of the Lord could be the better manifested. Paul at once entered upon a new stage in his relation to the trial: instead of simply

---

this inclination of your heart to sink down in patience, meekness, humility, and resignation to God, is truly giving up all that you are and all that you have from fallen Adam, it is perfectly leaving all you have to follow Christ; it is your highest act of faith in Him. Christ is nowhere but in these virtues; when they are there, He is in His own kingdom. Let this be the Christ you follow.

'The Spirit of divine love can have no birth in any fallen creature, till it wills and chooses to be dead to all self, in a patient, humble resignation to the power and mercy of God.

'I seek for all my salvation through the merits and mediation of the meek, humble, patient, suffering Lamb of God, who alone hath power to bring forth the blessed birth of these heavenly virtues in my soul. There is no possibility of salvation but in and by the birth of the meek, humble, patient, resigned Lamb of God in our souls. When the Lamb of God hath brought forth a real birth of His own meekness, humility, and full resignation to God in our souls, then it is the birthday of the Spirit of love in our souls, which, whenever we attain, will feast our souls with such peace and joy in God as will blot out the remembrance of everything that we called peace or joy before.

'This way to God is infallible. This infallibility is grounded in the twofold character of our Savior: 1. As He is the Lamb of God, a principle of all meekness and humility in the soul; 2. As He is the Light of heaven, and blesses eternal nature, and turns it into a kingdom of heaven, —when we are willing to get rest to our souls in meek, humble resignation to God, then it is that He, as the Light of God and heaven, joyfully breaks in upon us, turns our darkness into light, and begins that kingdom of God and of love within us, which will never have an end.' —See Wholly For God, pp 84-102. (The whole passage deserves careful study, showing most remarkably how the continual sinking down in humility before God is, from man's side, the only way to die to self. The whole dialogue has been published separately under the title Dying to Self: A Golden Dialogue. By William Law. With Notes by A.M., Nisbet & Co. Everyone who would study and practice humility will find in this golden dialogue what it is that hinders our humility, how we are to be delivered from it, and what the blessing of the Spirit of Love is that comes to the humble from Christ, the meek and lowly Lamb of God.

enduring it, *he most gladly gloried* in it; instead of asking for deliverance, *he took pleasure* in it. He had learned that the place of humiliation is the place of blessing, of power, of joy.

Every Christian virtually passes through these two stages in his pursuit of humility. In the first he fears and flees and seeks deliverance from all that can humble him. He has not yet learnt to seek humility at any cost. He has accepted the command to be humble, and seeks to obey it, though only to find how utterly he fails. He prays for humility, at times very earnestly; but in his secret heart he prays more, if not in word, then in wish, to be kept from the very things that will make him humble. He is not yet so in love with humility as the beauty of the Lamb of God, and the joy of heaven, that he would sell all to procure it. In his pursuit of it, and his prayer for it, there is still somewhat of a sense of burden and of bondage; to humble himself has not yet become the spontaneous expression of a life and a nature that is essentially humble. It has not yet become his joy and only pleasure. He cannot yet say, 'Most gladly do I glory in weakness, I take pleasure in whatever humbles me.'

But can we hope to reach the stage in which this will be the case? Undoubtedly. And what will it be that brings us there? *That* which brought Paul there—*a new revelation of the Lord Jesus.* Nothing but the presence of God can reveal and expel self. A clearer insight was to be given to Paul into the deep truth that the presence of Jesus will banish every desire to seek anything in ourselves, and will make us delight in every humiliation that prepares us for His fuller manifestation. Our humiliations lead us, in the experience of the presence and power of Jesus, to choose humility as our highest blessing. Let us try to learn the lessons the story of Paul teaches us.

We may have advanced believers, eminent teachers, men of heavenly experiences, who have not yet fully learnt the lesson of perfect humility, gladly glorying in weakness. We see this in Paul. The danger of exalting himself was coming very near. He knew not yet perfectly what it was to be nothing; to die, that Christ alone might live in him; to take pleasure in all that brought him low. It appears as if this were the highest lesson that he had to learn, full conformity to his Lord in that self-emptying where he gloried in weakness that God might be all.

The highest lesson a believer has to learn is humility. Oh that every Christian who seek to advance in holiness may remember this well! There may be intense consecration, and fervent zeal and heavenly experience, and yet, if it is not prevented by very special dealings of the Lord, there may be an unconscious self-exaltation with it all. Let us learn the lesson, —the highest holiness is the deepest humility; and let us remember that comes not of itself, but only as it is made matter of special dealing on the part of our faithful Lord and His faithful servant.

Let us look at our lives in the light of this experience, and see whether we gladly glory in weakness, whether we take pleasure, as Paul did, in injuries, in necessities, in distresses. Yes, let us ask whether we have learnt to regard a reproof, just or unjust, a reproach from friend or enemy, an injury, or trouble, or difficulty into which others bring us, as above all an opportunity of proving Jesus is all to us, how our own pleasure or honor are nothing, and how humiliation is in very truth what we take pleasure in. It is indeed blessed, the deep happiness of heaven, to be so free from self that whatever is said of us or done to us is lost and swallowed up, in the thought that Jesus is all.

Let us trust Him who took charge of Paul to take charge of us too. Paul needed special discipline, and with it special instruction, to learn, what was more precious than even the unutterable things he had heard in heaven—what it is to glory in weakness and lowliness. We need it, too, oh so much. He who cared for him will care for us too. He watches over us with a jealous, loving care, 'lest we exalt ourselves'. When we are doing so, He seeks to discover to us the evil, and deliver us from it. In trial and weakness and trouble He seeks to bring us low, until we so learn that His grace is all, as to take pleasure in the very thing that brings us and keeps us low. His strength made perfect in our weakness, His presence filling and satisfying our emptiness, becomes the secret of a humility that need never fail. It can, as Paul, in full sight of what God works in us, and through us, ever say, 'In nothing was I behind the chiefest apostles, *though I am nothing.'* His humiliations had led him to true humility, with its wonderful gladness and glorying and pleasure in all that humbles.

'Most gladly will I glory in my weaknesses, that the power of Christ may rest upon me; wherefore I take pleasure in weaknesses. 'The humble man has learnt the secret of abiding gladness. The weaker he feels, the lower he sinks; the greater his humiliations appear, the more the power and the presence of Christ are his portion, until, as he says, 'I am nothing,' the word of his Lord brings ever deeper joy: 'My grace is sufficient for thee.'

I feel as if I must once again gather up all in the two lessons: the danger of pride is greater and nearer than we think, and the grace for humility too.

The danger of pride is greater and nearer than we think, and that especially at the time of our highest experiences. The preacher of spiritual truth with an admiring congregation hanging on his lips, the gifted speaker on a Holiness platform expounding the secrets of the heavenly life, the Christian giving testimony to a blessed experience, the evangelist moving on as in triumph, and made a blessing to rejoicing multitudes, —no man knows the hidden, the unconscious danger to which these are exposed. Paul was in danger without knowing it; what Jesus did for him is written for our admonition, that we may know our danger and know our only safety. If ever it has been said of a teacher or professor of holiness, —he is so full of self; or, he does not practice what he preaches; or, his blessing has not made him humbler or gentler, —let it be said no more. Jesus, in whom we trust, can make us humble.

Yes, the grace for humility is greater and nearer, too, than we think. The humility of Jesus is our salvation: Jesus Himself is our humility. Our humility is His care and His work. His grace is sufficient for us, to meet the temptation of pride too. His strength will be perfected in our weakness. Let us choose to be weak, to be low, to be nothing. Let humility be to us joy and gladness. Let us gladly glory and take pleasure in weakness, in all that can humble us and keep us low; the power of Christ will rest upon us. Christ humbled Himself, therefore God exalted Him. Christ will humble us, and keep us humble; let us heartily consent, let us trustfully and joyfully accept all that humbles; the power of Christ will rest upon us. We shall find that the deepest humility is the secret of the truest happiness, of a joy that nothing can destroy.

Humility and Exaltation

'He that humbleth himself shall be exalted.' —LUKE xiv. 11, xviii. 13.
'God giveth grace to the humble. Humble yourself in the sight of the Lord, and He
    shall exalt you.' —JAS. iv. 10.
'Humble yourselves therefore under the mighty hand of God, that He may exalt you
    in due time.' —1 PET. v. 6.

JUST yesterday I was asked the question, How am I to conquer this pride? The answer; was simple. Two things are needed. Do what; God says is your work: humble yourself. Trust Him to do what He says is His work: He will exalt you.

The command is clear: humble yourself. That does not mean that it is your work to conquer and cast out the pride of your nature, and to form within yourself the lowliness of the holy Jesus. No, this is God's work; the very essence of that exaltation, wherein He lifts you up into the real likeness of the beloved Son. What the command does mean is this: take every opportunity of humbling yourself before God and man. In the faith of the grace that is already working in you; in the assurance of the more grace for victory that is coming; up to the light that conscience each time flashes upon the pride of the heart and its workings; notwithstanding all there may be of failure and falling, stand persistently as under the unchanging command: humble yourself. Accept with gratitude everything that God allows from within or without, from friend or enemy, in nature or in grace, to remind you of your need of humbling, and to help you to it. Reckon humility to be indeed the mother-virtue, your very first duty before God, the one perpetual safeguard of the soul, and set your heart upon it as the source of all blessing. The promise is divine and sure: He that humbleth himself shall be exalted. See that you do the one thing God asks: humble yourself. God will see that does the one thing He has promised. He will give more grace; He will exalt you in due time.

All God's dealings with man are characterized by two stages. There is the time of preparation, when command and promise, with the mingled experience of effort and impotence, of failure and partial success, with the holy expectancy of something better which these waken, train and discipline men for a higher stage. Then comes the time of fulfilment, when faith inherits the promise, and enjoys what it had so often struggled for in vain. This law holds good in every part of the Christian life, and in the pursuit of every separate virtue. And that because it is grounded in the very nature of things. In all that concerns our redemption, God must needs take the initiative. When that has been done, man's turn comes. In the effort after obedience and attainment, he must learn to know his impotence, in self-despair to die to himself, and so be fitted voluntarily and intelligently to receive from God the end, the completion of that of which he had accepted the beginning in ignorance. So, God who had been the Beginning, ere man rightly knew Him, or fully understood what His purpose was, is longed for and welcomed as the End, as the All in All.

It is even thus, too, in the pursuit of humility. To every Christian the command comes from the throne of God Himself: humble yourself. The earnest attempt to listen and obey will be rewarded—yes, rewarded—with the painful discovery of two things. The one, what depth of pride, that is of unwillingness to count oneself and to be counted nothing, to submit absolutely to God, there was, that one never knew. The other, what utter impotence there is in all our efforts, and in all our prayers too for God's help, to destroy the hideous monster. Blessed the man who now learns to put his hope in God, and to persevere, notwithstanding all the power of pride within him, in acts of humiliation before God and Men. We know the law of human nature: acts produce habits, habits breed dispositions, dispositions form the will, and the rightly-formed will is character. It is no otherwise in the work of grace. As acts, persistently repeated, beget habits and dispositions, and these strengthened the will, He who works both to will and to do comes with His mighty power and Spirit; and the humbling of the proud heart with which the' penitent saint cast himself so often before God, is rewarded with the 'more grace' of the humble heart, in which the Spirit of Jesus has conquered, and brought the new nature to its maturity, and He the meek and lowly One now dwells for ever.

Humble yourselves in the sight of the Lord, and He will exalt you. And wherein does the exaltation consist? The highest glory of the creature is in being only a vessel, to receive and enjoy and show forth the glory of God. It can do this only as it is willing to be nothing in itself, that God may be all. Water always fills first the lowest places. The lower, the emptier a man lies before God, the speedier and the fuller will be the inflow of the divine glory. The exaltation God promises is not, cannot be, any external thing apart from Himself: all that He has to give or can give is only more of Himself, Himself to take more complete possession. The exaltation is not, like an earthly prize, something arbitrary, in no necessary connection with the conduct to be rewarded. No, but it is in its very nature the effect and result of the humbling of ourselves. It is nothing but the gift of such a divine indwelling humility, such a conformity to and possession of the humility of the Lamb of God, as fits us for receiving fully the indwelling of God.

He that humbleth himself shall be exalted. Of the truth of these words Jesus Himself is the proof; of the certainty of their fulfilment to us He is the pledge. Let us take His yoke upon us and learn of Him, for He is meek and lowly of heart. If we are but willing to stoop to Him, as He has stooped to us, He will yet stoop to each one of us again, and we shall find ourselves not unequally yoked with Him. As we enter deeper into the fellowship of His humiliation, and either humble ourselves or bear the humbling of men, we can count upon it that the Spirit of His exaltation, 'the Spirit of God and of glory,' will rest upon us. The presence and the power of the glorified Christ will come to them that are of an humble spirit. When God can again have His rightful place in us, He will lift us up. Make His glory thy care in humbling thyself; He will make thy glory His care in perfecting thy humility, and breathing into thee, as thy abiding life, the very Spirit of His Son. As the all-pervading life of God possesses thee, there will be nothing so natural, and nothing so sweet, as to be nothing, with not a thought or wish for self, because all is occupied with Him who filleth all. 'Most gladly will I glory in my weakness, that the strength of Christ may rest upon me.'

Brother, have we not here the reason that our consecration and our faith have availed so little in the pursuit of holiness? It was by self and its strength that the work was done under the name of faith; it was for self and its happiness that God was called in; it was, unconsciously, but still truly, in self and its holiness that the soul rejoiced. We never knew that humility, absolute, abiding, Christlike humility and self-effacement, pervading and marking our whole life with God and man, was the most essential element of the life of the holiness we sought for.

It is only in the possession of God that I lose myself. As it is in the height and breadth and glory of the sunshine that the littleness of the mote playing in its beams is seen, even so humility is the taking our place in God's presence to be nothing but a mote dwelling in the sunlight of His love.

'How great is God! how small am I!
Lost, swallowed up in Love's immensity!
God only there, not I.'

May God teach us to believe that to be humble, to be nothing in His presence, is the highest attainment, and the fullest blessing of the Christian life. He speaks to us: 'I dwell in the high and holy place, and with him the is of a contrite and humble spirit.' Be this our portion!

> *'Oh, to be emptier, lowlier,*
> *Mean, unnoticed, and unknown,*
> *And to God a vessel holier,*
> *Filled with Christ, and Christ alone!'*

Endnote

A Secret of Secrets: Humility the Soul of True Prayer. —Till the spirit of the heart be renewed, till it is emptied of all earthly desires, and stands in an habitual hunger and thirst after God, which is the true spirit of prayer; till then, all our prayer will be, more or less, but too much like lessons given to scholars; and we shall mostly say them, only because we dare not neglect them. But be not discouraged; take the following advice, and then you may go to church without any danger of mere lip-labor or hypocrisy, although there should be a hymn or a prayer, whose language is higher than that of your heart. Do this: go to the church as the publican went to the temple; stand inwardly in the spirit of your mind in that form which he outwardly expressed, when he cast down his eyes, and could only say, 'God be merciful to me, a sinner.' Stand unchangeably, at least in your desire, in this form or state of heart; it will sanctify every petition that comes out of your mouth; and when anything is read or sung or prayed, that is more exalted than your heart is, if you make this an occasion of further sinking down in the spirit of the publican, you will then be helped, and highly blessed, by those prayers and praises which seem only to belong to a heart better than yours.

This, my friend, is a secret of secrets; it will help you to reap where you have not sown, and be a continual source of grace in your soul; for everything that inwardly stirs in you, or outwardly happens to you, becomes a real good to you, if it finds or excites in you this humble state of mind. For nothing is in vain, or without profit to the humble soul; it stands always in a state of divine growth; everything that falls upon it is like a dew of heaven to it. Shut up yourself, therefore, in this form of Humility; all good is enclosed in it; it is a water of heaven, that turns the fire of the fallen soul into the meekness of the divine life, and creates that oil, out of which the love to God and man gets its flame. Be enclosed, therefore, always in it; let it be as a garment wherewith you are always covered, and a girdle with which you are girt; breathe nothing but in and from its spirit; see nothing but with its eyes; hear nothing but with its ears. And then, whether you are in the church or out of the church, hearing the praises of God or receiving wrongs from men and the world, all will be edification, and everything will help forward your growth in the life of God. —*The Spirit of Prayer,* Pt. II. p. 121.

A Prayer for Humility

I will here give you an infallible touchstone, that will try all to the truth. It is this: retire from the world and all conversation, only for one month; neither write, nor read, nor debate anything with yourself; stop all the former workings of your heart and mind: and, with all the strength of your heart, stand all this month, as continually as you can, in the following form of prayer to God. Offer it frequently on your knees; but whether sitting, walking, or standing, be always inwardly longing, and earnestly praying this one prayer to God: 'That of His great goodness He would make known to you, and take from your heart, *every kind and form and degree of Pride,* whether it be from evil spirits, or your own corrupt nature; and that He would awaken in you the *deepest depth and truth of that Humility,* which can make you capable of His light and Holy Spirit.' Reject every thought, but that of waiting and praying in this matter from the bottom of your heart, with such truth and earnestness, as people in torment wish to pray and be delivered from it.... If you can and will give yourself up in truth and sincerity to this spirit of prayer, I will venture to affirm that, if you had twice as many evil spirits in you as Mary Magdalene had, they will all be cast out of you, and you will be forced with her to weep tears of love at the feet of the holy Jesus. —*The Spirit of Prayer,* Pt. II. p. 124.

Absolute Surrender

and Other Addresses

~ ※ ~

By *Andrew Murray*

"I am thine and all that I have." (1 Kings 20:1-4).

Absolute Surrender

"And Ben-hadad the king of Syria gathered all his host together: and there were thirty and two kings with him, and horses, and chariots: and he went up and besieged Samaria, and warred against it. And he sent messengers to Ahab king of Israel into the city, and said unto him, "Thus saith Ben-hadad, Thy silver and thy gold is mine; thy wives also and thy children, even the goodliest, are mine. And the king of Israel answered and said, My lord, O king, according to thy saying, I am thine and all that I have." (1 Kings 20:1-4).

What Ben Hadad asked was *absolute surrender*; and what Ahab gave was what was asked of him—*absolute surrender*. I want to use these words: "My lord, O king, according to thy saying, I am thine, and all that I have," as the words of absolute surrender with which every child of God ought to yield himself to his Father. We have heard it before, but we need to hear it very definitely—the condition of God's blessing is absolute surrender of all into His hands. Praise God! If our hearts are willing for that, there is no end to what God will do for us, and to the blessing God will bestow.

Absolute surrender—let me tell you where I got those words. I used them myself often, and you have heard them numberless times. But in Scotland once I was in a company where we were talking about the condition of Christ's Church, and what the great need of the Church and of believers is; and there was in our company a godly worker who has much to do in training workers, and I asked him what he would say was the great need of the Church, and the message that ought to be preached. He answered very quietly and simply and determinedly:

"Absolute surrender to God is the one thing."

The words struck me as never before. And that man began to tell how, in the workers with whom he had to deal, he finds that if they are sound on that point, even though they be backward, they are willing to be taught and helped, and they always improve; whereas others who are not sound there very often go back and leave the work. The condition for obtaining God's full blessing is *absolute surrender* to Him.

And now, I desire by God's grace to give to you this message—that your God in Heaven answers the prayers which you have offered for blessing on yourselves and for blessing on those around you by this one demand: *Are you willing to surrender yourselves absolutely into His hands?* What is our answer to be? God knows there are hundreds of hearts who have said it, and there are hundreds more who long to say it but hardly dare to do so. And there are hearts who have said it, but who have yet miserably failed, and who feel themselves condemned because they did not find the secret of the power to live that life. May God have a word for all!

Let me say, first of all, that God claims it from us.

God Expects Your Surrender

Yes, it has its foundation in the very nature of God. God cannot do otherwise. Who is God? He is the Fountain of life, the only Source of existence and power and goodness, and throughout the universe there is nothing good but what God works. God has created the sun, and the moon, and the stars, and the flowers, and the trees, and the grass; and are they not all absolutely surrendered to God? Do they not allow God to work in them just what He pleases? When God clothes the lily with its beauty, is it not yielded up, surrendered, given over to God as He works in its beauty? And God's redeemed children, oh, can you think that God can work His work if there is only half or a part of them surrendered? God cannot do it. God is life, and love, and blessing, and power, and infinite beauty, and God delights to communicate Himself to every child who is prepared to receive Him; but ah! this one lack of absolute surrender is just the thing that hinders God. And now He comes, and as God, He claims it.

You know in daily life what absolute surrender is. You know that everything has to be given up to its special, definite object and service. I have a pen in my pocket, and that pen is absolutely surrendered to the one work of writing, and that pen must be absolutely surrendered to my hand if I am to write properly with it. If another holds it partly, I cannot write properly. This coat is absolutely given up to me to cover my body. This building is entirely given up to religious services.

And now, do you expect that in your immortal being, in the divine nature that you have received by regeneration, God can work His work, every day and every hour, unless you are entirely given up to Him? God cannot. The Temple of Solomon was absolutely surrendered to God when it was dedicated to Him. And every one of us is a temple of God, in which God will dwell and work mightily on one condition—absolute surrender to Him. God claims it, God is worthy of it, and without it God cannot work His blessed work in us.

God not only claims it, but God will work it Himself.

God Accomplishes Your Surrender

I am sure there is many a heart that says: "Ah, but that absolute surrender implies so much!" Someone says: "Oh, I have passed through so much trial and suffering, and there is so much of the self-life still remaining, and I dare not face the entire giving of it up, because I know it will cause so much trouble and agony."

Alas! alas! that God's children have such thoughts of Him, such cruel thoughts. Oh, I come to you with a message, fearful and anxious one. God does not ask you to give the perfect surrender in your strength, or by the power of your will; God is willing to work it in you. Do we not read: "It is God that worketh in us, both to will and to do of his good pleasure" (Phil. 2:13)? And that is what we should seek for—to go on our faces before God, until our hearts learn to believe that the everlasting God Himself will come in to turn out what is wrong, to conquer what is evil, and to work what is well-pleasing in His blessed sight. God Himself will work it in you.

Look at the men in the Old Testament, like Abraham. Do you think it was by accident that God found that man, the father of the faithful and the Friend of God, and that it was Abraham himself, apart from God, who had such faith and such obedience and such devotion? You know it is not so. God raised him up and prepared him as an instrument for His glory.

Did not God say to Pharaoh: "For this cause have I raised thee up, for to show in thee my power" (Ex. 9:16)?

And if God said that of him, will not God say it far more of every child of His?

Oh, I want to encourage you, and I want you to cast away every fear. Come with that feeble desire; and if there is the fear which says: "Oh, my desire is not strong enough, I am not willing for everything that may come, I do not feel bold enough to say I can conquer everything"—I pray you, learn to know and trust your God now. Say: "My God, I am willing that Thou shouldst make me willing." If there is anything holding you back, or any sacrifice you are afraid of making, come to God now, and prove how gracious your God is, and be not afraid that He will command from you what He will not bestow.

God comes and offers to work this absolute surrender in you. All these searchings and hungerings and longings that are in your heart, I tell you they are the drawings of the divine magnet, Christ Jesus. He lived a life of absolute surrender, He has possession of you; He is living in your heart by His Holy Spirit. You have hindered and hindered Him terribly, but He desires to help you to get hold of Him entirely. And He comes and draws you now by His message and words. Will you not come and trust God to work in you that absolute surrender to Himself? Yes, blessed be God, He can do it, and He will do it.

God not only claims it and works it, but God accepts it when we bring it to Him.

God Accepts Your Surrender

God works it in the secret of our heart, God urges us by the hidden power of His Holy Spirit to come and speak it out, and we have to bring and to yield to Him that absolute surrender. But remember, when you come and bring God that absolute surrender, it may, as far as your feelings or your consciousness go, be a thing of great imperfection, and you may doubt and hesitate and say:

"Is it absolute?"

But, oh, remember there was once a man to whom Christ had said:

"If thou canst believe, all things are possible to him that believeth" (Mark 9:23).

And his heart was afraid, and he cried out:

"Lord, I believe, help thou mine unbelief" (Mark 9:24).

That was a faith that triumphed over the Devil, and the evil spirit was cast out. And if you come and say: "Lord, I yield myself in absolute surrender to my God," even though it be with a trembling heart and with the consciousness: "I do not feel the power, I do not feel the determination, I do not feel the assurance," it will succeed. Be not afraid, but come just as you are, and even in the midst of your trembling the power of the Holy Spirit will work.

Have you never yet learned the lesson that the Holy Spirit works with mighty power, while on the human side everything appears feeble? Look at the Lord Jesus Christ in Gethsemane. We read that He, "through the eternal Spirit" (Heb. 9:14), offered Himself a sacrifice unto God. The Almighty Spirit of God was enabling Him to do it. And yet what agony and fear and exceeding sorrow came over Him, and how He prayed! Externally, you can see no sign of the mighty power of the Spirit, but the Spirit of God was there. And even so, while you are feeble and fighting and trembling, in faith in the hidden work of God's Spirit do not fear, but yield yourself.

And when you do yield yourself in absolute surrender, let it be in the faith that God does now accept of it. That is the great point, and that is what we so often miss—that believers should be thus occupied with God in this matter of surrender. I pray you, be occupied with God. We want to get help, every one of us, so that in our daily life God shall be clearer to us, God shall have the right place, and be "all in all." And if we are to have that through life, let us begin now and look away from ourselves, and look up to God. Let each believe—while I, a poor worm on earth and a trembling child of God, full of failure and sin and fear, bow here, and no one knows what passes through my heart, and while I in simplicity say, O God, I accept Thy terms; I have pleaded for blessing on myself and others, I have accepted Thy terms of absolute surrender—while your heart says that in deep silence, remember there is a God present that takes note of it, and writes it down in His book, and there is a God present who at that very moment takes possession of you. You may not feel it, you may not realize it, but God takes possession if you will trust Him.

God not only claims it, and works it, and accepts it when I bring it, but God maintains it.

God Maintains Your Surrender

That is the great difficulty with many. People say: "I have often been stirred at a meeting, or at a convention, and I have consecrated myself to God, but it has passed away. I know it may last for a week or for a month, but away it fades, and after a time it is all gone."

But listen! It is because you do not believe what I am now going to tell you and remind you of. When God has begun the work of absolute surrender in you, and when God has accepted your surrender, then God holds Himself bound to care for it and to keep it. Will you believe that?

In this matter of surrender there are two: God and I—I a worm, God the everlasting and omnipotent Jehovah. Worm, will you be afraid to trust yourself to this mighty God now? God is willing. Do you not believe that He can keep you continually, day by day, and moment by moment?

Moment by moment I'm kept in His love;
Moment by moment I've life from above.

If God allows the sun to shine upon you moment by moment, without intermission, will not God let His life shine upon you every moment? And why have you not experienced it? Because you have not trusted God for it, and you do not surrender yourself absolutely to God in that trust.

A life of absolute surrender has its difficulties. I do not deny that. Yes, it has something far more than difficulties: it is a life that with men is absolutely impossible. But by the grace of God, by the power of God, by the power of the Holy Spirit dwelling in us, it is a life to which we are destined, and a life that is possible for us, praise God! Let us believe that God will maintain it.

Some of you have read the words of that aged saint who, on his ninetieth birthday, told of all God's goodness to him—I mean George Muller. What did he say he believed to be the secret of his happiness, and of all the blessing which God had given him? He said he believed there were two reasons. The one was that he had been enabled by grace to maintain a good conscience before God day by day; the other was, that he was a lover of God's Word. Ah, yes, a good conscience is complete obedience to God day by day, and fellowship with God every day in His Word, and prayer—that is a life of absolute surrender.

Such a life has two sides—on the one side, absolute surrender to work what God wants *you* to do; on the other side, to let God work what *He* wants to do.

First, *to do what God wants* you *to do.*

Give up yourselves absolutely to the will of God. You know something of that will; not enough, far from all. But say absolutely to the Lord God: "By Thy grace I desire to do Thy will in everything, every moment of every day." Say: "Lord God, not a word upon my tongue but for Thy glory, not a movement of my temper but for Thy glory, not an affection of love or hate in my heart but for Thy glory, and according to Thy blessed will."

Someone says: "Do you think that possible?"

I ask, What has God promised you, and what can God do to fill a vessel absolutely surrendered to Him? Oh, God wants to bless you in a way beyond what you expect. From the beginning, ear hath not heard, neither hath the eye seen, what God hath prepared for them that wait for Him (1 Cor. 2:9). God has prepared unheard-of things, blessings much more wonderful than you can imagine, more mighty than you can conceive. They are divine blessings. Oh, say now:

"I give myself absolutely to God, to His will, to do only what God wants."

It is God who will enable you to carry out the surrender.

And, on the other side, come and say: "I give myself absolutely to God, *to let Him work in me to will and to do of His good pleasure,* as He has promised to do."

Yes, the living God wants to work in His children in a way that we cannot understand, but that God's Word has revealed, and He wants to work in us every moment of the day. God is willing to maintain our life. Only let our absolute surrender be one of simple, childlike, and unbounded trust.

God Blesses When You Surrender

This absolute surrender to God will wonderfully bless.

What Ahab said to his enemy, King Ben-hadad—"My lord, O king, according to thy word I am thine, and all that I have"—shall we not say to our God and loving Father? If we do say it, God's blessing will come upon us. God wants us to be separate from the world; we are called to come out from the world that hates God. Come out for God, and say: "Lord, anything for Thee." If you say that with prayer, and speak that into God's ear, He will accept it, and He will teach you what it means.

I say again, God will bless you. You have been praying for blessing. But do remember, there must be absolute surrender. At every tea-table you see it. Why is tea poured into that cup? Because it is empty, and given up for the tea. But put ink, or vinegar, or wine into it, and will they pour the tea into the vessel? And can God fill you, can God bless you if you are not absolutely surrendered to Him? He cannot. Let us believe God has wonderful blessings for us, if we will but stand up for God, and say, be it with a trembling will, yet with a believing heart:

"O God, I accept Thy demands. I am thine and all that I have. Absolute surrender
is what my soul yields to Thee by divine grace."

You may not have such strong and clear feelings of deliverances as you would desire to have, but humble yourselves in His sight, and acknowledge that you have grieved the Holy Spirit by your self-will, self-confidence, and self-effort. Bow humbly before him in the confession of that, and ask him to break the heart and to bring you into the dust before Him. Then, as you bow before Him, just accept God's teaching that in your flesh "there dwelleth no good thing" (Rom. 7:18), and that nothing will help you except another life which must come in. You must deny self once for all. Denying self must every moment be the power of your life, and then Christ will come in and take possession of you.

When was Peter delivered? When was the change accomplished? The change began with Peter weeping, and the Holy Spirit came down and filled his heart.

God the Father loves to give us the power of the Spirit. We have the Spirit of God dwelling within us. We come to God confessing that, and praising God for it, and yet confessing how we have grieved the Spirit. And then we bow our knees to the Father to ask that He would strengthen us with all might by the Spirit in the inner man, and that He would fill us with His mighty power. And as the Spirit reveals Christ to us, Christ comes to live in our hearts forever, and the self-life is cast out.

Let us bow before God in humility, and in that humility confess before Him the state of the whole Church. No words can tell the sad state of the Church of Christ on earth. I wish I had words to speak what I sometimes feel about it. Just think of the Christians around you. I do not speak of nominal Christians, or of professing Christians, but I speak of hundreds and thousands of honest, earnest Christians who are not living a life in the power of God or to His glory. So little power, so little devotion or consecration to God, so little perception of the truth that a Christian is a man utterly surrendered to God's will! Oh, we want to confess the sins of God's people around us, and to humble ourselves. We are members of that sickly body, and the sickliness of the body will hinder us, and break us down, unless we come to God, and in confession separate ourselves from partnership with worldliness, with coldness toward each other, unless we give up ourselves to be entirely and wholly for God.

How much Christian work is being done in the spirit of the flesh and in the power of self! How much work, day by day, in which human energy—our will and our thoughts about the work—is continually manifested, and in which there is but little of waiting upon God, and upon the power of the Holy Spirit! Let us make confession. But as we confess the state of the Church and the feebleness and sinfulness of work for God among us, let us come back to ourselves. Who is there who truly longs to be delivered from the power of the self-life, who truly acknowledges that it is the power of self and the flesh, and who is willing to cast all at the feet of Christ? There is deliverance.

I heard of one who had been an earnest Christian, and who spoke about the "cruel" thought of separation and death. But you do not think that, do you? What are we to think of separation and death? This: death was the path to glory for Christ. For the joy set before Him He endured the cross. The cross was the birthplace of His everlasting glory. Do you love Christ? Do you long to be in Christ, and not like Him? Let death be to you the most desirable thing on earth—death to self, and fellowship with Christ. Separation—do you think it a hard thing to be called to be entirely free from the world, and by that separation to be united to God and His love, by separation to become prepared for living and walking with God every day? Surely one ought to say:

> *"Anything to bring me to separation, to death, for a life of full fellowship with God and Christ."*

Come and cast this self-life and flesh-life at the feet of Jesus. Then trust Him. Do not worry yourselves with trying to understand all about it, but come in the living faith that Christ will come into you with the power of His death and the power of His life; and then the Holy Spirit will bring the whole Christ—Christ crucified and risen and living in glory—into your heart.

"The Fruit of the Spirit is Love"

I want to look at the fact of a life filled with the Holy Spirit more from the practical side, and to show how this life will show itself in our daily walk and conduct.

Under the Old Testament you know the Holy Spirit often came upon men as a divine Spirit of revelation to reveal the mysteries of God, or for power to do the work of God. But He did not then dwell in them. Now, many just want the Old Testament gift of power for work, but know very little of the New Testament gift of the indwelling Spirit, animating and renewing the whole life. When God gives the Holy Spirit, His great object is the formation of a holy character. It is a gift of a holy mind and spiritual disposition, and what we need above everything else, is to say:

> *"I must have the Holy Spirit sanctifying my whole inner life if I am really to live for God's glory."*

You might say that when Christ promised the Spirit to the disciples, He did so that they might have power to be witnesses. True, but then they received the Holy Spirit in such heavenly power and reality that He took possession of their whole being at once and so fitted them as holy men for doing the work with power as they had to do it. Christ spoke of power to the disciples, but it was the Spirit filling their whole being that worked the power.

I wish now to dwell upon the passage found in Gal. 5:22:

> *"The fruit of the Spirit is love."*

We read that "Love is the fulfilling of the law" (Rom. 13:10), and my desire is to speak on love as a fruit of the Spirit with a twofold object. One is that this word may be a searchlight in our hearts, and give us a test by which to try all our thoughts about the Holy Spirit and all our experience of the holy life. Let us try ourselves by this word. Has this been our daily habit, to seek to be filled with the Holy Spirit as the Spirit of love? "The fruit of the Spirit is love." Has it been our experience that the more we have of the Holy Spirit the more loving we become? In claiming the Holy Spirit we should make this the first object of our expectation. The Holy Spirit comes as a Spirit of love.

Oh, if this were true in the Church of Christ how different her state would be! May God help us to get hold of this simple, heavenly truth that the fruit of the Spirit is a love which appears in the life, and that just as the Holy Spirit gets real possession of the life, the heart will be filled with real, divine, universal love.

One of the great causes why God cannot bless His Church is *the want of love*. When the body is divided, there cannot be strength. In the time of their great religious wars, when Holland stood out so nobly against Spain, one of their mottoes was: "Unity gives strength." It is only when God's people stand as one body, one before God in the fellowship of love, one toward another in deep affection, one before the world in a love that the world can see—it is only then that they will have power to secure the blessing which they ask of God. Remember that if a vessel that ought to be one whole is cracked into many pieces, it cannot be filled. You can take a potsherd, one part of a vessel, and dip out a little water into that, but if you want the vessel full, the vessel must be whole. That is literally true of Christ's Church, and if there is one thing we must pray for still, it is this: Lord, melt us together into one by the power of the Holy Spirit; let the Holy Spirit, who at Pentecost made them all of one heart and one soul, do His blessed work among us. Praise God, we can love each other in a divine love, for "the fruit of the Spirit is love." Give yourselves up to love, and the Holy Spirit will come; receive the Spirit, and He will teach you to love more.

God Is Love

Now, why is it that the fruit of the Spirit is love? *Because God is love* (1 John 4:8).

And what does that mean?

It is the very nature and being of God to delight in communicating Himself. God has no selfishness, God keeps nothing to Himself. God's nature is to be always giving. In the sun and the moon and the stars, in every flower you see it, in every bird in the air, in every fish in the sea. God communicates life to His creatures. And the angels around His throne, the seraphim and cherubim who are flames of fire—whence have they their glory? It is because God is love, and He imparts to them of His brightness and His blessedness. And we, His redeemed children—God delights to pour His love into us. And why? Because, as I said, God keeps nothing for Himself. From eternity God had His only begotten Son, and the Father gave Him all things, and nothing that God had was kept back. "God is love."

One of the old Church fathers said that we cannot better understand the Trinity than as a revelation of divine love—the Father, the loving One, the Fountain of love; the Son, the beloved one, the Reservoir of love, in whom the love was poured out; and the Spirit, the living love that united both and then overflowed into this world. The Spirit of Pentecost, the Spirit of the Father, and the Spirit of the Son is love. And when the Holy Spirit comes to us and to other men, will He be less a Spirit of love than He is in God? It cannot be; He cannot change His nature. The Spirit of God is love, and "the fruit of the Spirit is love."

Mankind Needs Love

Why is that so? That was the one great need of mankind, that was the thing which Christ's redemption came to accomplish: *to restore love to this world.*

When man sinned, why was it that he sinned? Selfishness triumphed—he sought self instead of God. And just look! Adam at once begins to accuse the woman of having led him astray. Love to God had gone, love to man was lost. Look again: of the first two children of Adam the one becomes a murderer of his brother.

Does not that teach us that sin had robbed the world of love? Ah! what a proof the history of the world has been of love having been lost! There may have been beautiful examples of love even among the heathen, but only as a little remnant of what was lost. One of the worst things sin did for man was to make him selfish, for selfishness cannot love.

The Lord Jesus Christ came down from Heaven as the Son of God's love. "God so loved the world that He gave His only begotten Son" (John 3:16). God's Son came to show what love is, and He lived a life of love here upon earth in fellowship with His disciples, in compassion over the poor and miserable, in love even to His enemies, and He died the death of love. And when He went to Heaven, whom did He send down? The Spirit of love, to come and banish selfishness and envy and pride, and bring the love of God into the hearts of men. "The fruit of the Spirit is love."

And what was the preparation for the promise of the Holy Spirit? You know that promise as found in the fourteenth chapter of John's Gospel. But remember what precedes in the thirteenth chapter. Before Christ promised the Holy Spirit, He gave a new commandment, and about that new commandment He said wonderful things. One thing was: "Even as I have loved you, so love ye one another." To them His dying love was to be the only law of their conduct and intercourse with each other. What a message to those fishermen, to those men full of pride and selfishness! "Learn to love each other," said Christ, "as I have loved you." And by the grace of God they did it. When Pentecost came, they were of one heart and one soul. Christ did it for them.

And now He calls us to dwell and to walk in love. He demands that though a man hate you, still you love him. True love cannot be conquered by anything in Heaven or upon the earth. The more hatred there is, the more love triumphs through it all and shows its true nature. This is the love that Christ commanded His disciples to exercise.

What more did He say? "By this shall all men know that ye are my disciples, if ye have love one to another" (John 13:35).

You all know what it is to wear a badge. And Christ said to His disciples in effect: "I give you a badge, and that badge is love. That is to be your mark. It is the only thing in Heaven or on earth by which men can know me."

Do we not begin to fear that love has fled from the earth? That if we were to ask the world: "Have you seen us wear the badge of love?" the world would say: "No; what we have heard of the Church of Christ is that there is not a place where there is no quarreling and separation." Let us ask God with one heart that we may wear the badge of Jesus' love. God is able to give it.

Love Conquers Selfishness

"The fruit of the Spirit is love." Why? Because *nothing but love can expel and conquer our selfishness.*

Self is the great curse, whether in its relation to God, or to our fellow-men in general, or to fellow-Christians, thinking of ourselves and seeking our own. Self is our greatest curse. But, praise God, Christ came to redeem us from self. We sometimes talk about deliverance from the self-life— and thank God for every word that can be said about it to help us—but I am afraid some people think deliverance from the self-life means that now they are going to have no longer any trouble in serving God; and they forget that deliverance from self-life means to be a vessel overflowing with love to everybody all the day.

And there you have the reason why many people pray for the power of the Holy Spirit, and they get something, but oh, so little! because they prayed for power for work, and power for blessing, but they have not prayed for power for full deliverance from self. That means not only the righteous self in intercourse with God, but the unloving self in intercourse with men. And there is deliverance. "The fruit of the Spirit is love." I bring you the glorious promise of Christ that He is able to fill our hearts with love.

A great many of us try hard at times to love. We try to force ourselves to love, and I do not say that is wrong; it is better than nothing. But the end of it is always very sad. "I fail continually," such a one must confess. And what is the reason? The reason is simply this: Because they have never learned to believe and accept the truth that the Holy Spirit can pour God's love into their heart. That blessed text; often it has been limited!—"The love of God is shed abroad in our hearts" (Rom. 5:5). It has often been understood in this sense: It means the love of God *to me.* Oh, what a limitation! That is only the beginning. The love of God is always the love of God in its entirety, in its fullness as an indwelling power, a love of God to me that leaps back to Him in love, and overflows to my fellow-men in love—God's love to me, and my love to God, and my love to my fellow-men. The three are one; you cannot separate them.

Do believe that the love of God can be shed abroad in your heart and mine so that we can love all the day.

"Ah!" you say, "how little I have understood that!"

Why is a lamb always gentle? Because that is its nature. Does it cost the lamb any trouble to be gentle? No. Why not? It is so beautiful and gentle. Has a lamb to study to be gentle? No. Why does that come so easy? It is its nature. And a wolf—why does it cost a wolf no trouble to be cruel, and to put its fangs into the poor lamb or sheep? Because that is its nature. It has not to summon up its courage; the wolf-nature is there.

And how can I learn to love? Never until the Spirit of God fills my heart with God's love, and I begin to long for God's love in a very different sense from which I have sought it so selfishly, as a comfort and a joy and a happiness and a pleasure to myself; never until I begin to learn that "God is love," and to claim it, and receive it as an indwelling power for self-sacrifice; never until I begin to see that my glory, my blessedness, is to be like God and like Christ, in giving up everything in myself for my fellow-men. May God teach us that! Oh, the divine blessedness of the love with which the Holy Spirit can fill our hearts! "The fruit of the Spirit is love."

Love Is God's Gift

Once again I ask, Why must this be so? And my answer is: *Without this we cannot live the daily life of love.*

How often, when we speak about the consecrated life, we have to speak about *temper*, and some people have sometimes said:

"You make too much of temper."

I do not think we can make too much of it. Think for a moment of a clock and of what its hands mean. The hands tell me what is within the clock, and if I see that the hands stand still, or that the hands point wrong, or that the clock is slow or fast, I say that something inside the clock is not working properly. And temper is just like the revelation that the clock gives of what is within. Temper is a proof whether the love of Christ is filling the heart, or not. How many there are who find it easier in church, or in prayer-meeting, or in work for the Lord—diligent, earnest work—to be holy and happy than in the daily life with wife and children; easier to be holy and happy outside the home than in it! Where is the love of God? In Christ. God has prepared for us a wonderful redemption in Christ, and He longs to make something supernatural of us. Have we learned to long for it, and ask for it, and expect it in its fullness?

Then there is the *tongue!* We sometimes speak of the tongue when we talk of the better life, and the restful life, but just think what liberty many Christians give to their tongues. They say:

"I have a right to think what I like."

When they speak about each other, when they speak about their neighbors, when they speak about other Christians, how often there are sharp remarks! God keep me from saying anything that would be unloving; God shut my mouth if I am not to speak in tender love. But what I am saying is a fact. How often there are found among Christians who are banded together in work, sharp criticism, sharp judgment, hasty opinion, unloving words, secret contempt of each other, secret condemnation of each other! Oh, just as a mother's love covers her children and delights in them and has the tenderest compassion with their foibles or failures, so there ought to be in the heart of every believer a motherly love toward every brother and sister in Christ. Have you aimed at that? Have you sought it? Have you ever pleaded for it? Jesus Christ said: "As I have loved you . . . love one another" (John 13:34). And He did not put that among the other commandments, but He said in effect:

"That is a new commandment, the one commandment: Love one another as I have loved you" (John 13:34).

It is in our daily life and conduct that the fruit of the Spirit is love. From that there comes all the graces and virtues in which love is manifested: joy, peace, longsuffering, gentleness, goodness; no sharpness or hardness in your tone, no unkindness or selfishness; meekness before God and man. You see that all these are the gentler virtues. I have often thought as I read those words in Colossians,

"Put on therefore as the elect of God, holy and beloved, bowels of mercies, kindness, humbleness of mind, meekness, longsuffering" (Col. 3:12), that if we had written this, we should have put in the foreground the manly virtues, such as zeal, courage, and diligence; but we need to see how the gentler, the most womanly virtues are especially connected with dependence upon the Holy Spirit. These are indeed heavenly graces. They never were found in the heathen world. Christ was needed to come from Heaven to teach us. Your blessedness is longsuffering, meekness, kindness; your glory is humility before God. The fruit of the Spirit that He brought from Heaven out of the heart of the crucified Christ, and that He gives in our heart, is first and foremost—love.

You know what John says: "No man hath seen God at any time. If we love one another, God dwelleth in us" (1 John 4:12). That is, I cannot see God, but as a compensation I can see my brother, and if I love him, God dwells in me. Is that really true? That I cannot see God, but I must love my brother, and God will dwell in me? Loving my brother is the way to real fellowship with God. You know what John further says in that most solemn test, "If a man say, I love God, and hateth his brother, he is a liar; for he that loveth not his brother whom he hath seen, how can he love God whom he hath not seen?" (1 John 4:20). There is a brother, a most unlovable man. He worries you every time you meet him. He is of the very opposite disposition to yours. You are a careful businessman, and you have to do with him in your business. He is most untidy, unbusiness-like. You say:

"I cannot love him."

Oh, friend, you have not learned the lesson that Christ wanted to teach above everything. Let a man be what he will, you are to love him. Love is to be the fruit of the Spirit all the day and every day. Yes, listen! If a man loves not his brother whom he hath seen—if you don't love that unlovable man whom you have seen, how can you love God whom you have not seen? You can deceive yourself with beautiful thoughts about loving God. You must prove your love to God by your love to your brother; that is the one standard by which God will judge your love to Him. If the love of God is in your heart you will love your brother. The fruit of the Spirit is love.

And what is the reason that God's Holy Spirit cannot come in power? Is it not possible?

You remember the comparison I used in speaking of the vessel. I can dip a little water into a potsherd, a bit of a vessel; but if a vessel is to be full, it must be unbroken. And the children of God, wherever they come together, to whatever church or mission or society they belong, must love each other intensely, or the Spirit of God cannot do His work. We talk about grieving the Spirit of God by worldliness and ritualism and formality and error and indifference, but, I tell you, the one thing above everything that grieves God's Spirit is this lack of love. Let every heart search itself, and ask that God may search it.

Our Love Shows God's Power

Why are we taught that "the fruit of the Spirit is love"? *Because the Spirit of God has come to make our daily life an exhibition of divine power and a revelation of what God can do for His children.*

In the second and the fourth chapters of Acts we read that the disciples were of one heart and of one soul. During the three years they had walked with Christ they never had been in that spirit. All Christ's teaching could not make them of one heart and one soul. But the Holy Spirit came from Heaven and shed the love of God in their hearts, and they were of one heart and one soul. The same Holy Spirit that brought the love of Heaven into their hearts must fill us too. Nothing less will do. Even as Christ did, one might preach love for three years with the tongue of an angel, but that would not teach any man to love unless the power of the Holy Spirit should come upon him to bring the love of Heaven into his heart.

Think of the church at large. What divisions! Think of the different bodies. Take the question of holiness, take the question of the cleansing blood, take the question of the baptism of the Spirit— what differences are caused among dear believers by such questions! That there are differences of opinion does not trouble me. We do not have the same constitution and temperament and mind. But how often hate, bitterness, contempt, separation, unlovingness are caused by the holiest truths of God's Word! Our doctrines, our creeds, have been more important than love. We often think we are valiant for the truth and we forget God's command to speak the truth *in love*. And it was so in the time of the Reformation between the Lutheran and Calvinistic churches. What bitterness there was then in regard to the Holy Supper, which was meant to be the bond of union among all believers! And so, down the ages, the very dearest truths of God have become mountains that have separated us.

If we want to pray in power, and if we want to expect the Holy Spirit to come down in power, and if we want indeed that God shall pour out His Spirit, we must enter into a covenant with God that we love one another with a heavenly love.

Are you ready for that? Only that is true love that is large enough to take in all God's children, the most unloving and unlovable, and unworthy, and unbearable, and trying. If my vow—absolute surrender to God—was true, then it must mean absolute surrender to the divine love to fill me; to be a servant of love to love every child of God around me. "The fruit of the Spirit is love."

Oh, God did something wonderful when He gave Christ, at His right hand, the Holy Spirit to come down out of the heart of the Father and His everlasting love. And how we have degraded the Holy Spirit into a mere power by which we have to do our work! God forgive us! Oh, that the Holy Spirit might be held in honor as a power to fill us with the very life and nature of God and of Christ!

Christian Work Requires Love

"The fruit of the Spirit is love." I ask once again, Why is it so? And the answer comes: *That is the only power in which Christians really can do their work.*

Yes, it is that we need. We want not only love that is to bind us to each other, but we want a divine love in our work for the lost around us. Oh, do we not often undertake a great deal of work, just as men undertake work of philanthropy, from a natural spirit of compassion for our fellow-men? Do we not often undertake Christian work because our minister or friend calls us to it? And do we not often perform Christian work with a certain zeal but without having had a baptism of love?

People often ask: "What is the baptism of fire?"

I have answered more than once: I know no fire like the fire of God, the fire of everlasting love that consumed the sacrifice on Calvary. The baptism of love is what the Church needs, and to get that we must begin at once to get down upon our faces before God in confession, and plead:

> "Lord, let love from Heaven flow down into my heart. I am giving up my life to
> pray and live as one who has given himself up for the everlasting love to
> dwell in and fill him."

Ah, yes, if the love of God were in our hearts, what a difference it would make! There are hundreds of believers who say:

> "I work for Christ, and I feel I could work much harder, but I have not the gift. I do
> not know how or where to begin. I do not know what I can do."

Brother, sister, ask God to baptize you with the Spirit of love, and love will find its way. Love is a fire that will burn through every difficulty. You may be a shy, hesitating man, who cannot speak well, but love can burn through everything. God fill us with love! We need it for our work.

You have read many a touching story of love expressed, and you have said, How beautiful! I heard one not long ago. A lady had been asked to speak at a Rescue Home where there were a number of poor women. As she arrived there and got to the window with the matron, she saw outside a wretched object sitting, and asked: "Who is that?"

The matron answered: "She has been into the house thirty or forty times, and she has always gone away again. Nothing can be done with her, she is so low and hard."

But the lady said: "She must come in."

The matron then said: "We have been waiting for you, and the company is assembled, and you have only an hour for the address."

The lady replied: "No, this is of more importance"; and she went outside where the woman was sitting and said: "My sister, what is the matter?"

"I am not your sister," was the reply.

Then the lady laid her hand on her, and said: "Yes, I am your sister, and I love you"; and so she spoke until the heart of the poor woman was touched.

The conversation lasted some time, and the company were waiting patiently. Ultimately the lady brought the woman into the room. There was the poor wretched, degraded creature, full of shame. She would not sit on a chair, but sat down on a stool beside the speaker's seat, and she let her lean against her, with her arms around the poor woman's neck, while she spoke to the assembled people. And that love touched the woman's heart; she had found one who really loved her, and that love gave access to the love of Jesus.

Praise God! there is love upon earth in the hearts of God's children; but oh, that there were more!

O God, baptize our ministers with a tender love, and our missionaries, and our Bible-readers, and our workers, and our young men's and young women's associations. Oh, that God would begin with us now, and baptize us with heavenly love!

Love Inspires Intercession

Once again. *It is only love that can fit us for the work of intercession.*

I have said that love must fit us for our work. Do you know what the hardest and the most important work is that has to be done for this sinful world? It is the work of intercession, the work of going to God and taking time to lay hold on Him.

A man may be an earnest Christian, an earnest minister, and a man may do good, but alas! how often he has to confess that he knows but little of what it is to tarry with God. May God give us the great gift of an intercessory spirit, a spirit of prayer and supplication! Let me ask you in the name of Jesus not to let a day pass without praying for all saints, and for all God's people.

I find there are Christians who think little of that. I find there are prayer unions where they pray for the members, and not for all believers. I pray you, take time to pray for the Church of Christ. It is right to pray for the heathen, as I have already said. God help us to pray more for them. It is right to pray for missionaries and for evangelistic work, and for the unconverted. But Paul did not tell people to pray for the heathen or the unconverted. Paul told them to pray for believers. Do make this your first prayer every day: "Lord, bless Thy saints everywhere."

The state of Christ's Church is indescribably low. Plead for God's people that He would visit them, plead for each other, plead for all believers who are trying to work for God. Let love fill your heart. Ask Christ to pour it out afresh into you every day. Try to get it into you by the Holy Spirit of God: I am separated unto the Holy Spirit, and the fruit of the Spirit is love. God help us to understand it.

May God grant that we learn day by day to wait more quietly upon Him. Do not wait upon God only for ourselves, or the power to do so will soon be lost; but give ourselves up to the ministry and the love of intercession, and pray more for God's people, for God's people round about us, for the Spirit of love in ourselves and in them, and for the work of God we are connected with; and the answer will surely come, and our waiting upon God will be a source of untold blessing and power. "The fruit of the Spirit is love."

Have you a lack of love to confess before God? Then make confession and say before Him, "O Lord, my lack of heart, my lack of love—I confess it." And then, as you cast that lack at His feet, believe that the blood cleanses you, that Jesus comes in His mighty, cleansing, saving power to deliver you, and that He will give His Holy Spirit.

"The fruit of the Spirit is love."

Separated unto the Holy Spirit

"Now there were in the church that was at Antioch certain prophets and teachers; as Barnabas, and Simeon that was called Niger, and Lucius of Cyrene, and Manaen . . . and Saul.

"As they ministered to the Lord, and fasted, the Holy Spirit said, Separate me Barnabas and Saul for the work whereunto I have called them.

"And when they had fasted and prayed, and laid their hands on them, they sent them away. So they, being sent forth by the Holy Spirit, departed unto Seleucia" (Acts 13:1-4).

In the story of our text we shall find some precious thoughts to guide us as to what God would have of us, and what God would do for us. The great lesson of the verses quoted is this: *The Holy Spirit is the director of the work of God upon the earth.* And what we should do if we are to work rightly for God, and if God is to bless our work, is to see that we stand in a right relation to the Holy Spirit, that we give Him every day the place of honor that belongs to Him, and that in all our work and (what is more) in all our private inner life, the Holy Spirit shall always have the first place. Let me point out to you some of the precious thoughts our passage suggests.

First of all, we see that *God has His own plans with regard to His kingdom.*

His church at Antioch had been established. God had certain plans and intentions with regard to Asia, and with regard to Europe. He had conceived them; they were His, and He made them known to His servants.

Our great Commander organizes every campaign, and His generals and officers do not always know the great plans. They often receive sealed orders, and they have to wait on Him for what He gives them as orders. God in Heaven has wishes, and a will, in regard to any work that ought to be done, and to the way in which it has to be done. Blessed is the man who gets into God's secrets and works under God.

Some years ago, at Wellington, South Africa, where I live, we opened a Mission Institute—what is counted there a fine large building. At our opening services the principal said something that I have never forgotten. He remarked:

"Last year we gathered here to lay the foundation-stone, and what was there then to be seen? Nothing but rubbish, and stones, and bricks, and ruins of an old building that had been pulled down. There we laid the foundation-stone, and very few knew what the building was that was to rise. No one knew it perfectly in every detail except one man, the architect. In his mind it was all clear, and as the contractor and the mason and the carpenter came to their work they took their orders from him, and the humblest laborer had to be obedient to orders, and the structure rose, and this beautiful building has been completed. And just so," he added, "this building that we open today is but laying the foundation of a work of which only God knows what is to become."

But God has His workers and His plans clearly mapped out, and our position is to wait, that God should communicate to us as much of His will as each time is needful.

We have simply to be faithful in obedience, carrying out His orders. God has a plan for His Church upon earth. But alas! we too often make our plan, and we think that we know what ought to be done. We ask God first to bless our feeble efforts, instead of absolutely refusing to go unless God goes before us. God has planned for the work and the extension of His kingdom. The Holy Spirit has had that work given in charge to Him. "The work whereunto I have called them." May God, therefore, help us all to be afraid of touching "the ark of God" except as we are led by the Holy Spirit.

Then the *second* thought—*God is willing and able to reveal to His servants what His will is.*

Yes, blessed be God, communications still come down from Heaven! As we read here what the Holy Spirit said, so the Holy Spirit will still speak to His Church and His people. In these later days He has often done it. He has come to individual men, and by His divine teaching He has led them out into fields of labor that others could not at first understand or approve, into ways and methods that did not recommend themselves to the majority. But the Holy Spirit does still in our time teach His people. Thank God, in our foreign missionary societies and in our home missions, and in a thousand forms of work, the guiding of the Holy Spirit is known, but (we are all ready, I think, to confess) *too little* known. We have not learned enough to wait upon Him, and so we should make a solemn declaration before God: O God, we want to wait more for Thee to show us Thy Will.

Do not ask God only for power. Many a Christian has his own plan of working, but God must send the power. The man works in his own will, and God must give the grace—the one reason why God often gives so little grace and so little success. But let us all take our place before God and say:

"What is done in the will of God, the strength of God will not be withheld from it;
what is done in the will of God must have the mighty blessing of God."
And so let our first desire be to have the will of God revealed.

If you ask me, Is it an easy thing to get these communications from Heaven, and to understand them? I can give you the answer. It is easy to those who are in right fellowship with Heaven, and who understand the art of waiting upon God in prayer.

How often we ask: How can a person know the will of God? And people want, when they are in perplexity, to pray very earnestly that God should answer them at once. But God can only reveal His will to a heart that is humble and tender and empty. God can only reveal His will in perplexities and special difficulties to a heart that has learned to obey and honor Him loyally in little things and in daily life.

That brings me to the *third* thought—*Note the disposition to which the Spirit reveals God's will.*

What do we read here? There were a number of men ministering to the Lord and fasting, and the Holy Spirit came and spoke to them. Some people understand this passage very much as they would in reference to a missionary committee of our day. We see there is an open field, and we have had our missions in other fields, and we are going to get on to that field. We have virtually settled that, and we pray about it. But the position was a very different one in those former days. I doubt whether any of them thought of Europe, for later on even Paul himself tried to go back into Asia, till the night vision called him by the will of God. Look at those men. God had done wonders. He had extended the Church to Antioch, and He had given rich and large blessing. Now, here were these men ministering to the Lord, serving Him with prayer and fasting. What a deep conviction they have—"It must all come direct from Heaven. We are in fellowship with the risen Lord; we must have a close union with Him, and somehow He will let us know what He wants." And there they were, empty, ignorant, helpless, glad and joyful, but deeply humbled.

"O Lord," they seem to say, "we are Thy servants, and in fasting and prayer we wait upon Thee. What is Thy will for us?"

Was it not the same with Peter? He was on the housetop, fasting and praying, and little did he think of the vision and the command to go to Caesarea. He was ignorant of what his work might be.

It is in hearts entirely surrendered to the Lord Jesus, in hearts separating themselves from the world, and even from ordinary religious exercises, and giving themselves up in intense prayer to look to their Lord—it is in such hearts that the heavenly will of God will be made manifest.

You know that word *fasting* occurs a second time (in the third verse): "They fasted and prayed." When you pray, you love to go into your closet, according to the command of Jesus, and shut the door. You shut out business and company and pleasure and anything that can distract, and you want to be alone with God. But in one way even the material world follows you there. You must eat. These men wanted to shut themselves out from the influences of the material and the visible, and they fasted. What they ate was simply enough to supply the wants of nature, and in the intensity of their souls they thought to give expression to their letting go of everything on earth in their fasting before God. Oh, may God give us that intensity of desire, that separation from everything, because we want to wait upon God, that the Holy Spirit may reveal to us God's blessed will.

The *fourth* thought—*What is now the will of God as the Holy Spirit reveals it?* It is contained in one phrase: *Separation unto the Holy Spirit.* That is the <u>keynote of the message from Heaven.</u>

"Separate me Barnabas and Saul for the work whereunto I have called them. The work is mine, and I care for it, and I have chosen these men and called them, and I want you who represent the Church of Christ upon earth to set them apart unto me."

Look at this heavenly message in its twofold aspect. The men were to be *set apart* to the Holy Spirit, and *the Church was to do this separating work.* The Holy Spirit could trust these men to do it in a right spirit. There they were abiding in fellowship with the heavenly, and the Holy Spirit could say to them, "Do the work of separating these men." And these were the men the Holy Spirit had prepared, and He could say of them, "Let them be separated unto me."

Here we come to the very root, to the very life of the need of Christian workers. The question is: What is needed that the power of God should rest upon us more mightily, that the blessing of God should be poured out more abundantly among those poor, wretched people and perishing sinners among whom we labor? And the answer from Heaven is:

"I want men separated unto the Holy Spirit."

What does that imply? You know that there are two spirits on earth. Christ said, when He spoke about the Holy Spirit: "The world cannot receive him" (John 14:17). Paul said: "We have received not the spirit of the world, but the Spirit that is of God" (1 Cor. 2:12). That is the great want in every worker—the spirit of the world going out, and the Spirit of God coming in to take possession of the inner life and of the whole being.

I am sure there are workers who often cry to God for the Holy Spirit to come upon them as a Spirit of power for their work, and when they feel that measure of power, and get blessing, they thank God for it. But God wants something more and something higher. God wants us to seek for the Holy Spirit as a Spirit of power in our own heart and life, to conquer self and cast out sin, and to work the blessed and beautiful image of Jesus into us.

There is a difference between the power of the Spirit as a gift, and the power of the Spirit for the grace of a holy life. A man may often have a measure of the power of the Spirit, but if there is not a large measure of the Spirit as the Spirit of grace and holiness, the defect will be manifest in his work. He may be made the means of conversion, but he never will help people on to a higher standard of spiritual life, and when he passes away, a great deal of his work may pass away too. But a man who is separated unto the Holy Spirit is a man who is given up to say:

"Father, let the Holy Spirit have full dominion over me, in my home, in my temper,
in every word of my tongue, in every thought of my heart, in every feeling
toward my fellow men; let the Holy Spirit have entire possession."

Is that what has been the longing and the covenant of your heart with your God—to be a man or a woman separated and given up unto the Holy Spirit? I pray you listen to the voice of Heaven. "Separate me," said the Holy Spirit. Yes, *separated* unto the Holy Spirit. May God grant that the Word may enter into the very depths of our being to search us, and if we discover that we have not come out from the world entirely, if God reveals to us that the self-life, self-will, self-exaltation are there, let us humble ourselves before Him.

Man, woman, brother, sister, you are a worker separated unto the Holy Spirit. Is that true? Has that been your longing desire? Has that been your surrender? Has that been what you have expected through faith in the power of our risen and almighty Lord Jesus? If not, here is the call of faith, and here is the key of blessing—*separated unto the Holy Spirit*. God write the word in our hearts!

I said the Holy Spirit spoke to that church as a church capable of doing that work. The Holy Spirit trusted them. God grant that our churches, our missionary societies, and our workers' unions, that all our directors and councils and committees may be men and women who are *fit for the work of separating workers unto the Holy Spirit.* We can ask God for that too.

Then comes my *fifth* thought, and it is this—*This holy partnership with the Holy Spirit in this work becomes a matter of consciousness and of action.*

These men, what did they do? They set apart Paul and Barnabas, and then it is written of the two that they, being sent forth by the Holy Spirit, went down to Seleucia. Oh, what fellowship! The Holy Spirit in Heaven doing part of the work, men on earth doing the other part. After the ordination of the men upon earth, it is written in God's inspired Word that they were sent forth by the Holy Spirit.

And see how this partnership calls to new prayer and fasting. They had for a certain time been ministering to the Lord and fasting, perhaps days; and the Holy Spirit speaks, and they have to do the work and to enter into partnership, and at once they come together for more prayer and fasting. That is the spirit in which they obey the command of their Lord. And that teaches us that it is not only in the beginning of our Christian work, but all along that we need to have our strength in prayer. If there is one thought with regard to the Church of Christ, which at times comes to me with overwhelming sorrow; if there is one thought in regard to my own life of which I am ashamed; if there is one thought of which I feel that the Church of Christ has not accepted it and not grasped it; if there is one thought which makes me pray to God: "Oh, teach us by Thy grace, new things"—it is the *wonderful power that prayer is meant to have in the kingdom*. We have so little availed ourselves of it.

We have all read the expression of Christian in Bunyan's great work, when he found he had the key in his breast that should unlock the dungeon. We have the key that can unlock the dungeon of atheism and of heathendom. But, oh! we are far more occupied with our work than we are with prayer. We believe more in speaking to men than we believe in speaking to God. Learn from these men that the work which the Holy Spirit commands must call us to new fasting and prayer, to new separation from the spirit and the pleasures of the world, to new consecration to God and to His fellowship. Those men gave themselves up to fasting and prayer, and if in all our ordinary Christian work there were more prayer, there would be more blessing in our own inner life. If we felt and proved and testified to the world that our only strength lay in keeping every minute in contact with Christ, every minute allowing God to work in us—if that were our spirit, would not, by the grace of God, our lives be holier? Would not they be more abundantly fruitful?

I hardly know a more solemn warning in God's Word than that which we find in the third chapter of Galatians, where Paul asked:

"Having begun in the Spirit, are ye now made perfect by the flesh?" (Gal. 3:3).

Do you understand what that means? A terrible danger in Christian work, just as in a Christian life that is begun with much prayer, begun in the Holy Spirit, is that it may be gradually shunted off on to the lines of the flesh; and the word comes: "Having begun in the Spirit, are ye now made perfect by the flesh?" In the time of our first perplexity and helplessness we prayed much to God, and God answered and God blessed, and our organization became perfected, and our band of workers became large; but gradually the organization and the work and the rush have so taken possession of us that the power of the Spirit, in which we began when we were a small company, has almost been lost. Oh, I pray you, note it well! It was with new prayer and fasting, with more prayer and fasting, that this company of disciples carried out the command of the Holy Spirit, "My soul, wait thou only upon God." That is our highest and most important work. The Holy Spirit comes in answer to believing prayer.

You know when the exalted Jesus had ascended to the throne, for ten days the footstool of the throne was the place where His waiting disciples cried to Him. And that is the law of the kingdom— the King upon the throne, the servants upon the footstool. May God find us there unceasingly!

Then comes the *last* thought—*What a wonderful blessing comes when the Holy Spirit is allowed to lead and to direct the work, and when it is carried on in obedience to Him!*

You know the story of the mission on which Barnabas and Saul were sent out. You know what power there was with them. The Holy Spirit sent them, and they went on from place to place with large blessing. The Holy Spirit was their leader further on. You recollect how it was by the Spirit that Paul was hindered from going again into Asia, and was led away over to Europe. Oh, the blessing that rested upon that little company of men, and upon their ministry unto the Lord!

I pray you, let us learn to believe that God has a blessing for us. The Holy Spirit, into whose hands God has put the work, has been called "the executive of the Holy Trinity." The Holy Spirit has not only power, but He has the Spirit of love. He is brooding over this dark world and every sphere of work in it, and He is willing to bless. And why is there not more blessing? There can be but one answer. We have not honored the Holy Spirit as we should have done. Is there one who can say that that is not true? Is not every thoughtful heart ready to cry: "God forgive me that I have not honored the Holy Spirit as I should have done, that I have grieved Him, that I have allowed self and the flesh and my own will to work where the Holy Spirit should have been honored! May God forgive me that I have allowed self and the flesh and the will actually to have the place that God wanted the Holy Spirit to have."

Oh, the sin is greater than we know! No wonder that there is so much feebleness and failure in the Church of Christ!

Peter's Repentance

"And the Lord turned, and looked upon Peter. And Peter remembered the word of the Lord, how he had said unto him, Before the cock crow, thou shalt deny me thrice. And Peter went out, and wept bitterly" (Luke 22:61, 62).

That was the turning-point in the history of Peter. Christ had said to him: "Thou canst not follow me now" (John 13:36). Peter was not in a fit state to follow Christ, because he had not been brought to an end of himself; he did not know himself, and he therefore could not follow Christ. But when he went out and wept bitterly, then came the great change. Christ previously said to him: "When thou art converted, strengthen thy brethren." Here is the point where Peter was converted from self to Christ.

I thank God for the story of Peter. I do not know a man in the Bible who gives us greater comfort. When we look at his character, so full of failures, and at what Christ made him by the power of the Holy Spirit, there is hope for every one of us. But remember, before Christ could fill Peter with the Holy Spirit and make a new man of him, he had to go out and weep bitterly; he had to be humbled. If we want to understand this, I think there are four points that we must look at. First, let us look at *Peter the devoted disciple of Jesus*; next, at *Peter as he lived the life of self*; then at *Peter in his repentance*; and last, at *what Christ made of Peter by the Holy Spirit.*

Peter the Devoted Disciple of Christ

Christ called Peter to forsake his nets, and follow Him. Peter did it at once, and he afterward could say rightly to the Lord:

"We have forsaken all and followed thee" (Matt. 19:27).

Peter was a man of *absolute surrender*; he gave up all to follow Jesus. Peter was also a man of *ready obedience*. You remember Christ said to him, "Launch out into the deep, and let down the net." Peter the fisherman knew there were no fish there, for they had been toiling all night and had caught nothing; but he said: "At thy word I will let down the net" (Luke 5:4, 5). He submitted to the word of Jesus. Further, he was a man of *great faith.* When he saw Christ walking on the sea, he said: "Lord, if it be thou, bid me come unto thee" (Matt. 14:28); and at the voice of Christ he stepped out of the boat and walked upon the water.

And Peter was a man of *spiritual insight.* When Christ asked the disciples: "Whom do ye say that I am?" Peter was able to answer: "Thou art the Christ, the Son of the living God." And Christ said: "Blessed art thou, Simon Barjona; for flesh and blood hath not revealed it unto thee, but my Father which is in heaven." And Christ spoke of him as the *rock* man, and of his having the keys of the kingdom. Peter was a splendid man, a devoted disciple of Jesus, and if he were living nowadays, everyone would say that he was an advanced Christian. And yet how much there was wanting in Peter!

Peter Living the Life of Self

You recollect that just after Christ had said to him: "Flesh and blood hath not revealed it unto thee, but my Father which is in heaven," Christ began to speak about His sufferings, and Peter dared to say: "Be it far from thee, Lord; this shall not be unto thee." Then Christ had to say:

"Get thee behind me, Satan; for thou savorest not the things that be of God, but those that be of men" (Matt. 16:22-23).

There was Peter in his self-will, trusting his own wisdom, and actually forbidding Christ to go and die. Whence did that come? Peter trusted in himself and his own thoughts about divine things. We see later on, more than once, that among the disciples there was a questioning who should be the greatest, and Peter was one of them, and he thought he had a right to the very first place. He sought his own honor even above the others. It was the life of self strong in Peter. He had left his boats and his nets, but not his old self.

When Christ had spoken to him about His sufferings, and said: "Get thee behind me, Satan," He followed it up by saying: "If any man will come after me, let him deny himself, and take up his cross, and follow me" (Matt. 16:24). No man can follow Him unless he do that. Self must be utterly denied. What does that mean? When Peter denied Christ, we read that he said three times: "I do not know the man"; in other words: "I have nothing to do with Him; He and I are no friends; I deny having any connection with Him." Christ told Peter that he must deny self. Self must be ignored, and its every claim rejected. That is the root of true discipleship; but Peter did not understand it, and could not obey it. And what happened? When the last night came, Christ said to him:

"Before the cock crow twice thou shalt deny me thrice."

But with what self-confidence Peter said:

"Though all should forsake thee, yet will not I. I am ready to go with thee, to prison and to death" (Mark 14:29; Luke 22:33).

Peter meant it honestly, and Peter really intended to do it; but Peter did not know himself. He did not believe he was as bad as Jesus said he was.

We perhaps think of individual sins that come between us and God, but what are we to do with that self-life which is all unclean—our very nature? What are we to do with that flesh that is entirely under the power of sin? Deliverance from that is what we need. Peter knew it not, and therefore it was that in his self-confidence he went forth and denied his Lord.

Notice how Christ uses that word *deny* twice. He said to Peter the first time, *"Deny self"*; He said to Peter the second time, *"Thou wilt deny me."* It is either of the two. There is no choice for us; we must either deny self or deny Christ. There are two great powers fighting each other—the self-nature in the power of sin, and Christ in the power of God. Either of these must rule within us.

It was self that made the Devil. He was an angel of God, but he wanted to exalt self. He became a Devil in hell. Self was the cause of the fall of man. Eve wanted something for herself, and so our first parents fell into all the wretchedness of sin. We their children have inherited an awful nature of sin.

Peter's Repentance

Peter denied his Lord thrice, and then the Lord looked upon him; and that look of Jesus broke the heart of Peter, and all at once there opened up before him the terrible sin that he had committed, the terrible failure that had come, and the depth into which he had fallen, and "Peter went out and wept bitterly."

Oh! who can tell what that repentance must have been? During the following hours of that night, and the next day, when he saw Christ crucified and buried, and the next day, the Sabbath—oh, in what hopeless despair and shame he must have spent that day!

"My Lord is gone, my hope is gone, and I denied my Lord. After that life of love, after that blessed fellowship of three years, I denied my Lord. God have mercy upon me!"

I do not think we can realize into what a depth of humiliation Peter sank then. But that was the turning point and the change; and on the first day of the week Christ was seen of Peter, and in the evening He met him with the others. Later on at the Lake of Galilee He asked him: "Lovest thou me?" until Peter was made sad by the thought that the Lord reminded him of having denied Him thrice; and said in sorrow, but in uprightness:

"Lord, thou knowest all things; thou knowest that I love thee" (John 21:17).

Peter Transformed

Now Peter was prepared for deliverance from self, and that is my last thought. You know Christ took him with others to the footstool of the throne, and bade them wait there; and then on the day of Pentecost the Holy Spirit came, and Peter was a changed man. I do not want you to think only of the change in Peter, in that boldness, and that power, and that insight into the Scriptures, and that blessing with which he preached that day. Thank God for that. But there was something for Peter deeper and better. Peter's whole nature was changed. The work that Christ began in Peter when He looked upon him, was perfected when he was filled with the Holy Spirit.

If you want to see that, read the First Epistle of Peter. You know wherein Peter's failings lay. When he said to Christ, in effect: "Thou never canst suffer; it cannot be"—it showed he had not a conception of what it was to pass through death into life. Christ said: *"Deny thyself,"* and in spite of that he denied his Lord. When Christ warned him: "Thou shalt deny me," and he insisted that he never would, Peter showed how little he understood what there was in himself. But when I read his epistle and hear him say: "If ye be reproached for the name of Christ, happy are ye, for the Spirit of God and of glory resteth upon you" (1 Pet. 4:14), then I say that it is not the old Peter, but that is the very Spirit of Christ breathing and speaking within him.

I read again how he says: "Hereunto ye are called, to suffer, even as Christ suffered" (1 Pet. 2:21). I understand what a change had come over Peter. Instead of denying Christ, he found joy and pleasure in having self denied and crucified and given up to the death. And therefore it is in the Acts we read that, when he was called before the Council, he could boldly say: "We must obey God rather than men" (Acts 5:29), and that he could return with the other disciples and rejoice that they were counted worthy to suffer for Christ's name.

You remember his self-exaltation; but now he has found out that "the ornament of a meek and quiet spirit is in the sight of God of great price." Again he tells us to be "subject one to another, and be clothed with humility" (1 Pet. 5:5).

Dear friend, I beseech you, look at Peter utterly changed—the self-pleasing, the self-trusting, the self-seeking Peter, full of sin, continually getting into trouble, foolish and impetuous, but now filled with the Spirit and the life of Jesus. Christ had done it for him by the Holy Spirit.

And now, what is my object in having thus very briefly pointed to the story of Peter? That story must be the history of every believer who is really to be made a blessing by God. That story is a prophecy of what everyone can receive from God in Heaven.

Now let us just glance hurriedly at what these lessons teach us.

The *first lesson* is this—You may be a very earnest, godly, devoted believer, in whom the power of the flesh is yet very strong.

That is a very solemn truth. Peter, before he denied Christ, had cast out devils and had healed the sick; and yet the flesh had power, and the flesh had room in him. Oh, beloved, we have to realize that it is just because there is so much of that self-life in us that the power of God cannot work in us as mightily as God is willing that it should work. Do you realize that the great God is longing to double His blessing, to give tenfold blessing through us? But there is something hindering Him, and that something is a proof of nothing but the self-life. We talk about the pride of Peter, and the impetuosity of Peter, and the self-confidence of Peter. It all rooted in that one word, *self.* Christ had said, "Deny self," and Peter had never understood, and never obeyed; and every failing came out of that.

What a solemn thought, and what an urgent plea for us to cry: O God, do reveal this to us, that none of us may be living the self-life! It has happened to many a one who had been a Christian for years, who had perhaps occupied a prominent position, that God found him out and taught him to find himself out, and he became utterly ashamed, falling down broken before God. Oh, the bitter shame and sorrow and pain and agony that came to him, until at last he found that there was deliverance! Peter went out and wept bitterly, and there may be many a godly one in whom the power of the flesh still rules.

And then my *second lesson* is—It is the work of our blessed Lord Jesus to reveal the power of self.

How was it that Peter, the carnal Peter, self-willed Peter, Peter with the strong self-love, ever became a man of Pentecost and the writer of his epistles? It was because Christ had him in charge, and Christ watched over him, and Christ taught and blessed him. The warnings that Christ had given him were part of the training; and last of all there came that look of love. In His suffering Christ did not forget him, but turned round and looked upon him, and "Peter went out and wept bitterly." And the Christ who led Peter to Pentecost is waiting today to take charge of every heart that is willing to surrender itself to Him.

Are there not some saying: "Ah! that is the mischief with me; it is always the self-life, and self-comfort, and self-consciousness, and self-pleasing, and self-will; how am I to get rid of it?"

My answer is: It is Christ Jesus who can rid you of it; none else but Christ Jesus can give deliverance from the power of self. And what does He ask you to do? He asks that you should humble yourself before Him.

Impossible with Man, Possible with God

"And he said, The things which are impossible with men are possible with God" (Luke 18:27).

Christ had said to the rich young ruler, "Sell all that thou hast . . . and come, follow me." The young man went away sorrowful. Christ then turned to the disciples, and said: "How hardly shall they that have riches enter into the kingdom of God!" The disciples, we read, were greatly astonished, and answered: "If it is so difficult to enter the kingdom, who, then, can be saved?" And Christ gave this blessed answer:

"The things which are impossible with men are possible with God."

The text contains two thoughts—that *in religion, in the question of salvation and of following Christ by a holy life, it is impossible for man to do it.* And then alongside that is the thought—*What is impossible with man is possible with God.*

The two thoughts mark the two great lessons that man has to learn in the religious life. It often takes a long time to learn the first lesson, that in religion man can do nothing, that salvation is impossible to man. And often a man learns that, and yet he does not learn the second lesson—what has been impossible to him is possible with God. Blessed is the man who learns both lessons! The learning of them marks stages in the Christian's life.

Man Cannot

The one stage is when a man is trying to do his utmost and fails, when a man tries to do better and fails again, when a man tries much more and always fails. And yet very often he does not even then learn the lesson: *With man it is impossible to serve God and Christ.* Peter spent three years in Christ's school, and he never learned that, *It is impossible,* until he had denied his Lord and went out and wept bitterly. Then he learned it.

Just look for a moment at a man who is learning this lesson. At first he fights against it; then he submits to it, but reluctantly and in despair; at last he accepts it willingly and rejoices in it. At the beginning of the Christian life the young convert has no conception of this truth. He has been converted, he has the joy of the Lord in his heart, he begins to run the race and fight the battle; he is sure he can conquer, for he is earnest and honest, and God will help him. Yet, somehow, very soon he fails where he did not expect it, and sin gets the better of him. He is disappointed; but he thinks: "I was not watchful enough, I did not make my resolutions strong enough." And again he vows, and again he prays, and yet he fails. He thought: "Am I not a regenerate man? Have I not the life of God within me?" And he thinks again: "Yes, and I have Christ to help me, I can live the holy life."

At a later period he comes to another state of mind. He begins to see such a life is impossible, but he does not accept it. There are multitudes of Christians who come to this point: "I cannot"; and then think God never expected them to do what they cannot do. If you tell them that God does expect it, it appears to them a mystery. A good many Christians are living a low life, a life of failure and of sin, instead of rest and victory, because they began to see: "I cannot, it is impossible." And yet they do not understand it fully, and so, under the impression, I cannot, they give way to despair. They will do their best, but they never expect to get on very far.

But God leads His children on to a third stage, when a man comes to take that, *It is impossible,* in its full truth, and yet at the same time says: "I must do it, and I will do it—it is impossible for man, and yet I must do it"; when the renewed will begins to exercise its whole power, and in intense longing and prayer begins to cry to God: "Lord, what is the meaning of this?—how am I to be freed from the power of sin?"

It is the state of the regenerate man in Romans 7. There you will find the Christian man trying his very utmost to live a holy life. God's law has been revealed to him as reaching down into the very depth of the desires of the heart, and the man can dare to say:

"I delight in the law of God after the inward man. To will what is good is present with me. My heart loves the law of God, and my will has chosen that law."

Can a man like that fail, with his heart full of delight in God's law and with his will determined to do what is right? Yes. That is what Romans 7 teaches us. There is something more needed. Not only must I delight in the law of God after the inward man, and will what God wills, but I need a divine omnipotence to work it in me. And that is what the apostle Paul teaches in Philippians 2:13:

"It is God which worketh in you, both to will and to do."

Note the contrast. In Romans 7, the regenerate man says: "To will is present with me, but to do—I find I cannot do. I will, but I cannot perform." But in Philippians 2, you have a man who has been led on farther, a man who understands that when God has worked the renewed will, God will give the power to accomplish what that will desires. Let us receive this as the first great lesson in the spiritual life: "It is impossible for me, my God; let there be an end of the flesh and all its powers, an end of self, and let it be my glory to be helpless."

Praise God for the divine teaching that makes us helpless!

When you thought of absolute surrender to God were you not brought to an end of yourself, and to feel that you could see how you actually could live as a man absolutely surrendered to God every moment of the day—at your table, in your house, in your business, in the midst of trials and temptations? I pray you learn the lesson now. If you felt you could not do it, you are on the right road, if you let yourselves be led. Accept that position, and maintain it before God: "My heart's desire and delight, O God, is absolute surrender, but I cannot perform it. It is impossible for me to live that life. It is beyond me." Fall down and learn that when you are utterly helpless, God will come to work in you not only to will, but also to do.

God Can

Now comes the second lesson. "The things which *are impossible with men are possible with God.*"

I said a little while ago that there is many a man who has learned the lesson, *It is impossible with men,* and then he gives up in helpless despair, and lives a wretched Christian life, without joy, or strength, or victory. And why? Because he does not humble himself to learn that other lesson: *With God all things are possible.*

Your religious life is every day to be a proof that God works impossibilities; your religious life is to be a series of impossibilities made possible and actual by God's almighty power. That is what the Christian needs. He has an almighty God that he worships, and he must learn to understand that he does not need a little of God's power, but he needs—with reverence be it said—the whole of God's omnipotence to keep him right, and to live like a Christian.

The whole of Christianity is a work of God's omnipotence. Look at the birth of Christ Jesus. That was a miracle of divine power, and it was said to Mary: "With God nothing shall be impossible." It was the omnipotence of God. Look at Christ's resurrection. We are taught that it was according to the exceeding greatness of His mighty power that God raised Christ from the dead.

Every tree must grow on the root from which it springs. An oak tree three hundred years old grows all the time on the one root from which it had its beginning. Christianity had its beginning in the omnipotence of God, and in every soul it must have its continuance in that omnipotence. All the possibilities of the higher Christian life have their origin in a new apprehension of Christ's power to work all God's will in us.

I want to call upon you now to come and worship an almighty God. Have you learned to do it? Have you learned to deal so closely with an almighty God that you know omnipotence is working in you? In outward appearance there is often so little sign of it. The apostle Paul said: "I was with you in weakness and in fear and in much trembling, and . . . my preaching was . . . in demonstration of the Spirit and of power." From the human side there was feebleness, from the divine side there was divine omnipotence. And that is true of every godly life; and if we would only learn that lesson better, and give a wholehearted, undivided surrender to it, we should learn what blessedness there is in dwelling every hour and every moment with an almighty God. Have you ever studied in the Bible the attribute of God's omnipotence? You know that it was God's omnipotence that created the world, and created light out of darkness, and created man. But have you studied God's omnipotence in the works of redemption?

Look at Abraham. When God called him to be the father of that people out of which Christ was to be born, God said to him: "I am God Almighty, walk before me and be thou perfect." And God trained Abraham to trust Him as the omnipotent One; and whether it was his going out to a land that he knew not, or his faith as a pilgrim midst the thousands of Canaanites—his faith said: This is my land—or whether it was his faith in waiting twenty-five years for a son in his old age, against all hope, or whether it was the raising up of Isaac from the dead on Mount Moriah when he was going to sacrifice him—Abraham believed God. He was strong in faith, giving glory to God, because he accounted Him who had promised able to perform.

The cause of the weakness of your Christian life is that you want to work it out partly, and to let God help you. And that cannot be. You must come to be utterly helpless, to let God work, and God will work gloriously. It is this that we need if we are indeed to be workers for God. I could go through Scripture and prove to you how Moses, when he led Israel out of Egypt; how Joshua, when he brought them into the land of Canaan; how all God's servants in the Old Testament counted upon the omnipotence of God doing impossibilities. And this God lives today, and this God is the God of every child of His. And yet we are some of us wanting God to give us a little help while we do our best, instead of coming to understand what God wants, and to say: "I can do nothing. God must and will do all." Have you said: "In worship, in work, in sanctification, in obedience to God, I can do nothing of myself, and so my place is to worship the omnipotent God, and to believe that He will work in me every moment"? Oh, may God teach us this! Oh, that God would by His grace show you what a God you have, and to what a God you have entrusted yourself—an omnipotent God, willing with His whole omnipotence to place Himself at the disposal of every child of His! Shall we not take the lesson of the Lord Jesus and say: "Amen; the things which are impossible with men are possible with God"?

Remember what we have said about Peter, his self-confidence, self-power, self-will, and how he came to deny his Lord. You feel, "Ah! there is the self-life, there is the flesh-life that rules in me!" And now, have you believed that there is deliverance from that? Have you believed that Almighty God is able so to reveal Christ in your heart, so to let the Holy Spirit rule in you, that the self-life shall not have power or dominion over you? Have you coupled the two together, and with tears of penitence and with deep humiliation and feebleness, cried out: "O God, it is impossible to me; man cannot do it, but, glory to Thy name, it is possible with God"? Have you claimed deliverance? Do it now. Put yourself afresh in absolute surrender into the hands of a God of infinite love; and as infinite as His love is His power to do it.

God Works in Man

But again, we came to the question of absolute surrender, and felt that that is the want in the Church of Christ, and that is why the Holy Spirit cannot fill us, and why we cannot live as people entirely separated unto the Holy Spirit; that is why the flesh and the self-life cannot be conquered. We have never understood what it is to be absolutely surrendered to God as Jesus was. I know that many a one earnestly and honestly says: "Amen, I accept the message of absolute surrender to God"; and yet thinks: "Will that ever be mine? Can I count upon God to make me one of whom it shall be said in Heaven and on earth and in Hell, he lives in absolute surrender to God?" Brother, sister, "the things which are impossible with men are possible with God." Do believe that when He takes charge of you in Christ, it is possible for God to make you a man of absolute surrender. And God is able to maintain that. He is able to let you rise from bed every morning of the week with that blessed thought directly or indirectly: "I am in God's charge. My God is working out my life for me."

Some are weary of thinking about sanctification. You pray, you have longed and cried for it, and yet it appeared so far off! The holiness and humility of Jesus—you are so conscious of how distant it is. Beloved friends, the one doctrine of sanctification that is scriptural and real and effectual is: "The things which are impossible with men are possible with God." God can sanctify men, and by His almighty and sanctifying power every moment God can keep them. Oh, that we might get a step nearer to our God now! Oh, that the light of God might shine, and that we might know our God better!

I could go on to speak about the life of Christ in us—living like Christ, taking Christ as our Savior from sin, and as our life and strength. It is God in Heaven who can reveal that in you. What does that prayer of the apostle Paul say: "That he would grant you according to riches of his glory"—it is sure to be something very wonderful if it is according to the riches of His glory—"to be strengthened with might by his Spirit in the inner man"? Do you not see that it is an omnipotent God working by His omnipotence in the heart of His believing children, so that Christ can become an indwelling Savior? You have tried to grasp it and to seize it, and you have tried to believe it, and it would not come. It was because you had not been brought to believe that "the things which are impossible with men are possible with God."

And so, I trust that the word spoken about love may have brought many to see that we must have an inflowing of love in quite a new way; our heart must be filled with life from above, from the Fountain of everlasting love, if it is going to overflow all the day; then it will be just as natural for us to love our fellow men as it is natural for the lamb to be gentle and the wolf to be cruel. Until I am brought to such a state that the more a man hates and speaks evil of me, the more unlikable and unlovable a man is, I shall love him all the more; until I am brought to such a state that the more the obstacles and hatred and ingratitude, the more can the power of love triumph in me—until I am brought to see that, I am not saying: "It is impossible with men." But if you have been led to say: "This message has spoken to me about a love utterly beyond my power; it is absolutely impossible"—then we can come to God and say: "It is possible with Thee."

Some are crying to God for a great revival. I can say that that is the prayer of my heart unceasingly. Oh, if God would only revive His believing people! I cannot think in the first place of the unconverted formalists of the Church, or of the infidels and skeptics, or of all the wretched and perishing around me, my heart prays in the first place: "My God, revive Thy Church and people." It is not for nothing that there are in thousands of hearts yearnings after holiness and consecration: it is a forerunner of God's power. God works *to will* and then He works *to do.* These yearnings are a witness and a proof that God has worked *to will.* Oh, let us in faith believe that the omnipotent God will work *to do* among His people more than we can ask. "Unto him," Paul said, "who is able to do exceeding abundantly above all that we ask or think. . . . unto him be glory." Let our hearts say that. Glory to God, the omnipotent One, who can do above what we dare to ask or think!

"The things which are impossible with men are possible with God." All around you there is a world of sin and sorrow, and the Devil is there. But remember, Christ is on the throne, Christ is stronger, Christ has conquered, and Christ will conquer. But wait on God. My text casts us down: "The things which are *impossible with men*"; but it ultimately lifts us up high—"are *possible with God.*" Get linked to God. Adore and trust Him as the omnipotent One, not only for your own life, but for all the souls that are entrusted to you. Never pray without adoring His omnipotence, saying: *"Mighty God, I claim Thine almightiness."* And the answer to the prayer will come, and like Abraham you will become strong in faith, giving glory to God, because you account Him who hath promised able to perform.

"O Wretched Man that I am!"

"O wretched man that I am! who shall deliver me from the body of this death? I thank God through Jesus Christ our Lord" (Romans 7:24, 25).

You know the wonderful place that this text has in the wonderful epistle to the Romans. It stands here at the end of the seventh chapter as the gateway into the eighth. In the first sixteen verses of the eighth chapter the name of the Holy Spirit is found sixteen times; you have there the description and promise of the life that a child of God can live in the power of the Holy Spirit. This begins in the second verse: "The law of the Spirit of life in Christ Jesus hath made me free from the law of sin and death" (Rom. 8:12). From that Paul goes on to speak of the great privileges of the child of God, who is to be led by the Spirit of God. The gateway into all this is in the twenty-fourth verse of the seventh chapter:

"O wretched man that I am!"

There you have the words of a man who has come to the end of himself. He has in the previous verses described how he had struggled and wrestled in his own power to obey the holy law of God, and had failed. But in answer to his own question he now finds the true answer and cries out: "I thank God through Jesus Christ our Lord." From that he goes on to speak of what that deliverance is that he has found.

I want from these words to describe the path by which a man can be led out of the spirit of bondage into the spirit of liberty. You know how distinctly it is said: "Ye have not received the spirit of bondage again to fear." We are continually warned that this is the great danger of the Christian life, to go again into bondage; and I want to describe the path by which a man can get out of bondage into the glorious liberty of the children of God. Rather, I want to describe the man himself.

First, these words are the language of a *regenerate* man; *second,* of an *impotent* man; *third,* of a *wretched* man; and *fourth,* of a man *on the borders of complete liberty.*

The Regenerate Man

There is much evidence of regeneration from the fourteenth verse of the chapter on to the twenty-third. "It is no more I that do it, but sin that dwelleth in me" (Rom. 7:17): that is the language of a regenerate man, a man who knows that his heart and nature have been renewed, and that sin is now a power in him that is not himself. "I delight in the law of the Lord after the inward man" (Rom. 7:22): that again is the language of a regenerate man. He dares to say when he does evil: "It is no more I that do it, but sin that dwelleth in me." It is of great importance to understand this.

In the first two great sections of the epistle, Paul deals with justification and sanctification. In dealing with justification, he lays the foundation of the doctrine in the teaching about sin, not in the singular, *sin,* but in the plural, *sins*—the actual transgressions. In the second part of the fifth chapter he begins to deal with sin, not as actual transgression, but as a power. Just imagine what a loss it would have been to us if we had not this second half of the seventh chapter of the Epistle to the Romans, if Paul had omitted in his teaching this vital question of the sinfulness of the believer. We should have missed the question we all want answered as to sin in the believer. What is the answer? The regenerate man is one in whom the will has been renewed, and who can say: "I delight in the law of God after the inward man."

The Impotent Man

Here is the great mistake made by many Christian people: they think that when there is a renewed will, it is enough; but that is not the case. This regenerate man tells us: *"I will to do what is good, but the power to perform I find not."* How often people tell us that if you set yourself determinedly, you can perform what you will! But this man was as determined as any man can be, and yet he made the confession: "To will is present with me; but how to perform that which is good, I find not" (Rom. 7:18).

But, you ask: "How is it God makes a regenerate man utter such a confession, with a right will, with a heart that longs to do good, and longs to do its very utmost to love God?"

Let us look at this question. What has God given us our will for? Had the angels who fell, in their own will, the strength to stand? Surely not. The will of the creature is nothing but an empty vessel in which the power of God is to be made manifest. The creature must seek in God all that it is to be. You have it in the second chapter of the epistle to the Philippians, and you have it here also, that God's work is to work in us both *to will* and *to do* of His good pleasure. Here is a man who appears to say: "God has not worked *to do* in me." But we are taught that God works both to will and to do. How is the apparent contradiction to be reconciled?

You will find that in this passage (Rom. 7:6-25) the name of the Holy Spirit does not occur once, nor does the name of Christ occur. The man is wrestling and struggling to fulfill God's law. Instead of the Holy Spirit and of Christ, the law is mentioned nearly twenty times. In this chapter, it shows a believer doing his very best to obey the law of God with his regenerate will. Not only this; but you will find the little words, *I, me, my,* occur more than forty times. It is the regenerate *I* in its impotence seeking to obey the law without being filled with the Spirit. This is the experience of almost every saint. After conversion a man begins to do his best, and he fails; but if we are brought into the full light, we need fail no longer. Nor need we fail at all if we have received the Spirit in His fullness at conversion.

God allows that failure that the regenerate man should be taught his own utter impotence. It is in the course of this struggle that there comes to us this sense of our utter sinfulness. It is God's way of dealing with us. He allows that man to strive to fulfill the law that, as he strives and wrestles, he may be brought to this: "I am a regenerate child of God, but I am utterly helpless to obey His law." See what strong words are used all through the chapter to describe this condition: "I am carnal, sold under sin" (Rom. 7:14); "I see another law in my members bringing me into captivity" (Rom. 7:23); and last of all, "O wretched man that I am! who shall deliver me from the body of this death?" (Rom. 7:24). This believer who bows here in deep contrition is utterly unable to obey the law of God.

The Wretched Man

Not only is the man who makes this confession a regenerate and an impotent man, but he is also a wretched man. He is utterly unhappy and miserable; and what is it that makes him so utterly miserable? It is because God has given him a nature that loves Himself. He is deeply wretched because he feels he is not obeying his God. He says, with brokenness of heart: "It is not I that do it, but I am under the awful power of sin, which is holding me down. It is I, and yet not I: alas! alas! it is myself; so closely am I bound up with it, and so closely is it intertwined with my very nature." Blessed be God when a man learns to say: "O wretched man that I am!" from the depth of his heart. He is on the way to the eighth chapter of Romans.

There are many who make this confession a pillow for sin. They say that if Paul had to confess his weakness and helplessness in this way, what are they that they should try to do better? So the call to holiness is quietly set aside. Would God that every one of us had learned to say these words in the very spirit in which they are written here! When we hear sin spoken of as the abominable thing that God hates, do not many of us wince before the word? Would that all Christians who go on sinning and sinning would take this verse to heart. If ever you utter a sharp word say: "O wretched man that I am!" And every time you lose your temper, kneel down and understand that it never was meant by God that this was to be the state in which His child should remain. Would God that we would take this word into our daily life, and say it every time we are touched about our own honor, and every time we say sharp things, and every time we sin against the Lord God, and against the Lord Jesus Christ in His humility, and in His obedience, and in His self-sacrifice! Would to God you could forget everything else, and cry out: "O wretched man that I am! who shall deliver me from the body of this death?"

Why should you say this whenever you commit sin? Because it is when a man is brought to this confession that deliverance is at hand.

And remember it was not only the sense of being impotent and taken captive that made him wretched, but it was above all the sense of sinning against his God. The law was doing its work, making sin *exceedingly sinful* in his sight. The thought of continually grieving God became utterly unbearable—it was this that brought forth the piercing cry: "O wretched man!" As long as we talk and reason about our impotence and our failure, and only try to find out what Romans 7 means, it will profit us but little; but when once *every sin* gives new intensity to the sense of wretchedness, and we feel our whole state as one of not only helplessness, but actual exceeding sinfulness, we shall be pressed not only to ask: "Who shall deliver us?" but to cry: "I thank God through Jesus Christ my Lord."

The Almost-Delivered Man

The man has tried to obey the beautiful law of God. He has loved it, he has wept over his sin, he has tried to conquer, he has tried to overcome fault after fault, but every time he has ended in failure.

What did he mean by "the body of this death"? Did he mean, my body when I die? Surely not. In the eighth chapter you have the answer to this question in the words: "If ye through the Spirit do mortify the deeds of the body, ye shall live." *That* is the body of death from which he is seeking deliverance.

And now he is on the brink of deliverance! In the twenty-third verse of the seventh chapter we have the words: "I see another law in my members, warring against the law of my mind, and bringing me into *captivity* to the law of sin which is in my members." It is a *captive* that cries: "O wretched man that I am! who shall deliver me from the body of this death?" He is a man who feels himself bound. But look to the contrast in the second verse of the eighth chapter: "The law of the Spirit of life in Christ Jesus hath *made me free* from the law of sin and death." That is the deliverance through Jesus Christ our Lord; the *liberty* to the captive which the Spirit brings. Can you keep captive any longer a man made free by the "law of the Spirit of life in Christ Jesus"?

But you say, the regenerate man, had not he the Spirit of Jesus when he spoke in the sixth chapter? Yes, *but he did not know what the Holy Spirit could do for him.*

God does not work by His Spirit as He works by a blind force in nature. He leads His people on as reasonable, intelligent beings, and therefore when He wants to give us that Holy Spirit whom He has promised, He brings us first to the end of self, to the conviction that though we have been striving to obey the law, we have failed. When we have come to the end of that, then He shows us that in the Holy Spirit we have the power of obedience, the power of victory, and the power of real holiness.

God works *to will*, and He is ready to work *to do*, but, alas! many Christians misunderstand this. They think because they have the will, it is enough, and that now they are able to do. This is not so. The new will is a permanent gift, an attribute of the new nature. The power to do is not a permanent gift, but must be each moment received from the Holy Spirit. It is the man who is conscious *of his own impotence as a believer* who will learn that by the Holy Spirit *he can live a holy life.* This man is on the brink of that great deliverance; the way has been prepared for the glorious eighth chapter. I now ask this solemn question: Where are you living? Is it with you, "O wretched man that I am! who shall deliver me?" with now and then a little experience of the power of the Holy Spirit? or is it, "I thank God through Jesus Christ! The law of the Spirit hath set me free from the law of sin and of death"?

What the Holy Spirit does is to give the victory. "If ye through the Spirit do mortify the deeds of the flesh, ye shall live" (Rom. 8:13). It is the Holy Spirit who does this—the third Person of the Godhead. He it is who, when the heart is opened wide to receive Him, comes in and reigns there, and mortifies the deeds of the body, day by day, hour by hour, and moment by moment.

I want to bring this to a point. Remember, dear friend, what we need is to come to decision and action. There are in Scripture two very different sorts of Christians. The Bible speaks in *Romans, Corinthians* and *Galatians* about yielding to the flesh; and that is the life of tens of thousands of believers. All their lack of joy in the Holy Spirit, and their lack of the liberty He gives, is just owing to the flesh. The Spirit is within them, but the flesh rules the life. To be led by the Spirit of God is what they need. Would God that I could make every child of His realize what it means that the everlasting God has given His dear Son, Christ Jesus, to watch over you every day, and that what you have to do is to trust; and that the work of the Holy Spirit is to enable you every moment to remember Jesus, and to trust Him! The Spirit has come to keep the link with Him unbroken every moment. Praise God for the Holy Spirit! We are so accustomed to think of the Holy Spirit as a luxury, for special times, or for special ministers and men. But the Holy Spirit is necessary for every believer, every moment of the day. Praise God you have Him, and that He gives you the full experience of the deliverance in Christ, as He makes you free from the power of sin.

Who longs to have the power and the liberty of the Holy Spirit? Oh, brother, bow before God in one final cry of despair:

> *"O God, must I go on sinning this way forever? Who shall deliver me, O wretched man that I am! from the body of this death?"*

Are you ready to sink before God in that cry and seek the power of Jesus to dwell and work in you? Are you ready to say: "I thank God through Jesus Christ"?

What good does it do that we go to church or attend conventions, that we study our Bibles and pray, unless our lives are filled with the Holy Spirit? That is what God wants; and nothing else will enable us to live a life of power and peace. You know that when a minister or parent is using the catechism, when a question is asked an answer is expected. Alas! how many Christians are content with the question put here: "O wretched man that I am! who shall deliver me from the body of this death?" but never give the answer. Instead of answering, they are silent. Instead of saying: "I thank God through Jesus Christ our Lord," they are forever repeating the question without the answer. If you want the path to the full deliverance of Christ, and the liberty of the Spirit, the glorious liberty of the children of God, take it through the seventh chapter of Romans; and then say: "I thank God through Jesus Christ our Lord." Be not content to remain ever groaning, but say: "I, a wretched man, thank God, through Jesus Christ. Even though I do not see it all, I am going to praise God."

There is deliverance, there is the liberty of the Holy Spirit. The kingdom of God is "joy in the Holy Spirit" (Rom. 14:17).

"Having Begun in the Spirit"

The words from which I wish to address you, you will find in the epistle to the Galatians, the third chapter, the third verse; let us read the second verse also: "This only would I learn of you, Received ye the Spirit by the works of the law, or by the hearing of faith? Are ye so foolish?" And then comes my text—"Having begun in the Spirit, are ye now made perfect by the flesh?"

When we speak of the quickening or the deepening or the strengthening of the spiritual life, we are thinking of something that is feeble and wrong and sinful; and it is a great thing to take our place before God with the confession:

"Oh, God, our spiritual life is not what it should be!"

May God work that in your heart, reader.

As we look round about on the church we see so many indications of feebleness and of failure, and of sin, and of shortcoming, that we are compelled to ask: Why is it? Is there any necessity for the church of Christ to be living in such a low state? Or is it actually possible that God's people should be living always in the joy and strength of their God?

Every believing heart must answer: It *is* possible.

Then comes the great question: Why is it, how is it to be accounted for, that God's church as a whole is so feeble, and that the great majority of Christians are not living up to their privileges? There must be a reason for it. Has God not given Christ His Almighty Son to be the Keeper of every believer, to make Christ an ever-present reality, and to impart and communicate to us all that we have in Christ? God has given His Son, and God has given His Spirit. How is it that believers do not live up to their privileges?

We find in more than one of the epistles a very solemn answer to that question. There are epistles, such as the first to the Thessalonians, where Paul writes to the Christians, in effect: "I want you to grow, to abound, to increase more and more." They were young, and there were things lacking in their faith, but their state was so far satisfactory, and gave him great joy, and he writes time after time: "I pray God that you may abound more and more; I write to you to increase more and more" (1 Thes. 4:1,10). But there are other epistles where he takes a very different tone, especially the epistles to the Corinthians and to the Galatians, and he tells them in many different ways what the one reason was, that they were not living as Christians ought to live; many were under the power of the flesh. My text is one example. He reminds them that by the preaching of faith they had received the Holy Spirit. He had preached Christ to them; they had accepted that Christ and had received the Holy Spirit in power. But what happened? Having begun in the Spirit, they tried to perfect the work that the Spirit had begun in the flesh by their own effort. We find the same teaching in the epistle to the Corinthians.

Now, we have here a solemn discovery of what the great want is in the church of Christ. God has called the church of Christ to live in the power of the Holy Spirit, and the church is living for the most part in the power of human flesh, and of will and energy and effort apart from the Spirit of God. I doubt not that that is the case with many individual believers; and oh, if God will use me to give you a message from Him, my one message will be this: "If the church will return to acknowledge that the Holy Spirit is her strength and her help, and if the church will return to give up everything, and wait upon God to be filled with the Spirit, her days of beauty and gladness will return, and we shall see the glory of God revealed among us." This is my message to every individual believer: "Nothing will help you unless you come to understand that you must live every day under the power of the Holy Spirit."

God wants you to be a living vessel in whom the power of the Spirit is to be manifested every hour and every moment of your life, and God will enable you to be that.

Now let us try to learn that this word to the Galatians teaches us—some very simple thoughts. It shows us how (1) *the beginning of the Christian life is receiving the Holy Spirit.* It shows us (2) *what great danger there is of forgetting that we are to live by the Spirit, and not live after the flesh.* It shows us (3) *what are the fruits and the proofs of our seeking perfection in the flesh.* And then it suggests to us (4) *the way of deliverance from this state.*

Receiving the Holy Spirit

First of all, Paul says: *"Having begun in the Spirit."* Remember, the apostle not only preached justification by faith, but he preached something more. He preached this—the epistle is full of it—that justified men cannot live but by the Holy Spirit, and that therefore God gives to every justified man the Holy Spirit to seal him. The apostle says to them in effect more than once:

"How did you receive the Holy Spirit? Was it by the preaching of the law, or by the preaching of faith?"

He could point back to that time when there had been a mighty revival under his teaching. The power of God had been manifested, and the Galatians were compelled to confess:

"Yes, we have got the Holy Spirit: accepting Christ by faith, by faith we received the Holy Spirit."

Now, it is to be feared that there are many Christians who hardly know that when they believed, they received the Holy Spirit. A great many Christians can say: "I received pardon and I received peace." But if you were to ask them: "Have you received the Holy Spirit?" they would hesitate, and many, if they were to say Yes, would say it with hesitation; and they would tell you that they hardly knew what it was, since that time, to walk in the power of the Holy Spirit. Let us try and take hold of this great truth: The beginning of the true Christian life is to receive the Holy Spirit. And the work of every Christian minister is that which was the work of Paul—to remind his people that they received the Holy Spirit, and must live according to His guidance and in His power.

If those Galatians who received the Holy Spirit in power were tempted to go astray by that terrible danger of perfecting in the flesh what had been begun in the Spirit, how much more danger do those Christians run who hardly ever know that they have received the Holy Spirit, or who, if they know it as a matter of belief, hardly ever think of it and hardly ever praise God for it!

Neglecting the Holy Spirit

But now look, in the second place, at *the great danger.*

You all know what shunting is on a railway. A locomotive with its train may be run in a certain direction, and the points at some place may not be properly opened or closed, and unobservingly it is shunted off to the right or to the left. And if that takes place, for instance, on a dark night, the train goes in the wrong direction, and the people might never know it until they have gone some distance.

And just so God gives Christians the Holy Spirit with this intention, that every day all their life should be lived in the power of the Spirit. A man cannot live one hour a godly life unless by the power of the Holy Spirit. He may live a proper, consistent life, as people call it, an irreproachable life, a life of virtue and diligent service; but to live a life acceptable to God, in the enjoyment of God's salvation and God's love, to live and walk in the power of the new life—he cannot do it unless he be guided by the Holy Spirit every day and every hour.

But now listen to the danger. The Galatians received the Holy Spirit, but what was begun by the Spirit they tried to perfect in the flesh. How? They fell back again under Judaizing teachers who told them they must be circumcised. They began to seek their religion in external observances. And so Paul uses that expression about those teachers who had them circumcised, that "they sought to glory in their flesh" (Gal. 6:13).

You sometimes hear the expression used, *religious flesh.* What is meant by that? It is simply an expression made to give utterance to this thought: My human nature and my human will and my human effort can be very active in religion, and after being converted, and after receiving the Holy Spirit, I may begin in my own strength to try to serve God.

I may be very diligent and doing a great deal, and yet all the time it is more the work of human flesh than of God's Spirit. What a solemn thought, that man can, without noticing it, be shunted off from the line of the Holy Spirit on to the line of the flesh; that he can be most diligent and make great sacrifices, and yet it is all in the power of the human will! Ah, the great question for us to ask of God in self-examination is that we may be shown whether our religious life is lived more in the power of the flesh than in the power of the Holy Spirit. A man may be a preacher, he may work most diligently in his ministry, a man may be a Christian worker, and others may tell of him that he makes great sacrifices, and yet you can feel there is a want about it. You feel that he is not a spiritual man; there is no spirituality about his life. How many Christians there are about whom no one would ever think of saying: "What a spiritual man he is!" Ah! there is the weakness of the Church of Christ. It is all in that one word—*flesh*.

Now, the flesh may manifest itself in many ways. It may be manifested in fleshly wisdom. My mind may be most active about religion. I may preach or write or think or meditate, and delight in being occupied with things in God's Book and in God's Kingdom; and yet the power of the Holy Spirit may be markedly absent. I fear that if you take the preaching throughout the Church of Christ and ask why there is, alas! so little converting power in the preaching of the Word, why there is so much work and often so little result for eternity, why the Word has so little power to build up believers in holiness and in consecration—the answer will come: It is the absence of the power of the Holy Spirit. And why is this? There can be no other reason but that the flesh and human energy have taken the place that the Holy Spirit ought to have. That was true of the Galatians, it was true of the Corinthians. You know Paul said to them: "I cannot speak to you as to spiritual men; you ought to be spiritual men, but you are carnal." And you know how often in the course of his epistles he had to reprove and condemn them for strife and for divisions.

Lacking the Fruit of the Holy Spirit

A third thought: *What are the proofs or indications that a church like the Galatians, or a Christian, is serving God in the power of the flesh—is perfecting in the flesh what was begun in the Spirit?*

The answer is very easy. Religious self-effort always ends in sinful flesh. What was the state of those Galatians? Striving to be justified by the works of the law. And yet they were quarreling and in danger of devouring one another. Count up the expressions that the apostle uses to indicate their want of love, and you will find more than twelve—envy, jealousy, bitterness, strife, and all sorts of expressions. Read in the fourth and fifth chapters what he says about that. You see how they tried to serve God in their own strength, and they failed utterly. All this religious effort resulted in failure. The power of sin and the sinful flesh got the better of them, and their whole condition was one of the saddest that could be thought of.

This comes to us with unspeakable solemnity. There is a complaint everywhere in the Christian Church of the want of a high standard of integrity and godliness, even among the professing members of Christian churches. I remember a sermon which I heard preached on commercial morality. And, oh, if we speak not only of the commercial morality or immorality, but if we go into the homes of Christians, and if we think of the life to which God has called His children, and which He enables them to live by the Holy Spirit, and if we think of how much, nevertheless, there is of unlovingness and temper and sharpness and bitterness, and if we think how much there is very often of strife among the members of churches, and how much there is of envy and jealousy and sensitiveness and pride, then we are compelled to say: "Where are marks of the presence of the Spirit of the Lamb of God?" Wanting, sadly wanting!

Many people speak of these things as though they were the natural result of our feebleness and cannot well be helped. Many people speak of these things as sins, yet have given up the hope of conquering them. Many people speak of these things in the church around them, and do not see the least prospect of ever having the things changed. There is no prospect until there comes a radical change, until the Church of God begins to see that every sin in the believer comes from the flesh, from a fleshly life midst our religious activities, from a striving in self-effort to serve God. Until we learn to make confession, and until we begin to see, we must somehow or other get God's Spirit in power back to His Church, we must fail. Where did the Church begin in Pentecost? There they began in the Spirit. But, alas, how the Church of the next century went off into the flesh! They thought to perfect the Church in the flesh.

Do not let us think, because the blessed Reformation restored the great doctrine of justification by faith, that the power of the Holy Spirit was then fully restored. If it is our faith that God is going to have mercy on His Church in these last ages, it will be because the doctrine and the truth about the Holy Spirit will not only be studied, but sought after with a whole heart; and not only because that truth will be sought after, but because ministers and congregations will be found bowing before God in deep abasement with one cry: "We have grieved God's Spirit; we have tried to be Christian churches with as little as possible of God's Spirit; we have not sought to be churches filled with the Holy Spirit."

All the feebleness in the Church is owing to the refusal of the Church to obey its God.

And why is that so? I know your answer. You say: "We are too feeble and too helpless, and we try to obey, and we vow to obey, but somehow we fail."

Ah, yes, *you fail because you do not accept the strength of God.* God alone can work out His will in you. You cannot work out God's will, but His Holy Spirit can; and until the Church, until believers grasp this, and cease trying by human effort to do God's will, and wait upon the Holy Spirit to come with all His omnipotent and enabling power, the Church will never be what God wants her to be, and what God is willing to make of her.

Yielding to the Holy Spirit

I come now to my last thought, the question: *What is the way to restoration?*

Beloved friend, the answer is simple and easy. If that train has been shunted off, there is nothing for it but to come back to the point at which it was led away. The Galatians had no other way in returning but to come back to where they had gone wrong, to come back from all religious effort in their own strength, and from seeking anything by their own work, and to yield themselves humbly to the Holy Spirit. There is no other way for us as individuals.

Is there any brother or sister whose heart is conscious: "Alas! my life knows but little of the power of the Holy Spirit"? I come to you with God's message that you can have no conception of what your life would be in the power of the Holy Spirit. It is too high and too blessed and too wonderful, but I bring you the message that just as truly as the everlasting Son of God came to this world and wrought His wonderful works, that just as truly as on Calvary He died and wrought out your redemption by His precious blood, so, just as truly, can the Holy Spirit come into your heart that with His divine power He may sanctify you and enable you to do God's blessed will, and fill your heart with joy and with strength. But, alas! we have forgotten, we have grieved, we have dishonored the Holy Spirit, and He has not been able to do His work. But I bring you the message: The Father in Heaven loves to fill His children with His Holy Spirit. God longs to give each one individually, separately, the power of the Holy Spirit for daily life. The command comes to us individually, unitedly. God wants us as His children to arise and place our sins before Him, and to call upon Him for mercy. Oh, are ye so foolish? Having begun in the Spirit, are ye perfecting in the flesh that which was begun in the Spirit? Let us bow in shame, and confess before God how our fleshly religion, our self-effort, and self-confidence, have been the cause of every failure.

I have often been asked by young Christians: "Why is it that I fail so? I did so solemnly vow with my whole heart, and did desire to serve God; why have I failed?"

To such I always give the one answer: "My dear friend, you are trying to do in your own strength what Christ alone can do in you."

And when they tell me: "I am sure I knew Christ alone could do it, I was not trusting in myself," my answer always is:

> *"You were trusting in yourself or you could not have failed. If you had trusted Christ, He could not fail."*

Oh, this perfecting in the flesh what was begun in the Spirit runs far deeper through us than we know. Let us ask God to reveal to us that it is only when we are brought to utter shame and emptiness that we shall be prepared to receive the blessing that comes from on high.

And so I come with these two questions. Are you living, beloved brother-minister—I ask it of every minister of the Gospel—are you living under the power of the Holy Spirit? Are you living as an anointed, Spirit-filled man in your ministry and your life before God? O brethren, our place is an awful one. We have to show people what God will do for us, not in our words and teaching, but in our life. God help us to do it!

I ask it of every member of Christ's Church and of every believer: Are you living a life under the power of the Holy Spirit day by day, or are you attempting to live without that? Remember you cannot. Are you consecrated, given up to the Spirit to work in you and to live in you? Oh, come and confess every failure of temper, every failure of tongue however small, every failure owing to the absence of the Holy Spirit and the presence of the power of self. Are you consecrated, are you given up to the Holy Spirit?

If your answer is No, then I come with a second question—Are you *willing* to be consecrated? Are you willing to give up yourself to the power of the Holy Spirit?

You well know that the human side of consecration will not help you. I may consecrate myself a hundred times with all the intensity of my being, and that will not help me. What will help me is this—that God from Heaven accepts and seals the consecration.

And now are you willing to give yourselves up to the Holy Spirit? You can do it now. A great deal may still be dark and dim, and beyond what we understand, and you may feel nothing; but come. God alone can effect the change. God alone, who gave us the Holy Spirit, can restore the Holy Spirit in power into our life. God alone can "strengthen us with might by his Spirit in the inner man." And to every waiting heart that will make the sacrifice, and give up everything, and give time to cry and pray to God, the answer will come. The blessing is not far off. Our God delights to help us. He will enable us to perfect, not in the flesh, but in the Spirit, what was begun in the Spirit.

Kept by the Power of God

The words from which I speak, you will find in 1 Peter 1:5. The third, fourth and fifth verses are: "Blessed be the God and Father of our Lord Jesus Christ, which . . . hath begotten us again unto a lively hope by the resurrection of Jesus Christ from the dead, to an inheritance incorruptible . . . reserved in heaven for you, who are kept by the power of God through faith unto salvation." The words of my text are: "Kept by the power of God through faith."

There we have two wonderful, blessed truths about the keeping by which a believer is kept unto salvation. One truth is, *Kept by the power of God*; and the other truth is, *Kept through faith.* We should look at the two sides—at God's side and His almighty power, offered to us to be our Keeper every moment of the day; and at the human side, we having nothing to do but in faith to let God do His keeping work. We are begotten again to an inheritance kept in Heaven for us; and we are kept here on earth by the power of God. We see there is a double keeping—*the inheritance kept for me in Heaven,* and *I on earth kept for the inheritance* there.

Now, as to the first part of this keeping, there is no doubt and no question. God keeps the inheritance in Heaven very wonderfully and perfectly, and it is waiting there safely. And the same God keeps me for the inheritance. That is what I want to understand.

You know it is very foolish of a father to take great trouble to have an inheritance for his children, and to keep it for them, if he does not keep them for it. What would you think of a man spending his whole time and making every sacrifice to amass money, and as he gets his tens of thousands, you ask him why it is that he sacrifices himself so, and his answer is: "I want to leave my children a large inheritance, and I am keeping it for them"—if you were then to hear that that man takes no trouble to educate his children, that he allows them to run upon the street wild, and to go on in paths of sin and ignorance and folly, what would you think of him? Would not you say: "Poor man! he is keeping an inheritance for his children, but he is not keeping or preparing his children for the inheritance"! And there are so many Christians who think: "My God is keeping the inheritance for me"; but they cannot believe: "My God is keeping me for that inheritance." The same power, the same love, the same God doing the double work.

Now, I want to speak about a work God does upon us—keeping us for the inheritance. I have already said that we have two very simple truths: the one the divine side—*we are kept by the power of God*; the other, the human side—*we are kept through faith.*

Kept by the Power of God

Look at the divine side: Christians are kept by the power of God.

Keeping Includes All

Think, first of all, that *this keeping is all-inclusive.*

What is kept? *You* are kept. How much of you? The whole being. Does God keep one part of you and not another? No. Some people have an idea that this is a sort of vague, general keeping, and that God will keep them in such a way that when they die they will get to Heaven. But they do not apply that word kept to everything in their being and nature. And yet that is what God wants.

Here I have a watch. Suppose that this watch had been borrowed from a friend, and he said to me: "When you go to Europe, I will let you take it with you, but mind you keep it safely and bring it back."

And suppose I damaged the watch, and had the hands broken, and the face defaced, and some of the wheels and springs spoiled, and took it back in that condition, and handed it to my friend; he would say: "Ah, but I gave you that watch on condition that you would keep it."

"Have I not kept it? There is the watch."

"But I did not want you to keep it in that general way, so that you should bring me back only the shell of the watch, or the remains. I expected you to keep every part of it."

And so God does not want to keep us in this general way, so that at the last, somehow or other, we shall be saved as by fire, and just get into Heaven. But the keeping power and the love of God applies to every particular of our being.

There are some people who think God will keep them in spiritual things, but not in temporal things. This latter, they say, lies outside of His line. Now, God sends you to work in the world, but He did not say: "I must now leave you to go and earn your own money, and to get your livelihood for yourself." He knows you are not able to keep yourself. But God says: "My child, there is no work you are to do, and no business in which you are engaged, and not a cent which you are to spend, but I, your Father, will take that up into my keeping." God not only cares for the spiritual, but for the temporal also. The greater part of the life of many people must be spent, sometimes eight or nine or ten hours a day, amid the temptations and distractions of business; but God will care for you there. The keeping of God includes all.

There are other people who think: "Ah! in time of trial God keeps me, but in times of prosperity I do not need His keeping; then I forget Him and let Him go." Others, again, think the very opposite. They think: "In time of prosperity, when things are smooth and quiet, I am able to cling to God, but when heavy trials come, somehow or other my will rebels, and God does not keep me then."

Now, I bring you the message that in prosperity as in adversity, in the sunshine as in the dark, your God is ready to keep you all the time.

Then again, there are others who think of this keeping thus: "God will keep me from doing very great wickedness, but there are small sins I cannot expect God to keep me from. There is the sin of temper. I cannot expect God to conquer that."

When you hear of some man who has been tempted and gone astray or fallen into drunkenness or murder, you thank God for His keeping power.

"I might have done the same as that man," you say, "if God had not kept me." And you believe He kept you from drunkenness and murder.

And why do you not need believe that God can keep you from outbreaks of temper? You thought that this was of less importance; you did not remember that the great commandment of the New Testament is—"Love one another as I have loved you" (John 13:34). And when your temper and hasty judgment and sharp words came out, you sinned against the highest law—the law of God's love. And yet you say: "God will not, God cannot"—no, you will not say, God cannot; but you say, "God does not keep me from that." You perhaps say: "He can; but there is something in me that cannot attain to it, and which God does not take away."

I want to ask you, Can believers live a holier life than is generally lived? Can believers experience the keeping power of God all the day, to keep them from sin? Can believers be kept in fellowship with God? And I bring you a message from the Word of God, in these words: *Kept by the power of God.* There is no qualifying clause to them. The meaning is, that if you will entrust yourself entirely and absolutely to the omnipotence of God, He will delight to keep you.

Some people think that they never can get so far as that every word of their mouth should be to the glory of God. But it is what God wants of them, it is what God expects of them. God is willing to set a watch at the door of their mouth, and if God will do that, cannot He keep their tongue and their lips? He can; and that is what God is going to do for them that trust Him. God's keeping is all-inclusive, and let everyone who longs to live a holy life think out all their needs, and all their weaknesses, and all their shortcomings, and all their sins, and say deliberately: "Is there any sin that my God cannot keep me from?" And the heart will have to answer: "No; God can keep me from every sin."

Keeping Requires Power

Second, if you want to understand this keeping, remember that it is not only an all-inclusive keeping, but it is an almighty keeping.

I want to get that truth burned into my soul; I want to worship God until my whole heart is filled with the thought of His omnipotence. God is almighty, and the Almighty God offers Himself to work in my heart, to do the work of keeping me; and I want to get linked with Omnipotence, or rather, linked to the Omnipotent One, to the living God, and to have my place in the hollow of His hand. You read the Psalms, and you think of the wonderful thoughts in many of the expressions that David uses; as, for instance, when he speaks about God being *our God, our Fortress, our Refuge, our strong Tower, our Strength* and *our Salvation.* David had very wonderful views of how the everlasting God is Himself the hiding place of the believing soul, and of how He takes the believer and keeps him in the very hollow of His hand, in the secret of His pavilion, under the shadow of His wings, under His very feathers. And there David lived. And oh, we who are the children of Pentecost, we who have known Christ and His blood and the Holy Spirit sent down from Heaven, why is it we know so little of what it is to walk tremblingly step by step with the Almighty God as our Keeper?

Have you ever thought that in every action of grace in your heart you have the whole omnipotence of God engaged to bless you? When I come to a man and he bestows upon me a gift of money, I get it and go away with it. He has given me something of his; the rest he keeps for himself. But that is not the way with the power of God. God can part with nothing of His own power, and therefore I can experience the power and goodness of God only so far as I am in contact and fellowship with Himself; and when I come into contact and fellowship with Himself, I come into contact and fellowship with the whole omnipotence of God, and have the omnipotence of God to help me every day.

A son has, perhaps, a very rich father, and as the former is about to commence business the father says: "You can have as much money as you want for your undertaking." All the father has is at the disposal of the son. And that is the way with God, your Almighty God. You can hardly take it in; you feel yourself such a little worm. His omnipotence needed to keep a little worm! Yes, His omnipotence is needed to keep every little worm that lives in the dust, and also to keep the universe, and therefore His omnipotence is much more needed in keeping your soul and mine from the power of sin.

Oh, if you want to grow in grace, do learn to begin here. In all your judgings and meditations and thoughts and deeds and questionings and studies and prayers, learn to be kept by your Almighty God. What is Almighty God not going to do for the child that trusts Him? The Bible says: "Above all that we can ask or think" (Eph. 3:20). It is Omnipotence you must learn to know and trust, and then you will live as a Christian ought to live. How little we have learned to study God, and to understand that a godly life is a life full of God, a life that loves God and waits on Him, and trusts Him, and allows Him to bless it! We cannot do the will of God except by the power of God. God gives us the first experience of His power to prepare us to long for more, and to come and claim all that He can do. God help us to trust Him every day.

Keeping Is Continuous

Another thought. This keeping is not only all-inclusive and omnipotent, but also continuous and unbroken.

People sometimes say: "For a week or a month God has kept me very wonderfully: I have lived in the light of His countenance, and I cannot say what joy I have not had in fellowship with Him. He has blessed me in my work for others. He has given me souls, and at times I felt as if I were carried heavenward on eagle wings. But it did not continue. It was too good; it could not last." And some say: "It was necessary that I should fall to keep me humble." And others say: "I know it was my own fault; but somehow you cannot always live up in the heights."

Oh, beloved, why is it? Can there be any reason why the keeping of God should not be continuous and unbroken? Just think. All life is in unbroken continuity. If my life were stopped for half an hour I would be dead, and my life gone. Life is a continuous thing, and the life of God is the life of His Church, and the life of God is His almighty power working in us. And God comes to us as the Almighty One, and without any condition He offers to be my Keeper, and His keeping means that day by day, moment by moment, God is going to keep us.

If I were to ask you the question: "Do you think God is able to keep you one day from actual transgression?" you would answer: "I not only know He is able to do it, but I think He has done it. There have been days in which He has kept my heart in His holy presence, when, though I have always had a sinful nature within me, He has kept me from conscious, actual transgression."

Now, if He can do that for an hour or a day, why not for two days? Oh! let us make God's omnipotence as revealed in His Word the measure of our expectations. Has God not said in His Word: "I, the Lord, do keep it, and will water it every moment" (Isa. 27:3)? What can that mean? Does "every moment" *mean* every moment? Did God promise of that vineyard or red wine that *every moment* He would water it so that the heat of the sun and the scorching wind might never dry it up? Yes. In South Africa they sometimes make a graft, and above it they tie a bottle of water, so that now and then there shall be a drop to saturate what they have put about it. And so the moisture is kept there unceasingly until the graft has had time to stroke, and resist the heat of the sun.

Will our God, in His tenderhearted love toward us, not keep us every moment when He has promised to do so? Oh! if we once got hold of the thought: Our whole spiritual life is to be God's doing—"It is God that worketh in us to will and to do of his good pleasure" (Phil. 2:13)—when once we get faith to expect that from God, God will do all for us.

The keeping is to be continuous. Every morning God will meet you as you wake. It is not a question: If I forgot to wake in the morning with the thought of Him, what will come of it? If you trust your waking to God, God will meet you in the morning as you wake with His divine sunshine and love, and He will give you the consciousness that through the day you have got God to take charge of you continuously with His almighty power. And God will meet you the next day and every day; and never mind if in the practice of fellowship there comes failure sometimes. If you maintain your position and say: "Lord, I am going to expect Thee to do Thy utmost, and I am going to trust Thee day by day to keep me absolutely," your faith will grow stronger and stronger, and you will know the keeping power of God in unbrokenness.

Kept Through Faith

And now the other side—*Believing.* "Kept by the power of God *through faith.*" How must we look at this faith?

Faith Implies Helplessness

Let me say, first of all, that this faith means utter impotence and helplessness before God.

At the bottom of all faith there is a feeling of helplessness. If I have a bit of business to transact, perhaps to buy a house, the lawyer must do the work of getting the transfer of the property in my name and making all the arrangements. I cannot do that work, and in trusting that agent I confess I cannot do it. And so faith always means helplessness. In many cases it means: I can do it with a great deal of trouble, but another can do it better. But in most cases it is utter helplessness; another must do it for me. And that is the secret of the spiritual life. A man must learn to say: "I give up everything; I have tried and longed and thought and prayed, but failure has come. God has blessed me and helped me, but still, in the long run, there has been so much of sin and sadness." What a change comes when a man is thus broken down into utter helplessness and self-despair, and says: "I can do nothing!"

Remember Paul. He was living a blessed life, and he had been taken up into the third Heaven, and then the thorn in the flesh came, "a messenger of Satan to buffet me." And what happened? Paul could not understand it, and he prayed the Lord three times to take it away; but the Lord said, in effect:

"No; it is possible that you might exalt yourself, and therefore I have sent you this trial to keep you weak and humble."

And Paul then learned a lesson that he never forgot, and that was—to rejoice in his infirmities. He said that the weaker he was the better it was for him, for when he was weak, he was strong in his Lord Christ.

Do you want to enter what people call "the higher life"? Then go a step lower down. I remember Dr. Boardman telling how that once he was invited by a gentleman to go to see a factory where they made fine shot, and I believe the workmen did so by pouring down molten lead from a great height. This gentleman wanted to take Dr. Boardman up to the top of the tower to see how the work was done. The doctor came to the tower, he entered by the door, and began going upstairs; but when he had gone a few steps the gentleman called out:

"That is the wrong way. You must come down this way; that stair is locked up."

The gentleman took him downstairs a good many steps, and there an elevator was ready to take him to the top; and he said:

"I have learned a lesson that going down is often the best way to get up."

Ah, yes, God will have to bring us very low down; there will have to come upon us a sense of emptiness and despair and nothingness. It is when we sink down in utter helplessness that the everlasting God will reveal Himself in His power, and that our hearts will learn to trust God alone.

What is it that keeps us from trusting Him perfectly?

Many a one says: "I believe what you say, but there is one difficulty. If my trust were perfect and always abiding, all would come right, for I know God will honor trust. But how am I to get that trust?"

My answer is: "By the death of self. The great hindrance to trust is self-effort. So long as you have got your own wisdom and thoughts and strength, you cannot fully trust God. But when God breaks you down, when everything begins to grow dim before your eyes, and you see that you understand nothing, then God is coming near, and if you will bow down in nothingness and wait upon God, He will become all."

As long as we are something, God cannot be all, and His omnipotence cannot do its full work. That is the beginning of faith—utter despair of self, a ceasing from man and everything on earth, and finding our hope in God alone.

Faith Is Rest

And then, next, we must understand that faith is rest.

In the beginning of the faith-life, faith is struggling; but as long as faith is struggling, faith has not attained its strength. But when faith in its struggling gets to the end of itself, and just throws itself upon God and rests on Him, then comes joy and victory.

Perhaps I can make it plainer if I tell the story of how the Keswick Convention began. Canon Battersby was an evangelical clergyman of the Church of England for more than twenty years, a man of deep and tender godliness, but he had not the consciousness of rest and victory over sin, and often was deeply sad at the thought of stumbling and failure and sin. When he heard about the possibility of victory, he felt it was desirable, but it was as if he could not attain it. On one occasion, he heard an address on "Rest and Faith" from the story of the nobleman who came from Capernaum to Cana to ask Christ to heal his child. In the address it was shown that the nobleman believed that Christ could help him in a general way, but he came to Jesus a good deal by way of an experiment. He hoped Christ would help him, but he had not any assurance of that help. But what happened? When Christ said to him: "Go thy way, for thy child liveth," that man believed the word that Jesus spoke; he rested in that word. He had no proof that his child was well again, and he had to walk back seven hours' journey to Capernaum. He walked back, and on the way met his servant, and got the first news that the child was well, that at one o'clock on the afternoon of the previous day, at the very time that Jesus spoke to him, the fever left the child. That father rested upon the word of Jesus and His work, and he went down to Capernaum and found his child well; and he praised God, and became with his whole house a believer and disciple of Jesus.

Oh, friends, that is faith! When God comes to me with the promise of His keeping, and I have nothing on earth to trust in, I say to God: "Thy word is enough; kept by the power of God." That is faith, that is rest.

When Canon Battersby heard that address, he went home that night, and in the darkness of the night found rest. He rested on the word of Jesus. And the next morning, in the streets of Oxford, he said to a friend: "I have found it!" Then he went and told others, and asked that the Keswick Convention might be begun, and those at the convention with himself should testify simply what God had done.

It is a great thing when a man comes to rest on God's almighty power for every moment of his life, in prospect of temptations to temper and haste and anger and unlovingness and pride and sin. It is a great thing in prospect of these to enter into a covenant with the omnipotent Jehovah, not on account of anything that any man says, or of anything that my heart feels, but on the strength of the Word of God: "Kept by the power of God through faith."

Oh, let us say to God that we are going to test Him to the very uttermost. Let us say: We ask Thee for nothing more than Thou canst give, but we want nothing less. Let us say: My God, let my life be a proof of what the omnipotent God can do. Let these be the two dispositions of our souls every day—deep helplessness, and simple, childlike rest.

Faith Needs Fellowship

That brings me to just one more thought in regard to faith—faith implies fellowship with God.

Many people want to take the Word and believe that, and they find they cannot believe it. Ah, no! you cannot separate God from His Word. No goodness or power can be received separate from God, and if you want to get into this life of godliness, you *must* take time for fellowship with God.

People sometimes tell me: "My life is one of such scurry and bustle that I have no time for fellowship with God." A dear missionary said to me: "People do not know how we missionaries are tempted. I get up at five o'clock in the morning, and there are the natives waiting for their orders for work. Then I have to go to the school and spend hours there; and then there is other work, and sixteen hours rush along, and I hardly get time to be alone with God."

Ah! there is the lack. I pray you, remember two things. I have not told you to trust the omnipotence of God as a thing, and I have not told you to trust the Word of God as a written book, but I have told you to go to the God of omnipotence and the God of the Word. Deal with God as that nobleman dealt with the living Christ. Why was he able to believe the word that Christ spoke to him? Because in the very eyes and tones and voice of Jesus, the Son of God, he saw and heard something which made him feel that he could trust Him. And that is what Christ can do for you and me. Do not try to stir and arouse faith from within. How often I have tried to do that, and made a fool of myself! You cannot stir up faith from the depths of your heart. Leave your heart, and look into the face of Christ, and listen to what He tells you about how He will keep you. Look up into the face of your loving Father, and take time every day with Him, and begin a new life with the deep emptiness and poverty of a man who has got nothing, and who wants to get everything from Him—with the deep restfulness of a man who rests on the living God, the omnipotent Jehovah—and try God, and prove Him if He will not open the windows of Heaven and pour out a blessing that there shall not be room to receive it.

I close by asking if you are willing to experience to the very full the heavenly keeping for the heavenly inheritance? Robert Murray M'Cheyne says, somewhere: "Oh, God, make me as holy as a pardoned sinner can be made." And if that prayer is in your heart, come now, and let us enter into a covenant with the everlasting and omnipotent Jehovah afresh, and in great helplessness, but in great restfulness place ourselves in His hands. And then as we enter into our covenant, let us have the one prayer—that we may believe fully that the everlasting God is going to be our Companion, holding our hand every moment of the day; our Keeper, watching over us without a moment's interval; our Father, delighting to reveal Himself in our souls always. He has the power to let the sunshine of His love be with us all the day. Do not be afraid because you have got your business that you cannot have God with you always. Learn the lesson that the natural sun shines upon you all the day, and you enjoy its light, and wherever you are you have got the sun; God takes care that it shines upon you. And God will take care that His own divine light shines upon you, and that you shall abide in that light, if you will only trust Him for it. Let us trust God to do that with a great and entire trust.

Here is the omnipotence of God, and here is faith reaching out to the measure of that omnipotence. Shall we not say: "All that that omnipotence can do, I am going to trust my God for"? Are not the two sides of this heavenly life wonderful? God's omnipotence covers me, and my will in its littleness rests in that omnipotence, and rejoices in it!

Moment by moment, I'm kept in His love;

Moment by moment, I've life from above;
Looking to Jesus, the glory doth shine;
Moment by moment, Oh, Lord, I am Thine!

"Ye are the Branches"

An Address to Christian Workers

Everything depends on our being right ourselves in Christ. If I want good apples, I must have a good apple tree; and if I care for the health of the apple tree, the apple tree will give me good apples. And it is just so with our Christian life and work. *If our life with Christ be right,* all will come right. There may be the need of instruction and suggestion and help and training in the different departments of the work; all that has value. But in the long run, the greatest essential is to have the full life in Christ—in other words, to have Christ in us, working through us. I know how much there often is to disturb us, or to cause anxious questionings; but the Master has such a blessing for every one of us, and such perfect peace and rest, and such joy and strength, if we can only come into, and be kept in, the right attitude toward Him.

I will take my text from the parable of the Vine and the Branches, in John 15:5: "I am the vine, ye are the branches." Especially these words: "Ye are the branches."

What a simple thing it is to be a branch, the branch of a tree, or the branch of a vine! The branch grows out of the vine, or out of the tree, and there it lives and grows, and in due time, bears fruit. It has no responsibility except just to receive from the root and stem sap and nourishment. And if we only by the Holy Spirit knew our relationship to Jesus Christ, our work would be changed into the brightest and most heavenly thing upon earth. Instead of there ever being soul-weariness or exhaustion, our work would be like a new experience, linking us to Jesus as nothing else can. For, alas! is it not often true that our work comes between us and Jesus? What folly! The very work that He has to do in me, and I for Him, I take up in such a way that it separates me from Christ. Many a laborer in the vineyard has complained that he has too much work, and not time for close communion with Jesus, and that his usual work weakens his inclination for prayer, and that his too much intercourse with men darkens the spiritual life. Sad thought, that the bearing of fruit should separate the branch from the vine! That must be because we have looked upon our work as something other than the branch bearing fruit. May God deliver us from every false thought about the Christian life.

Now, just a few thoughts about this blessed branch-life.

Absolute Dependence

In the first place, it is a life of absolute dependence. The branch has nothing; it just depends upon the vine for everything. *Absolute dependence* is one of the most solemn and precious of thoughts. A great German theologian wrote two large volumes some years ago to show that the whole of Calvin's theology is summed up in that one principle of *absolute dependence* upon God; and he was right. Another great writer has said that *absolute, unalterable dependence upon God* alone is the essence of the religion of angels, and should be that of men also. God is everything to the angels, and He is willing to be everything to the Christian. If I can learn every moment of the day to depend upon God, everything will come right. You will get the higher life if you depend absolutely upon God.

Now, here we find it with the vine and the branches. Every vine you ever see, or every bunch of grapes that comes upon your table, let it remind you that the branch is absolutely dependent on the vine. The vine has to do the work, and the branch enjoys the fruit of it.

What has the vine to do? It has to do a great work. It has to send its roots out into the soil and hunt under the ground—the roots often extend a long way out—for nourishment, and to drink in the moisture. Put certain elements of manure in certain directions, and the vine sends its roots there, and then in its roots or stems it turns the moisture and manure into that special sap which is to make the fruit that is borne. The vine does the work, and the branch has just to receive from the vine the sap, which is changed into grapes. I have been told that at Hampton Court, London, there is a vine that sometimes bore a couple of thousand bunches of grapes, and people were astonished at its large growth and rich fruitage. Afterward it was discovered what was the cause of it. Not so very far away runs the River Thames, and the vine had stretched its roots away hundreds of yards under the ground, until it had come to the riverside, and there in all the rich slime of the riverbed it had found rich nourishment, and obtained moisture, and the roots had drawn the sap all that distance up and up into the vine, and as a result there was the abundant, rich harvest. The vine had the work to do, and the branches had just to depend upon the vine, and receive what it gave.

Is that literally true of my Lord Jesus? Must I understand that when I have to work, when I have to preach a sermon, or address a Bible class, or to go out and visit the poor, neglected ones, that all the responsibility of the work is on Christ?

That is exactly what Christ wants you to understand. Christ wants that in all your work, the very foundation should be the simple, blessed consciousness: Christ must care for all.

And how does He fulfill the trust of that dependence? He does it by sending down the Holy Spirit—not now and then only as a special gift, for remember the relationship between the vine and the branches is such that hourly, daily, unceasingly there is the living connection maintained. The sap does not flow for a time, and then stop, and then flow again, but from moment to moment the sap flows from the vine to the branches. And just so, my Lord Jesus wants me to take that blessed position as a worker, and morning by morning and day by day and hour by hour and step by step, in every work I have to go out to just to abide before Him in the simple utter helplessness of one who knows nothing, and is nothing, and can do nothing. Oh, beloved workers, study that word *nothing.* You sometimes sing: "Oh, to be nothing, nothing"; but have you really studied that word and prayed every day, and worshiped God, in the light of it? Do you know the blessedness of that word *nothing*?

If I am something, then God is not everything; but when I become *nothing,* God can become *all*, and the everlasting God in Christ can reveal Himself fully. That is the higher life. We need to become nothing. Someone has well said that the seraphim and cherubim are flames of fire because they know they are nothing, and they allow God to put His fullness and His glory and brightness into them. Oh, become nothing in deep reality, and, as a worker, study only one thing—to become poorer and lower and more helpless, that Christ may work all in you.

Workers, here is your first lesson: learn to be nothing, learn to be helpless. The man who has got something is not absolutely dependent; but the man who has got nothing is absolutely dependent. Absolute dependence upon God is the secret of all power in work. The branch has nothing but what it gets from the vine, and you and I can have nothing but what we get from Jesus.

Deep Restfulness

But second, the life of the branch is not only a life of entire dependence, but of deep restfulness.

That little branch, if it could think, and if it could feel, and if it could speak—that branch away in Hampton Court vine, or on some of the million vines that we have in South Africa, in our sunny land—if we could have a little branch here today to talk to us, and if we could say: "Come, branch of the vine, I want to learn from you how I can be a true branch of the living Vine," what would it answer? The little branch would whisper:

"Man, I hear that you are wise, and I know that you can do a great many wonderful things. I know you have much strength and wisdom given to you but I have one lesson for you. With all your hurry and effort in Christ's work you never prosper. The first thing you need is to come and rest in your Lord Jesus. That is what I do. Since I grew out of that vine I have spent years and years, and all I have done is just to rest in the vine. When the time of spring came I had no anxious thought or care. The vine began to pour its sap into me, and to give the bud and leaf. And when the time of summer came I had no care, and in the great heat I trusted the vine to bring moisture to keep me fresh. And in the time of harvest, when the owner came to pluck the grapes, I had no care. If there was anything in the grapes not good, the owner never blamed the branch, the blame was always on the vine. And if you would be a true branch of Christ, the living Vine, just rest on Him. Let Christ bear the responsibility."

You say: "Won't that make me slothful?"

I tell you it will not. No one who learns to rest upon the living Christ can become slothful, for the closer your contact with Christ the more of the Spirit of His zeal and love will be borne in upon you. But, oh, begin to work in the midst of your entire dependence by adding to that *deep restfulness*. A man sometimes tries and tries to be dependent upon Christ, but he worries himself about this absolute dependence; he tries and he cannot get it. But let him sink down into entire restfulness every day.

> *In Thy strong hand I lay me down.*
> *So shall the work be done;*
> *For who can work so wondrously*
> *As the Almighty One?*

Worker, take your place every day at the feet of Jesus, in the blessed peace and rest that come from the knowledge —

> *I have no care, my cares are His!*
> *I have no fear, He cares for all my fears.*

Come, children of God, and understand that it is the Lord Jesus who wants to work through you. You complain of the lack of fervent love. It will come from Jesus. He will give the divine love in your heart with which you can love people. That is the meaning of the assurance: "The love of God is shed abroad in our hearts by the Holy Spirit" (Rom. 5:5); and of that other word: "The love of Christ constraineth us" (2 Cor. 5:14). Christ can give you a fountain of love, so that you cannot help loving the most wretched and the most ungrateful, or those who have wearied you hitherto. Rest in Christ, who can give wisdom and strength, and you do not know how that restfulness will often prove to be the very best part of your message. You plead with people and you argue, and they get the idea: "There is a man arguing and striving with me." They only feel: "Here are two men dealing with each other." But if you will let the deep rest of God come over you, the rest in Christ Jesus, the peace and rest and holiness of Heaven, that restfulness will bring a blessing to the heart, even more than the words you speak.

Much Fruitfulness

But third, the branch teaches a lesson of much fruitfulness.

The Lord Jesus Christ repeated that word *fruit* often in that parable. He spoke, first, of *fruit,* and then of *more fruit,* and then of *much fruit.* Yes, you are ordained not only to bear fruit, but to bear *much fruit.* "Herein is my Father glorified, *that ye bear much fruit*" (John 15:8). In the first place, Christ said: "I am the Vine, and my Father is the Husbandman. My Father is the Husbandman who has charge of me and you." He who will watch over the connection between Christ and the branches is God; and it is in the power of God through Christ we are to bear fruit.

Oh, Christians, you know this world is perishing for the want of workers. And it lacks not only more workers—the workers are saying, some more earnestly than others: "We need not only more workers, but we need our workers to have a new power, a different life; that we workers should be able to bring more blessing." Children of God, I appeal to you. You know what trouble you take, say, in a case of sickness. You have a beloved friend apparently in danger of death, and nothing can refresh that friend so much as a few grapes, and they are out of season; but what trouble you will take to get the grapes that are to be the nourishment of this dying friend! And, oh, there are around you people who never go to church, and so many who go to church, but do not know Christ. And yet the heavenly grapes, the grapes of the heavenly Vine, are not to be had at any price, except as the child of God bears them out of his inner life in fellowship with Christ. Except the children of God are filled with the sap of the heavenly Vine, except they are filled with the Holy Spirit and the love of Jesus, they cannot bear much of the real heavenly grape. We all confess there is a great deal of work, a great deal of preaching and teaching and visiting, a great deal of machinery, a great deal of earnest effort of every kind; but there is not much manifestation of the power of God in it.

What is lacking? There is lacking the close connection between the worker and the heavenly Vine. Christ, the heavenly Vine, has blessings that He could pour on tens of thousands who are perishing. Christ, the heavenly Vine, has power to provide the heavenly grapes. But "Ye are the branches," and you cannot bear heavenly fruit unless you are in close connection with Jesus Christ.

Do not confound *work* and *fruit.* There may be a good deal of work for Christ that is not the fruit of the heavenly Vine. Do not seek for work only. Oh! study this question of fruit-bearing. It means the very life and the very power and the very spirit and the very love within the heart of the Son of God—it means the heavenly Vine Himself coming into your heart and mine.

You know there are different sorts of grapes, each with a different name, and every vine provides exactly that peculiar aroma and juice which gives the grape its particular flavor and taste. Just so, there is in the heart of Christ Jesus a life, and a love, and a Spirit, and a blessing, and a power for men, that are entirely heavenly and divine, and that will come down into our hearts. Stand in close connection with the heavenly Vine and say:

"Lord Jesus, nothing less than the sap that flows through Thyself, nothing less than
the Spirit of Thy divine life is what we ask. Lord Jesus, I pray Thee let Thy
Spirit flow through me in all my work for Thee."

I tell you again that the sap of the heavenly Vine is nothing but the Holy Spirit. The Holy Spirit is the life of the heavenly Vine, and what you must get from Christ is nothing less than a strong inflow of the Holy Spirit. You need it exceedingly, and you want nothing more than that. Remember that. Do not expect Christ to give a bit of strength here, and a bit of blessing yonder, and a bit of help over there. As the vine does its work in giving its own peculiar sap to the branch, so expect Christ to give His own Holy Spirit into your heart, and then you will bear much fruit. And if you have only begun to bear fruit, and are listening to the word of Christ in the parable, "more fruit," "much fruit," remember that in order that you should bear more fruit you just require more of Jesus in your life and heart.

We ministers of the Gospel, how we are in danger of getting into a condition of work, work, work! And we pray over it, but the freshness and buoyancy and joy of the heavenly life are not always present. Let us seek to understand that the life of the branch is a life of much fruit, because it is a life rooted in Christ, the living, heavenly Vine.

Close Communion

And fourth, the life of the branch is a life of close communion.

Let us again ask: What has the branch to do? You know that precious, inexhaustible word that Christ used: Abide. Your life is to be an abiding life. And how is the abiding to be? It is to be just like the branch in the vine, abiding every minute of the day. There are the branches, in close communion, in unbroken communion, with the vine, from January to December. And cannot I live every day—it is to me an almost terrible thing that we should ask the question—cannot I live in abiding communion with the heavenly Vine?

You say: "But I am so much occupied with other things."

You may have ten hours' hard work daily, during which your brain has to be occupied with temporal things; God orders it so. But the abiding work is the work of the heart, not of the brain, the work of the heart clinging to and resting in Jesus, a work in which the Holy Spirit links us to Christ Jesus. Oh, do believe that deeper down than the brain, deep down in the inner life, you can abide in Christ, so that every moment you are free the consciousness will come:

"Blessed Jesus, I am still in Thee."

If you will learn for a time to put aside other work and to get into this abiding contact with the heavenly Vine, you will find that fruit will come.

What is the application to our life of this abiding communion? What does it mean?

It means *close fellowship with Christ in secret prayer.* I am sure there are Christians who do long for the higher life, and who sometimes have got a great blessing, and have at times found a great inflow of heavenly joy and a great outflow of heavenly gladness; and yet after a time it has passed away. They have not understood that close personal actual communion with Christ is an absolute necessity for daily life. Take time to be alone with Christ. Nothing in Heaven or earth can free you from the necessity for that, if you are to be happy and holy Christians.

Oh! how many Christians look upon it as a burden and a tax, and a duty, and a difficulty to be often alone with God! That is the great hindrance to our Christian life everywhere. We need more quiet fellowship with God, and I tell you in the name of the heavenly Vine that you cannot be healthy branches, branches into which the heavenly sap can flow, unless you take plenty of time for communion with God. If you are not willing to sacrifice time to get alone with Him, and to give Him time every day to work in you, and to keep up the link of connection between you and Himself, He cannot give you that blessing of His unbroken fellowship. Jesus Christ asks you to live in close communion with Him. Let every heart say: "O, Christ, it is this I long for, it is this I choose." And He will gladly give it to you.

Absolute Surrender

And then finally, the life of the branch is a life of absolute surrender.

This word, absolute surrender, is a great and solemn word, and I believe we do not understand its meaning. But yet the little branch preaches it.

"Have you anything to do, little branch, besides bearing grapes?"

"No, *nothing.*"

"Are you fit for nothing?"

Fit for nothing! The Bible says that a bit of vine cannot even be used as a pen; it is fit for nothing but to be burned.

"And now, what do you understand, little branch, about your relationship to the vine?"

"My relationship is just this: I am utterly given up to the vine, and the vine can give me as much or as little sap as it chooses. Here I am at its disposal and the vine can do with me what it likes."

Oh, friends, we need this absolute surrender to the Lord Jesus Christ. The more I speak, the more I feel that this is one of the most difficult points to make clear, and one of the most important and needful points to explain—what this absolute surrender is. It is often an easy thing for a man or a number of men to come out and offer themselves up to God for entire consecration, and to say: "Lord, it is my desire to give up myself entirely to Thee." That is of great value, and often brings very rich blessing. But the one question I ought to study quietly is What is meant by *absolute surrender*?

It means that, as literally as Christ was given up entirely to God, I am given up entirely to Christ. Is that too strong? Some think so. Some think that never can be; that just as entirely and absolutely as Christ gave up His life to do nothing but seek the Father's pleasure, and depend on the Father absolutely and entirely, I am to do nothing but to seek the pleasure of Christ. But that is actually true. Christ Jesus came to breathe His own Spirit into us, to make us find our very highest happiness in living entirely for God, just as He did. Oh, beloved brethren, if that is the case, then I ought to say:

> *"Yes, as true as it is of that little branch of the vine, so true, by God's grace, I would have it to be of me. I would live day by day that Christ may be able to do with me what He will."*

Ah! here comes the terrible mistake that lies at the bottom of so much of our own religion. A man thinks:

> *"I have my business and family duties, and my relationships as a citizen, and all this I cannot change. And now alongside all this I am to take in religion and the service of God, as something that will keep me from sin. God help me to perform my duties properly!"*

This is not right. When Christ came, He came and bought the sinner with His blood. If there was a slave market here and I were to buy a slave, I should take that slave away to my own house from his old surroundings, and he would live at my house as my personal property, and I could order him about all the day. And if he were a faithful slave, he would live as having no will and no interests of his own, his one care being to promote the well-being and honor of his master. And in like manner I, who have been bought with the blood of Christ, have been bought to live every day with the one thought—How can I please my Master?

Oh, we find the Christian life so difficult because we seek for God's blessing while we live in our own will. We should be glad to live the Christian life according to our own liking. We make our own plans and choose our own work, and then we ask the Lord Jesus to come in and take care that sin shall not conquer us too much, and that we shall not go too far wrong; we ask Him to come in and give us so much of His blessing. But our relationship to Jesus ought to be such that we are entirely at His disposal, and every day come to Him humbly and straightforwardly and say:

"Lord, is there anything in me that is not according to Thy will, that has not been ordered by Thee, or that is not entirely given up to Thee?"

Oh, if we would wait and wait patiently, I tell you what the result would be. There would spring up a relationship between us and Christ so close and so tender that we should afterward be amazed at how we formerly could have lived with the idea: "I am surrendered to Christ." We should feel how far distant our intercourse with Him had previously been, and that He can, and does indeed, come and take actual possession of us, and gives unbroken fellowship all the day. The branch calls us to absolute surrender.

I do not speak now so much about the giving up of sins. There are people who need that, people who have got violent tempers, bad habits, and actual sins which they from time to time commit, and which they have never given up into the very bosom of the Lamb of God. I pray you, if you are branches of the living Vine, do not keep one sin back. I know there are a great many difficulties about this question of holiness. I know that all do not think exactly the same with regard to it. That would be to me a matter of comparative indifference if I could see that all are honestly longing to be free from every sin. But I am afraid that unconsciously there are in hearts often compromises with the idea that we cannot be without sin, we must sin a little every day; we cannot help it. Oh, that people would actually cry to God: "Lord, do keep me from sin!" Give yourself utterly to Jesus, and ask Him to do His very utmost for you in keeping you from sin.

There is a great deal in our work, in our church and our surroundings that we found in the world when we were born into it, and it has grown all around us, and we think that it is all right, it cannot be changed. We do not come to the Lord Jesus and ask Him about it. Oh! I advise you, Christians, *bring everything into relationship with Jesus* and say:

"Lord, everything in my life has to be in most complete harmony with my position as a branch of Thee, the blessed Vine."

Let your surrender to Christ be absolute. I do not understand that word *surrender* fully; it gets new meanings every now and then; it enlarges immensely from time to time. But I advise you to speak it out: "Absolute surrender to Thee, O Christ, is what I have chosen." And Christ will show you what is not according to His mind, and lead you on to deeper and higher blessedness.

In conclusion, let me gather up all in one sentence. Christ Jesus said: "I am the Vine, ye are the branches." In other words: "I, the living One who have so completely given myself to you, am the Vine. You cannot trust me *too much*. I am the Almighty Worker, full of a divine life and power." You are the branches of the Lord Jesus Christ. If there is in your heart the consciousness that you are not a strong, healthy, fruit-bearing branch, not closely linked with Jesus, not living in Him as you should be—then listen to Him say: "I am the Vine, I will receive you, I will draw you to myself, I will bless you, I will strengthen you, I will fill you with my Spirit. I, the Vine, have taken you to be my branches, I have given myself utterly to you; children, give yourselves utterly to me. I have surrendered myself as God absolutely to you; I became man and died for you that I might be entirely yours. Come and surrender yourselves entirely to be mine."

What shall our answer be? Oh, let it be a prayer from the depths of our heart, that the living Christ may take each one of us and link us close to Himself. Let our prayer be that He, the living Vine, shall so link each of us to Himself that we shall go away with our hearts singing: "He is my Vine, and I am His branches—I want nothing more—now I have the everlasting Vine." Then, when you get alone with Him, worship and adore Him, praise and trust Him, love Him and wait for His love. "Thou art my Vine, and I am Thy branch. It is enough, my soul is satisfied."

Glory to His blessed name!

Lord, Teach Us to Pray

~ ※ ~

By *Andrew Murray*

1896

LORD, TEACH US TO PRAY

OR

THE ONLY TEACHER.

The disciples had been with Christ, and seen Him pray. They had learnt to understand something of the connection between His wondrous life in public, and His secret life of prayer. They had learnt to believe in Him as a Master in the art of prayer—none could pray like Him. And so they came to Him with the request, 'Lord, teach us to pray.' And in after years they would have told us that there were few things more wonderful or blessed that He taught them than His lessons on prayer.

And now still it comes to pass, as He is praying in a certain place, that disciples who see Him thus engaged feel the need of repeating the same request, 'Lord, teach us to pray.' As we grow in the Christian life, the thought and the faith of the Beloved Master in His never-failing intercession becomes evermore precious, and the hope of being *Like Christ* in His intercession gains an attractiveness before unknown. And as we see Him pray, and remember that there is none who can pray like Him, and none who can teach like Him, we feel the petition of the disciples, 'Lord, teach us to pray,' is just what we need. And as we think how all He is and has, how He Himself is our very own, how He is Himself our life, we feel assured that we have but to ask, and He will be delighted to take us up into closer fellowship with Himself, and teach us to pray even as He prays.

Come, my brothers! Shall we not go to the Blessed Master and ask Him to enroll our names too anew in that school which He always keeps open for those who long to continue their studies in the Divine art of prayer and intercession? Yes, let us this very day say to the Master, as they did of old, 'Lord, teach us to pray.' As we meditate we shall find each word of the petition we bring to be full of meaning.

'Lord, teach us *to pray*.' Yes, *to pray*. This is what we need to be taught. Though in its beginnings prayer is so simple that the feeble child can pray, yet it is at the same time the highest and holiest work to which man can rise. It is fellowship with the Unseen and Most Holy One. The powers of the eternal world have been placed at its disposal. It is the very essence of true religion, the channel of all blessings, the secret of power and life. Not only for ourselves, but for others, for the Church, for the world, it is to prayer that God has given the right to take hold of Him and His strength. It is on prayer that the promises wait for their fulfilment, the kingdom for its coming, the glory of God for its full revelation. And for this blessed work, how slothful and unfit we are. It is only the Spirit of God can enable us to do it aright. How speedily we are deceived into a resting in the form, while the power is wanting. Our early training, the teaching of the Church, the influence of habit, the stirring of the emotions—how easily these lead to prayer which has no spiritual power, and avails but little. True prayer, that takes hold of God's strength, that availeth much, to which the gates of heaven are really opened wide—who would not cry, Oh for some one to teach me thus to pray?

Jesus has opened a school, in which He trains His redeemed ones, who specially desire it, to have power in prayer. Shall we not enter it with the petition, Lord! it is just this we need to be taught! O teach us to *pray*.

'Lord, teach *us* to pray.' Yes, *us*, Lord. We have read in Thy Word with what power Thy believing people of old used to pray, and what mighty wonders were done in answer to their prayers. And if this took place under the Old Covenant, in the time of preparation, how much more wilt Thou not now, in these days of fulfilment, give Thy people this sure sign of Thy presence in their midst. We have heard the promises given to Thine apostles of the power of prayer in Thy name, and have seen how gloriously they experienced their truth: we know for certain, they can become true to us too. We hear continually even in these days what glorious tokens of Thy power Thou dost still give to those who trust Thee fully. Lord! these all are men of like passions with ourselves; teach *us* to pray so too. The promises are for us, the powers and gifts of the heavenly world are for us. O teach *us* to pray so that we may receive abundantly. To us too Thou hast entrusted Thy work, on our prayer too the coming of Thy kingdom depends, in our prayer too Thou canst glorify Thy name; 'Lord, teach us to pray.' Yes, us, Lord; we offer ourselves as learners; we would indeed be taught of Thee. 'Lord, teach *us* to pray.'

'Lord, *teach* us to pray.' Yes, we feel the need now of being *taught* to pray. At first there is no work appears so simple; later on, none that is more difficult; and the confession is forced from us:

We know not how to pray as we ought. It is true we have God's Word, with its clear and sure promises; but sin has so darkened our mind, that we know not always how to apply the Word. In spiritual things we do not always seek the most needful things, or fail in praying according to the law of the sanctuary. In temporal things we are still less able to avail ourselves of the wonderful liberty our Father has given us to ask what we need. And even when we know what to ask, how much there is still needed to make prayer acceptable. It must be to the glory of God, in full surrender to His will, in full assurance of faith, in the name of Jesus, and with a perseverance that, if need be, refuses to be denied. All this must be learned. It can only be learned in the school of much prayer, for practice makes perfect. Amid the painful consciousness of ignorance and unworthiness, in the struggle between believing and doubting, the heavenly art of effectual prayer is learnt. Because, even when we do not remember it, there is One, the Beginner and Finisher of faith and prayer, who watches over our praying, and sees to it that *in all who trust Him for it* their education in the school of prayer shall be carried on to perfection. Let but the deep undertone of all our prayer be the teachableness that comes from a sense of ignorance, and from faith in Him as a perfect teacher, and we may be sure we shall be taught, we shall learn to pray in power. Yes, we may depend upon it, He *teaches* to pray.

'*Lord*, teach us to pray.' None can teach like Jesus, none but Jesus; therefore we call on Him, 'Lord, teach us to pray.' A pupil needs a teacher, who knows his work, who has the gift of teaching, who in patience and love will descend to the pupil's needs. Blessed be God! Jesus is all this and much more. He knows what prayer is. It is Jesus, praying Himself, who teaches to pray. He knows what prayer is. He learned it amid the trials and tears of His earthly life. In heaven it is still His beloved work: His life there is prayer. Nothing delights Him more than to find those whom He can take with Him into the Father's presence, whom He can clothe with power to pray down God's blessing on those around them, whom He can train to be His fellow-workers in the intercession by which the kingdom is to be revealed on earth. He knows how to teach. Now by the urgency of felt need, then by the confidence with which joy inspires. Here by the teaching of the Word, there by the testimony of another believer who knows what it is to have prayer heard. By His Holy Spirit, He has access to our heart, and teaches us to pray by showing us the sin that hinders the prayer, or giving us the assurance that we please God. He teaches, by giving not only thoughts of what to ask or how to ask, but by breathing within us the very spirit of prayer, by living within us as the Great Intercessor. We may indeed and most joyfully say, 'Who teacheth like Him?' Jesus never taught His disciples how to preach, only how to pray. He did not speak much of what was needed to preach well, but much of praying well. To know how to speak to God is more than knowing how to speak to man. Not power with men, but power with God is the first thing. Jesus loves to teach us how to pray.

What think you, my beloved fellow-disciples! would it not be just what we need, to ask the Master for a month to give us a course of special lessons on the art of prayer? As we meditate on the words He spake on earth, let us yield ourselves to His teaching in the fullest confidence that, with such a teacher, we shall make progress. Let us take time not only to meditate, but to pray, to tarry at the foot of the throne, and be trained to the work of intercession. Let us do so in the assurance that amidst our stammerings and fears He is carrying on His work most beautifully. He will breathe His own life, which is all prayer, into us. As He makes us partakers of His righteousness and His life, He will of His intercession too. As the members of His body, as a holy priesthood, we shall take part in His priestly work of pleading and prevailing with God for men. Yes, let us most joyfully say, ignorant and feeble though we be, 'Lord, teach us to pray.'

'Lord, Teach Us To Pray.'

~ ※ ~

Blessed Lord! who ever livest to pray, Thou canst teach me too to pray, me to live ever to pray. In this Thou lovest to make me share Thy glory in heaven, that I should pray without ceasing, and ever stand as a priest in the presence of my God.

Lord Jesus! I ask Thee this day to enroll my name among those who confess that they know not how to pray as they ought, and especially ask Thee for a course of teaching in prayer. Lord! teach me to tarry with Thee in the school, and give Thee time to train me. May a deep sense of my ignorance, of the wonderful privilege and power of prayer, of the need of the Holy Spirit as the Spirit of prayer, lead me to cast away my thoughts of what I think I know, and make me kneel before Thee in true teachableness and poverty of spirit.

And fill me, Lord, with the confidence that with such a teacher as Thou art I shall learn to pray. In the assurance that I have as my teacher, Jesus, who is ever praying to the Father, and by His prayer rules the destinies of His Church and the world, I will not be afraid. As much as I need to know of the mysteries of the prayer-world, Thou wilt unfold for me. And when I may not know, Thou wilt teach me to be strong in faith, giving glory to God.

Blessed Lord! Thou wilt not put to shame Thy scholar who trusts Thee, nor, by Thy grace, would he Thee either. Amen.

'IN SPIRIT AND TRUTH'

OR

THE TRUE WORSHIPPERS.

'The hour cometh, and now is, when the true worshippers shall worship the Father in spirit and truth: for such doth the Father seek to be His worshippers. God is a Spirit: and they that worship Him must worship Him in spirit and truth.'—John iv. 23, 24.

These words of Jesus to the woman of Samaria are His first recorded teaching on the subject of prayer. They give us some wonderful first glimpses into the world of prayer. The Father *seeks* worshippers: our worship satisfies His loving heart and is a joy to Him. He seeks *true worshippers*, but finds many not such as He would have them. True worship is that which is *in spirit and truth. The Son has come* to open the way for this worship in spirit and in truth, and teach it us. And so one of our first lessons in the school of prayer must be to understand what it is to pray in spirit and in truth, and to know how we can attain to it.

To the woman of Samaria our Lord spoke of a threefold worship. There is, first, the ignorant worship of the Samaritans: 'Ye worship that which ye know not.' The second, the intelligent worship of the Jew, having the true knowledge of God: 'We worship that which we know; for salvation is of the Jews.' And then the new, the spiritual worship which He Himself has come to introduce: 'The hour is coming, and is now, when the true worshippers shall worship the Father in spirit and truth.' From the connection it is evident that the words 'in spirit and truth' do not mean, as is often thought, earnestly, from the heart, in sincerity. The Samaritans had the five books of Moses and some knowledge of God; there was doubtless more than one among them who honestly and earnestly sought God in prayer. The Jews had the true full revelation of God in His word, as thus far given; there were among them godly men, who called upon God with their whole heart. And yet not 'in spirit and truth,' in the full meaning of the words. Jesus says, *'The hour is coming, and now is:'* it is only in and through Him that the worship of God will be in spirit and truth.

Among Christians one still finds the three classes of worshippers. Some who in their ignorance hardly know what they ask: they pray earnestly, and yet receive but little. Others there are, who have more correct knowledge, who try to pray with all their mind and heart, and often pray most earnestly, and yet do not attain to the full blessedness of worship in spirit and truth. It is into this third class we must ask our Lord Jesus to take us; we must be taught of Him how to worship in spirit and truth. This alone is spiritual worship; this makes us worshippers such as the Father seeks. In prayer everything will depend on our understanding well and practicing the worship in spirit and truth.

'God is *a Spirit* and they that worship Him must worship Him *in spirit* and truth.' The first thought suggested here by the Master is that there must be harmony between God and His worshippers; such as God is, must His worship be. This is according to a principle which prevails throughout the universe: we look for correspondence between an object and the organ to which it reveals or yields itself. The eye has an inner fitness for the light, the ear for sound. The man who would truly worship God, would find and know and possess and enjoy God, must be in harmony with Him, must have a capacity for receiving Him. Because God *is Spirit*, we must worship *in spirit*. As God is, so His worshipper.

And what does this mean? The woman had asked our Lord whether Samaria or Jerusalem was the true place of worship. He answers that henceforth worship is no longer to be limited to a certain place: 'Woman, believe Me, *the hour cometh* when neither in this mountain, nor in Jerusalem, shall ye worship the Father.' As God is Spirit, not bound by space or time, but in His infinite perfection always and everywhere the same, so His worship would henceforth no longer be confined by place or form, but spiritual as God Himself is spiritual. A lesson of deep importance. How much our Christianity suffers from this, that it is confined to certain times and places. A man who seeks to pray earnestly in the church or in the closet, spends the greater part of the week or the day in a spirit entirely at variance with that in which he prayed. His worship was the work of a fixed place or hour, not of his whole being. God is a spirit: He is the Everlasting and Unchangeable One; what He is, He is always and in truth. Our worship must even so be in spirit and truth: His worship must be the spirit of our life; our life must be worship in spirit as God is Spirit.

'God is a Spirit: and they that worship Him must worship Him in spirit and truth.' The second thought that comes to us is that this worship in the spirit must come from God Himself. God is Spirit: He alone has Spirit to give. It was for this He sent His Son, to fit us for such spiritual worship, by giving us the Holy Spirit. It is of His own work that Jesus speaks when He says twice, 'The hour cometh,' and then adds, 'and is now.' He came to baptize with the Holy Spirit; the Spirit could not stream forth till He was glorified (*John i. 33, vii. 37, 38, xvi. 7*). It was when He had made an end of sin, and entering into the Holiest of all with His blood, had there on our behalf *received* the Holy Spirit (*Acts ii. 33*), that He could send Him down to us as the Spirit of the Father. It was when Christ had redeemed us, and we in Him had received the position of children, that the Father sent forth the Spirit of His Son into our hearts to cry, 'Abba, Father.' The worship in spirit is the worship of the Father in the Spirit of Christ, the Spirit of Sonship.

This is the reason why Jesus here uses the name of Father. We never find one of the Old Testament saints personally appropriate the name of child or call God his Father. The worship *of the Father* is only possible to those to whom the Spirit of the Son has been given. The worship *in spirit* is only possible to those to whom the Son has revealed the Father, and who have received the spirit of Sonship. It is only Christ who opens the way and teaches the worship in spirit.

And *in truth*. That does not only mean, *in sincerity*. Nor does it only signify, in accordance with the truth of God's Word. The expression is one of deep and Divine meaning. Jesus is 'the only-begotten of the Father, *full of* grace and *truth*.' 'The law was given by Moses; grace and *truth came* by Jesus Christ.' Jesus says, '*I am the truth* and the life.' In the Old Testament all was shadow and promise; Jesus brought and gives the reality, *the substance*, of things hoped for. In Him the blessings and powers of the eternal life are our actual possession and experience. Jesus is full of grace and truth; the Holy Spirit is the Spirit of truth; through Him the grace that is in Jesus is ours indeed, and truth a positive communication out of the Divine life. And so worship in spirit is worship *in truth*; actual living fellowship with God, a real correspondence and harmony between the Father, who is a Spirit, and the child praying in the spirit.

What Jesus said to the woman of Samaria, she could not at once understand. Pentecost was needed to reveal its full meaning. We are hardly prepared at our first entrance into the school of prayer to grasp such teaching. We shall understand it better later on. Let us only begin and take the lesson as He gives it. We are carnal and cannot bring God the worship He seeks. But Jesus came to give the Spirit: He has given Him to us. Let the disposition in which we set ourselves to pray be what Christ's words have taught us. Let there be the deep confession of our inability to bring God the worship that is pleasing to Him; the childlike teachableness that waits on Him to instruct us; the simple faith that yields itself to the breathing of the Spirit. Above all, let us hold fast the blessed truth—we shall find that the Lord has more to say to us about it—that the knowledge of the Fatherhood of God, the revelation of His infinite Fatherliness in our hearts, the faith in the infinite love that gives us His Son and His Spirit to make us children, is indeed the secret of prayer in spirit and truth. This is the new and living way Christ opened up for us. To have Christ the Son, and *The Spirit of the Son*, dwelling within us, and revealing the Father, this makes us true, spiritual worshippers.

'Lord, Teach Us To Pray.'
~ ※ ~

Blessed Lord! I adore the love with which Thou didst teach a woman, who had
refused Thee a cup of water, what the worship of God must be. I rejoice in the
assurance that Thou wilt no less now instruct Thy disciple, who comes to
Thee with a heart that longs to pray in spirit and in truth. O my Holy Master!
do teach me this blessed secret.

Teach me that the worship in spirit and truth is not of man, but only comes from
Thee; that it is not only a thing of times and seasons, but the outflowing of a
life in Thee. Teach me to draw near to God in prayer under the deep
impression of my ignorance and my having nothing in myself to offer Him,
and at the same time of the provision Thou, my Savior, makest for the Spirit's
breathing in my childlike stammerings. I do bless Thee that in Thee I am a

child, and have a child's liberty of access; that in Thee I have the spirit of Sonship and of worship of truth. Teach me, above all, Blessed Son of the Father, how it is the revelation of the Father that gives confidence in prayer; and let the infinite Fatherliness of God's Heart be my joy and strength for a life of prayer and of worship. Amen.

PRAY TO THY FATHER WHICH IS IN SECRET

OR

ALONE WITH GOD.

*'But thou, when thou prayest, enter into thine inner chamber, and having shut thy
door, pray to thy Father which is in secret, and thy Father which seeth in
secret shall recompense thee.'—Matt. vi. 6.*

After Jesus had called His first disciples He gave them their first public teaching in the Sermon on the Mount. He there expounded to them the kingdom of God, its laws and its life. In that kingdom God is not only King, but Father; He not only gives all, but is Himself all. In the knowledge and fellowship of Him alone is its blessedness. Hence it came as a matter of course that the revelation of prayer and the prayer-life was a part of His teaching concerning the New Kingdom He came to set up. Moses gave neither command nor regulation with regard to prayer: even the prophets say little directly of the duty of prayer; it is Christ who teaches to pray.

And the first thing the Lord teaches His disciples is that they must have a secret place for prayer; every one must have some solitary spot where he can be alone with his God. Every teacher must have a schoolroom. We have learnt to know and accept Jesus as our only teacher in the school of prayer. He has already taught us at Samaria that worship is no longer confined to times and places; that worship, spiritual true worship, is a thing of the spirit and the life; the whole man must in his whole life be worship in spirit and truth. And yet He wants each one to choose for himself the fixed spot where He can daily meet him. That inner chamber, that solitary place, is Jesus' schoolroom. That spot may be anywhere; that spot may change from day to day if we have to change our abode; but that secret place there must be, with the quiet time in which the pupil places himself in the Master's presence, to be by Him prepared to worship the Father. There alone, but there most surely, Jesus comes to us to teach us to pray.

A teacher is always anxious that his schoolroom should be bright and attractive, filled with the light and air of heaven, a place where pupils long to come, and love to stay. In His first words on prayer in the Sermon on the Mount, Jesus seeks to set the inner chamber before us in its most attractive light. If we listen carefully, we soon notice what the chief thing is He has to tell us of our tarrying there. Three times He uses the name of Father: 'Pray to *thy Father*;' '*Thy Father* shall recompense thee;' *Your Father* knoweth what things ye have need of.' The first thing in closet-prayer is: I must meet my Father. The light that shines in the closet must be: the light of the Father's countenance. The fresh air from heaven with which Jesus would have filled the atmosphere in which I am to breathe and pray, is: God's Father-love, God's infinite Fatherliness. Thus each thought or petition we breathe out will be simple, hearty, childlike trust in the Father. This is how the Master teaches us to pray: He brings us into the Father's living presence. What we pray there must avail. Let us listen carefully to hear what the Lord has to say to us.

First, '*Pray to thy Father which is in secret*.' God is a God who hides Himself to the carnal eye. As long as in our worship of God we are chiefly occupied with our own thoughts and exercises, we shall not meet Him who is a Spirit, the unseen One. But to the man who withdraws himself from all that is of the world and man, and prepares to wait upon God alone, the Father will reveal Himself. As he forsakes and gives up and shuts out the world, and the life of the world, and surrenders himself to be led of Christ into the secret of God's presence, the light of the Father's love will rise upon him. The secrecy of the inner chamber and the closed door, the entire separation from all around us, is an image of, and so a help to, that inner spiritual sanctuary, the secret of God's tabernacle, within the veil, where our spirit truly comes into contact with the Invisible One. And so we are taught, at the very outset of our search after the secret of effectual prayer, to remember that it is in the inner chamber, where we are alone with the Father, that we shall learn to pray aright. The Father is in secret: in these words Jesus teaches us where He is waiting us, where He is always to be found. Christians often complain that private prayer is not what it should be. They feel weak and sinful, the heart is cold and dark; it is as if they have so little to pray, and in that little no faith or joy. They are discouraged and kept from prayer by the thought that they cannot come to the Father as they ought or as they wish. Child of God! listen to your Teacher. He tells you that when you go to private prayer your first thought must be: The Father is in secret, the Father waits me there. Just because your heart is cold and prayerless, get you into the presence of the loving Father. As a father pitieth his children, so the Lord pitieth you. Do not be thinking of how little you have to bring God, but of how much He wants to give you. Just place yourself before, and look up into, His face; think of His love, His wonderful, tender, pitying love. Just tell Him how sinful and cold and dark all is: it is the Father's loving heart will give light and warmth to yours. O do what Jesus says: Just shut the door, and pray to thy Father, which is in secret. Is it not wonderful? to be able to go alone with God, the infinite God. And then to look up and say: My Father!

'*And thy Father, which seeth in secret, will recompense thee.*' Here Jesus assures us that secret prayer cannot be fruitless: its blessing will show itself in our life. We have but in secret, alone with God, to entrust our life before men to Him; He will reward us openly; He will see to it that the answer to prayer be made manifest in His blessing upon us. Our Lord would thus teach us that as infinite Fatherliness and Faithfulness is that with which God meets us in secret, so on our part there should be the childlike simplicity of faith, the confidence that our prayer does bring down a blessing. 'He that cometh to God must believe that *He is a rewarder* of them that seek Him.' Not on the strong or the fervent feeling with which I pray does the blessing of the closet depend, but upon the love and the power of the Father to whom I there entrust my needs. And therefore the Master has but one desire: Remember your Father is, and sees and hears in secret; go there and stay there, and go again from there in the confidence: He will recompense. Trust Him for it; depend upon Him: prayer to the Father cannot be vain; He will reward you openly.

Still further to confirm this faith in the Father-love of God, Christ speaks a third word: '*Your Father knoweth what things ye have need of before ye ask Him.*' At first sight it might appear as if this thought made prayer less needful: God knows far better than we what we need. But as we get a deeper insight into what prayer really is, this truth will help much to strengthen our faith. It will teach us that we do not need, as the heathen, with the multitude and urgency of our words, to compel an unwilling God to listen to us. It will lead to a holy thoughtfulness and silence in prayer as it suggests the question: Does my Father really know that I need this? It will, when once we have been led by the Spirit to the certainty that our request is indeed something that, according to the Word, we do need for God's glory, give us wonderful confidence to say, My Father knows I need it and must have it. And if there be any delay in the answer, it will teach us in quiet perseverance to hold on: Father! Thou knowest I need it. O the blessed liberty and simplicity of a child that Christ our Teacher would fain cultivate in us, as we draw near to God: let us look up to the Father until His Spirit works it in us. Let us sometimes in our prayers, when we are in danger of being so occupied with our fervent, urgent petitions, as to forget that the Father knows and hears, let us hold still and just quietly say: My Father sees, my Father hears, my Father knows; it will help our faith to take the answer, and to say: We know that we have the petitions we have asked of Him.

And now, all ye who have anew entered the school of Christ to be taught to pray, take these lessons, practice them, and trust Him to perfect you in them. Dwell much in the inner chamber, with the door shut—shut in from men, shut up with God; it is there the Father waits you, it is there Jesus will teach you to pray. To be alone in secret with the Father: this be your highest joy. To be assured that the Father will openly reward the secret prayer, so that it cannot remain unblessed: this be your strength day by day. And to know that the Father knows that you need what you ask, this be your liberty to bring every need, in the assurance that your God will supply it according to His riches in glory in Christ Jesus.

'Lord, Teach Us To Pray.'
~ ※ ~

Blessed Savior! with my whole heart I do bless Thee for the appointment of the inner chamber, as the school where Thou meetest each of Thy pupils alone, and revealest to him the Father. O my Lord! strengthen my faith so in the Father's tender love and kindness, that as often as I feel sinful or troubled, the first instinctive thought may be to go where I know the Father waits me, and where prayer never can go unblessed. Let the thought that He knows my need before I ask, bring me, in great restfulness of faith, to trust that He will give what His child requires. O let the place of secret prayer become to me the most beloved spot on earth.

And, Lord! hear me as I pray that Thou wouldest everywhere bless the closets of Thy believing people. Let Thy wonderful revelation of a Father's tenderness free all young Christians from every thought of secret prayer as a duty or a burden, and lead them to regard it as the highest privilege of their life, a joy and a blessing. Bring back all who are discouraged, because they cannot find ought to bring Thee in prayer. O give them to understand that they have only to come with their emptiness to Him who has all to give, and delights to do it. Not, what they have to bring the Father, but what the Father waits to give them, be their one thought.

And bless especially the inner chamber of all Thy servants who are working for Thee, as the place where God's truth and God's grace is revealed to them, where they are daily anointed with fresh oil, where their strength is renewed, and the blessings are received in faith, with which they are to bless their fellow-men. Lord, draw us all in the closet nearer to Thyself and the Father. Amen.

'AFTER THIS MANNER PRAY'

OR

THE MODEL PRAYER.

'After this manner therefore pray ye: Our Father which art in heaven.'—Matt. vi. 9.

Every teacher knows the power of example. He not only tells the child what to do and how to do it, but shows him how it really can be done. In condescension to our weakness, our Heavenly Teacher has given us the very words we are to take with us as we draw near to our Father. We have in them a form of prayer in which there breathe the freshness and fulness of the Eternal Life. So simple that the child can lisp it, so divinely rich that it comprehends all that God can give. A form of prayer that becomes the model and inspiration for all other prayer, and yet always draws us back to itself as the deepest utterance of our souls before our God.

'Our Father which art in heaven!' To appreciate this word of adoration aright, I must remember that none of the saints had in Scripture ever ventured to address God as their Father. The invocation places us at once in the center of the wonderful revelation the Son came to make of His Father as our Father too. It comprehends the mystery of redemption—Christ delivering us from the curse that we might become the children of God. The mystery of regeneration—the Spirit in the new birth giving us the new life. And the mystery of faith—ere yet the redemption is accomplished or understood, the word is given on the lips of the disciples to prepare them for the blessed experience still to come. The words are the key to the whole prayer, to all prayer. It takes time, it takes life to study them; it will take eternity to understand them fully. The knowledge of God's Father-love is the first and simplest, but also the last and highest lesson in the school of prayer. It is in the personal relation to the living God, and the personal conscious fellowship of love with Himself, that prayer begins. It is in the knowledge of God's Fatherliness, revealed by the Holy Spirit, that the power of prayer will be found to root and grow. In the infinite tenderness and pity and patience of the infinite Father, in His loving readiness to hear and to help, the life of prayer has its joy. O let us take time, until the Spirit has made these words to us spirit and truth, filling heart and life: 'Our Father which art in heaven.' Then we are indeed within the veil, in the secret place of power where prayer always prevails.

'Hallowed be Thy name.' There is something here that strikes us at once. While we ordinarily first bring our own needs to God in prayer, and then think of what belongs to God and His interests, the Master reverses the order. First, *Thy* name, *Thy* kingdom, *Thy* will; then, give *us*, forgive *us*, lead *us*, deliver *us*. The lesson is of more importance than we think. In true worship the Father must be first, must be all. The sooner I learn to forget myself in the desire that He may be glorified, the richer will the blessing be that prayer will bring to myself. No one ever loses by what he sacrifices for the Father.

This must influence all our prayer. There are two sorts of prayer: personal and intercessory. The latter ordinarily occupies the lesser part of our time and energy. This may not be. Christ has opened the school of prayer specially to train intercessors for the great work of bringing down, by their faith and prayer, the blessings of His work and love on the world around. There can be no deep growth in prayer unless this be made our aim. The little child may ask of the father only what it needs for itself; and yet it soon learns to say, Give some for sister too. But the grown-up son, who only lives for the father's interest and takes charge of the father's business, asks more largely, and gets all that is asked. And Jesus would train us to the blessed life of consecration and service, in which our interests are all subordinate to the Name, and the Kingdom, and the Will of the Father. O let us live for this, and let, on each act of adoration, Our Father! there follow in the same breath, *Thy* Name, *Thy* Kingdom, *Thy* Will;—for this we look up and long.

'Hallowed be Thy name.' What name? This new name of Father. The word *Holy* is the central word of the Old Testament; the *name* Father of the New. In this name of Love all the holiness and glory of God are now to be revealed. And how is the name to be hallowed? By God Himself: *'I will hallow* My great name which ye have profaned.' Our prayer must be that in ourselves, in all God's children, in presence of the world, God Himself would reveal the holiness, the Divine power, the hidden glory of the name of Father. The Spirit of the Father is the *Holy* Spirit: it is only when we yield ourselves to be led *of Him*, that the name will be *hallowed* in our prayer and our lives. Let us learn the prayer: 'Our Father, hallowed be Thy name.'

'*Thy kingdom come.*' The Father is a King and has a kingdom. The son and heir of a king has no higher ambition than the glory of his father's kingdom. In time of war or danger this becomes his passion; he can think of nothing else. The children of the Father are here in the enemy's territory, where the kingdom, which is in heaven, is not yet fully manifested. What more natural than that, when they learn to hallow the Father-name, they should long and cry with deep enthusiasm: 'Thy kingdom come.' The coming of the kingdom is the one great event on which the revelation of the Father's glory, the blessedness of His children, the salvation of the world depends. On our prayers too the coming of the kingdom waits. Shall we not join in the deep longing cry of the redeemed: 'Thy kingdom come'? Let us learn it in the school of Jesus.

'*Thy will be done, as in heaven, so on earth.*' This petition is too frequently applied alone to the *suffering* of the will of God. In heaven God's will is *done*, and the Master teaches the child to ask that the will may be done on earth just as in heaven: in the spirit of adoring submission and ready obedience. Because the will of God is the glory of heaven, the doing of it is the blessedness of heaven. As the will is done, the kingdom of heaven comes into the heart. And wherever faith has accepted the Father's love, obedience accepts the Father's will. The surrender to, and the prayer for a life of heaven-like obedience, is the spirit of childlike prayer.

'*Give us this day our daily bread.*' When first the child has yielded himself to the Father in the care for His Name, His Kingdom, and His Will, he has full liberty to ask for his daily bread. A master cares for the food of his servant, a general of his soldiers, a father of his child. And will not the Father in heaven care for the child who has in prayer given himself up to His interests? We may indeed in full confidence say: Father, I live for Thy honor and Thy work; I know Thou carest for me. Consecration to God and His will gives wonderful liberty in prayer for temporal things: the whole earthly life is given to the Father's loving care.

'*And forgive us our debts as we also have forgiven our debtors.*' As bread is the first need of the body, so forgiveness for the soul. And the provision for the one is as sure as for the other. We are children, but sinners too; our right of access to the Father's presence we owe to the precious blood and the forgiveness it has won for us. Let us beware of the prayer for forgiveness becoming a formality: only what is really confessed is really forgiven. Let us in faith accept the forgiveness as promised: as a spiritual reality, an actual transaction between God and us, it is the entrance into all the Father's love and all the privileges of children. Such forgiveness, as a living experience, is impossible without a forgiving spirit to others: as *forgiven* expresses the heavenward, so *forgiving* the earthward, relation of God's child. In each prayer to the Father I must be able to say that I know of no one whom I do not heartily love.

'*And lead us not into temptation, but deliver us from the evil one.*' Our daily bread, the pardon of our sins, and then our being kept from all sin and the power of the evil one, in these three petitions all our personal need is comprehended. The prayer for bread and pardon must be accompanied by the surrender to live in all things in holy obedience to the Father's will, and the believing prayer in everything to be kept by the power of the indwelling Spirit from the power of the evil one.

Children of God! it is thus Jesus would have us to pray to the Father in heaven. O let His Name, and Kingdom, and Will, have the first place in our love; His providing, and pardoning, and keeping love will be our sure portion. So the prayer will lead us up to the true child-life: the Father all to the child, the Father all for the child. We shall understand how Father and child, the *Thine* and the *Our*, are all one, and how the heart that begins its prayer with the God-devoted Thine, will have the power in faith to speak out the Our too. Such prayer will, indeed, be the fellowship and interchange of love, always bringing us back in trust and worship to Him who is not only the Beginning but the End: 'For thine is the kingdom, and the power, and the glory, for ever, Amen.' Son of the Father, teach us to pray, 'Our Father.'

'Lord, Teach Us To Pray.'

~ ※ ~

O Thou who art the only-begotten Son, teach us, we beseech Thee, to pray, 'Our Father.' We thank Thee, Lord, for these Living Blessed Words which Thou hast given us. We thank Thee for the millions who in them have learnt to know and worship the Father, and for what they have been to us. Lord! it is as if we needed days and weeks in Thy school with each separate petition; so deep and full are they. But we look to Thee to lead us deeper into their meaning: do it, we pray Thee, for Thy Name's sake; Thy name is Son of the Father.

Lord! Thou didst once say: 'No man knoweth the Father save the Son, and he to whom the Son willeth to reveal Him.' And again: 'I made known unto them Thy name, and will make it known, that the love wherewith Thou hast loved Me may be in them.' Lord Jesus! reveal to us the Father. Let His name, His infinite Father-love, the love with which He loved Thee, according to Thy prayer, BE IN US. Then shall we say aright, 'Our Father!' Then shall we apprehend Thy teaching, and the first spontaneous breathing of our heart will be: 'Our Father, Thy Name, Thy Kingdom, Thy Will.' And we shall bring our needs and our sins and our temptations to Him in the confidence that the love of such a Father cares for all.

Blessed Lord! we are Thy scholars, we trust Thee; do teach us to pray, 'Our Father.' Amen.

Waiting on God

Daily Messages for a Month

~ ※ ~

By *Andrew Murray*

1897

'Wait Thou only upon God.'

'My soul, wait thou only upon God.' –Ps. 62:5
'A God... which worketh for him that waiteth for Him.' –Isa. 64:4(R.V.)

'WAIT only upon God;' my soul, be still,
And let thy God unfold His perfect will,
Thou fain[1] would'st follow Him throughout this year,
Thou fain with listening heart His voice would'st hear,
Thou fain would'st be a passive instrument
Possessed by God, and ever Spirit-sent
Upon His service sweet—then be thou still
For only thus can He in thee fulfil
His heart's desire. Oh, hinder not His hand
From fashioning the vessel He hath planned.
'Be silent unto God,' and thou shalt know
The quiet, holy calm He doth bestow
On these who wait on Him; so shalt thou bear
His promises, and His life and light e'en where
The night is darkest, and thine earthly days
Shall shew His love, and sound His glorious praise
And He will work with head unfettered, free
His high and holy purposes through thee.
First on thee must that hand of power be turned,
Till in His love's strong fire thy dross is burned,
And thou come forth a vessel for thy Lord,
So frail and empty, yet, since He hath poured
Into thine emptiness His life, His love
Henceforth through thee the power of God shall move
And He will work *for* thee. Stand still and see
The victories thy God will gain for thee;
So silent, yet so irresistible,
Thy God shall do the thing impossible.
Oh, question not henceforth what thou canst do;
Thou canst do *naught*. But He will carry through
The work where human energy had failed
Where all thy best endeavors had availed
Thee nothing. Then, my soul, wait and be still;
Thy God shall work for thee His perfect will.
If thou will take no less, *His best* shall be
Thy portion now and through eternity.

—FREDA HANBURY

Extract from Address in Exeter Hall

May 31st 1895

I HAVE been surprised at nothing more than at the letters that have come to me from missionaries and others from all parts of the world, devoted men and women, testifying to the need they feel in their work of being helped to a deeper and a clearer insight into all that Christ could be

---

[1] Fain: 'with pleasure'

to them. Let us look to God to reveal Himself among His people in a measure very few have realized. Let us expect great things of our God. At all our conventions and assemblies too little time is given to waiting on God. Is He not willing to put things right in His own divine way? Has the life of God's people reached the utmost limit of what God is willing to do for them? Surely not. We want to wait on Him; to put away our experiences, however blessed they have been; our conceptions of truth, however sound and scriptural we think they seem; our plans, however needful and suitable they appear; and give God time and place to show us what He could, what He will do. God has new developments and new resources. He can do new things, unheard of things. Let us enlarge our hearts and not limit Him. 'When Thou camest down, Thou didst terrible things we looked not for; the mountains flowed down at Thy presence.'

—A. M.

Preface

PREVIOUS to my leaving for England last year, I had been much impressed by the thought of how, in all our religion, personal and public, we need more of God. I had felt that we needed to train our people in their worship more to wait on God, and to make the cultivation of a deeper sense of His presence, of more direct contact with Him, of entire dependence on Him, a definite aim of our ministry. At a 'welcome' breakfast in Exeter Hall, I gave very simple expression to this thought in connection with all our religious work. I have already said elsewhere that I was surprised at the response the sentiment met with. I saw that God's Spirit had been working the same desire in many hearts.

The experiences of the past year, both personal and public, have greatly deepened the conviction. It is as if I myself am only beginning to see the deepest truth concerning God, and our relation to Him, center in this waiting on God, and how very little, in our life and work, we have been surrounded by its spirit. The following pages are the outcome of my conviction, and of the desire to direct the attention of all God's people to the one great remedy for all our needs. More than half the pieces were written on board ship; I fear they bear the marks of being somewhat crude and hasty. I have felt, in looking them over, as if I could wish to write them over again. But this I cannot now do. And so I send them out with the prayer that He who loves to use the feeble may give His blessing with them.

I do not know if it will be possible for me to put into a few words what are the chief things we need to learn. In a note at the close of the book on Law I have mentioned some. But what I want to say here is this: The great lack of our religion is, *we do not know God.* The answer to every complaint of feebleness and failure, the message to every congregation or convention seeking instruction on holiness, ought to be simply, What is the matter: *Have you not God?* If you really believe in God, He will put all right. God is willing and able by His Holy Spirit. Cease from expecting the least good from yourself, or the least help from anything there is in man, and just yield yourself unreservedly to God to work in you: He will do all for you.

How simple this looks! And yet this is the gospel we so little know. I feel ashamed as I send forth these very defective meditations; I can only cast them on the love of my brethren, and of our God. May He use them to draw us all to Himself, to learn in practice and experience the blessed art of Waiting only upon God. Would God that we might get some right conception of what the influence would be of a life given, not in thought, or imagination, or effort, but in the power of the Holy Spirit, wholly to waiting upon God.

With my greeting in Christ to all God's saints it has been my privilege to meet, and no less to those I have not met, I subscribe myself, your brother and servant,

ANDREW MURRAY.
Wellington
3rd March 1896

Day 1: The God of Our Salvation.

'My soul waiteth only upon God[1]; from Him cometh my salvation.'—*Ps. 62:1(R.V.).*

IF salvation indeed comes from God, and is entirely His work, just as our creation was, it follows, as a matter of course, that our first and highest duty is to wait on Him to do that work as it pleases Him. Waiting becomes then the only way to the experience of a full salvation, the only way, truly, to know God as the God of our salvation. All the difficulties that are brought forward as keeping us back from full salvation, have their cause in this one thing: the defective knowledge and practice of waiting upon God. All that the Church and its members need for the manifestation of the mighty power of God in the world, is the return to our true place, the place that belongs to us, both in creation and redemption, the place of absolute and unceasing dependence upon God. Let us strive to see what the elements are that make up this most blessed and needful waiting upon God: it may help us to discover the reasons why this grace is so little cultivated, and to feel how infinitely desirable it is that the Church, that we ourselves, should at any price learn its blessed secret.

The deep need for this waiting on God lies equally in the nature of man and the nature of God. God, as Creator, formed man, to be a vessel in which He could show forth His power and goodness. Man was not to have in himself a fountain of life, or strength, or happiness: the ever-living and only living One was each moment to be the Communicator to him of all that he needed. Man's glory and blessedness was not to be independent, or dependent upon himself, but dependent on a God of such infinite riches and love. Man was to have the joy of receiving every moment out of the fulness of God. This was his blessedness as an unfallen creature.

When he fell from God, he was still more absolutely dependent on Him. There was not the slightest hope of his recovery out of his state of death, but in God, His power and mercy. It is God alone who began the work of redemption; it is God alone who continues and carries it on each moment in each individual believer. Even in the regenerate man there is no power of goodness in himself: he has and can have nothing that he does not each moment receive; and waiting on God is just as indispensable, and must be just as continuous and unbroken, as the breathing that maintains his natural life.

It is, then, because Christians do not know in their relation to God of their own absolute poverty and helplessness, that they have no sense of the need of absolute and unceasing dependence, or of the unspeakable blessedness of continual waiting on God. But when once a believer begins to see it, and consent to it, that he by the Holy Spirit must each moment receive what God each moment works, waiting on God becomes his brightest hope and joy. As he appreciates how God, as God, as Infinite Love, delights to impart His own nature to His child as fully as He can, how God is not weary of each moment keeping charge of his life and strength, he wonders that he ever thought otherwise of God than as a God to be waited on all the day. God unceasingly giving and working; His child unceasingly waiting and receiving: this is the blessed life.

'Truly my soul waiteth upon God; from Him cometh my salvation.' First we wait on God for salvation. Then we learn that salvation is only to bring us to God, and teach us to wait on Him. Then we find what is better still, that waiting on God is itself the highest salvation. It is the ascribing to Him the glory of being All; it is the experiencing that He is All to us. May God teach us the blessedness of waiting on Him.

'My soul, wait thou only upon God!'

Day 2: The Keynote of Life.

'I have waited for Thy salvation, O Lord!'—*Gen. 49:18.*

IT is not easy to say exactly in what sense Jacob used these words, in the midst of his prophecies in regard to the future of his sons. But they do certainly indicate that both for himself and for them his expectation was from God alone. It was God's salvation he waited for; a salvation which God had promised and which God Himself alone could work out. He knew himself and his sons to be under God's charge. Jehovah the Everlasting God would show in them what His saving power is and does. The words point forward to that wonderful history of redemption which is not

---

[1] Or, 'is silent unto God'

yet finished, and to the glorious future in eternity. They suggest to us how there is no salvation but God's salvation, and how waiting on God for that, whether for our personal experience, or in wider circles, is our first duty, our true blessedness.

Let us think of ourselves, and the inconceivably glorious salvation God has wrought for us in Christ, and is now purposing to work out and to perfect in us by His Spirit. Let us meditate until we somewhat realize that every participation of this great salvation, from moment to moment, must be the work of God Himself. God cannot part with His grace, or goodness, or strength, as an external thing that He gives us, as He gives the raindrops from heaven. No; He can only give it, and we can only enjoy it, as He works it Himself directly and unceasingly. And the only reason that He does not work it more effectively and continuously is, that we do not let Him. We hinder Him either by our indifference or by our self-effort, so that He cannot do what He would. What He asks of us, in the way of surrender, and obedience, and desire, and trust, is all comprised in this one word: waiting on Him, waiting for His salvation. It combines the deep sense of our entire helplessness of ourselves to work what is divinely good, and the perfect confidence that our God will work it all in His divine power.

Again, I say, let us meditate on the divine glory of the salvation God purposes working out in us, until we know the truth it implies. Our heart is the scene of a divine operation more wonderful than Creation. We can do as little towards the work as towards creating the world, except as God works in us to will and to do. God only asks of us to yield, to consent, to wait upon Him, and He will do it all. Let us meditate and be still, until we see how appropriate and right and blessed it is that God alone do all, and our soul will of itself sink down in deep humility to say: 'I have waited for Thy salvation, O Lord.' And the deep blessed background of all our praying and working will be: 'Truly my soul waiteth upon God.'

The application of the truth to wider circles, to those we labor among or intercede for, to the Church of Christ around us, or throughout the world, is not difficult. There can be no good but what God works; to wait upon God, and have the heart filled with faith in His working, and in that faith to pray for His mighty power to come down, is our only wisdom. Oh for the eyes of our heart to be opened to see God working in ourselves and in others, and to see how blessed it is to worship and just to wait for His salvation!

Our private and public prayer are our chief expression of our relation to God: it is in them chiefly that our waiting upon God must be exercised. If our waiting begin by quieting the activities of nature, and being still before God; if it bows and seeks to see God in His universal and almighty operation, alone able and always ready to work all good; if it yields itself to Him in the assurance that He is working and will work in us; if it maintains the place of humility and stillness and surrender, until God's Spirit has quickened the faith that He will perfect His work: it will indeed become the strength and the joy of the soul. Life will become one deep blessed cry: 'I have waited for Thy salvation, O Lord.'

'My soul, wait thou only upon God!'

Day 3: The True Place of the Creature.

'These wait all upon Thee;
That Thou mayest give them their meat in due season.
That Thou givest unto them, they gather;
Thou openest Thine hand, they are satisfied with good.
Ps. 104:27, 28(R.V.).

THIS Psalm, in praise of the Creator, has been speaking of the birds and the beasts of the forest; of the young lions, and man going forth to his work; of the great sea, wherein are things creeping innumerable, both small and great beasts. And it sums up the whole relation of all creation to its Creator, and its continuous and universal dependence upon Him in the one word: *'These all wait upon Thee!'* Just as much as it was God's work to create, it is His work to maintain. As little as the creature could create itself, is it left to provide for itself. The whole creation is ruled by the one unalterable law of—*waiting upon God!*

The word is the simple expression of that for the sake of which alone the creature was brought into existence, the very groundwork of its constitution. The one object for which God gave life to creatures was that in them He might prove and show forth His wisdom, power, and goodness, in His being each moment their life and happiness, and pouring forth unto them, according to their capacity, the riches of his goodness and power. And just as this is the very place and nature of God, to be unceasingly the supplier of every want in the creature, so the very place and nature of the creature is nothing but this—to wait upon God and receive from Him what He alone can give, what He delights to give. (See note on Law, *The Power of the Spirit*.)

If we are in this little book at all to appreciate what *waiting on God* is to be to the believer, to practice it and to experience its blessedness, it is of consequence that we begin at the very beginning, and see the deep reasonableness of the call that comes to us. We shall understand how the duty is no arbitrary command. We shall see how it is not only rendered necessary by our sin and helplessness. It is simply and truly our restoration to our original destiny and our highest nobility, to our true place and glory as creatures blessedly dependent on the All-Glorious God.

If once our eyes are opened to this precious truth, all Nature will become a preacher, reminding us of the relationship which, founded in creation, is now taken up in grace. As we read this Psalm, and learn to look upon all life in Nature as continually maintained by God Himself, waiting on God will be seen to be the very necessity of our being. As we think of the young lions and the ravens crying to Him, of the birds and the fish and every insect waiting on Him, until He give them their meat in due season, we shall see that it is the very nature and glory of God that He is a God who is to be waited on. Every thought of what Nature is, and what God is, will give new force to the call: 'Wait thou only upon God.'

'These all wait upon Thee, that thou may *give*.' It is God who gives all: let this faith enter deeply into our hearts. Ere yet we fully understand all that is implied in our waiting upon God, and ere we ever have been able to cultivate the habit, let the truth enter our souls: waiting on God, unceasing and entire dependence upon Him, is, in heaven and earth, the one only true religion, the one unalterable and all-comprehensive expression for the true relationship to the ever-blessed One in whom we live.

Let us resolve at once that it shall be the one characteristic of our life and worship, a continual, humble, trustful waiting upon God. We may rest assured that He who made us for Himself, that He might give Himself to us and in us, that He will never disappoint us. In waiting on Him we shall find rest and joy and strength, and the supply of every need.

'My soul, wait thou only upon God!'

Day 4: For Supplies.

'The Lord upholdeth all that fall,
And raiseth up all those that be bowed down.
The eyes of all wait upon Thee;
And Thou givest them their meat in due season.'
—Ps. 145:14, 15.

PSALM 104 is a Psalm of Creation, and the words, *'These all wait upon Thee,'* were used with reference to the animal creation. Here we have a Psalm of the Kingdom, and *'The eyes of all wait upon Thee'* appears especially to point to the needs of God's saints, of all that fall and them that be bowed down. What the universe and the animal creation does unconsciously, God's people are to do intelligently and voluntarily. Man is to be the interpreter of Nature. He is to prove that there is nothing more noble or more blessed in the exercise of our free will than to use it in waiting upon God.

If an army has been sent out to march into an enemy's country, and tidings are received that it is not advancing, the question is at once asked, what may be the cause of delay. The answer will very often be: 'Waiting for supplies.' All the stores of provisions or clothing or ammunition have not arrived; without these it dare not proceed. It is no otherwise in the Christian life: day by day, at every step, we need our supplies from above. And there is nothing so needful as to cultivate that spirit of dependence on God and of confidence in Him, which refuses to go on without the needed supply of grace and strength.

If the question be asked, whether this be anything different from what we do when we pray, the answer is, that there may be much praying with but very little waiting on God. In praying we are often occupied with ourselves, with our own needs, and our own efforts in the presentation of them. In waiting upon God, the first thought is of *the God upon whom we wait*. We enter His presence, and feel we need just to be quiet, so that He, as God, can overshadow us with Himself. God longs to reveal Himself, to fill us with Himself. Waiting on God gives Him time in His own way and divine power to come to us.

It is especially at the time of prayer that we ought to set ourselves to cultivate this spirit.

Before you pray, bow quietly before God, just to remember and realize who He is, how near He is, how certainly He can and will help. Just be still before Him, and allow His Holy Spirit to waken and stir up in your soul the childlike disposition of absolute dependence and confident expectation. Wait upon God as a Living Being, as the Living God, who notices you, and is just longing to fill you with His salvation. Wait on God until you know you have met Him; prayer will then become so different.

And when you are praying, let there be intervals of silence, reverent stillness of soul, in which you yield yourself to God, in case He may have aught He wishes to teach you or to work in you. Waiting on Him will become the most blessed part of prayer, and the blessing thus obtained will be doubly precious as the fruit of such fellowship with the Holy One. God has so ordained it, in harmony with His holy nature, and with ours, that waiting on Him should be the honor we give Him. Let us bring Him the service gladly and truthfully; He will reward it abundantly.

'The eyes of all wait upon Thee, and Thou givest them their meat in due season.' Dear soul, God provides in Nature for the creatures He has made: how much more will He provide in Grace for those He has redeemed. Learn to say of every want, and every failure, and every lack of needful grace: I have waited too little upon God, or He would have given me in due season all I needed. And say then too—

'My soul, wait thou only upon God!'

Day 5: For Instruction.

'Shew me thy ways, O Lord; Teach me Thy paths.
Teach me Thy paths.
Lead me in Thy truth, and teach me;
For Thou art the God of my salvation;
On Thee do I wait all the day.'—Ps. 25:4, 5.

'I SPOKE of an army, on the point of entering an enemy's territories, answering the question as to the cause of delay: *'Waiting for supplies.'* The answer might also have been: *'Waiting for instructions,'* or, *'Waiting for orders.'* If the last dispatch had not been received, with the final orders of the commander-in-chief, the army dared not move. Even so in the Christian life: as deep as the need of *waiting for supplies*, is that of *waiting for instructions.'*

See how beautifully this comes out in Ps. 25. The writer knew and loved God's law exceedingly, and meditated in that law day and night. But he knew that this was not enough. He knew that for the right spiritual apprehension of the truth, and for the right personal application of it to his own peculiar circumstances, he needed a direct divine teaching.

The psalm has at all times been a very favorite one, because of its reiterated expression of the felt need of the Divine teaching, and of the childlike confidence that that teaching would be given. Study the psalm until your heart is filled with the two thoughts—the absolute need, the absolute certainty of divine guidance. And notice, then, how entirely it is in this connection that he speaks, *'On Thee do I wait all the day.'* Waiting for guidance, waiting for instruction, all the day, is a very blessed part of waiting upon God.

The Father in heaven is so interested in His child, and so longs to have his life at every step in His will and His love, that He is willing to keep his guidance entirely in His own hand. He knows so well that we are unable to do what is really holy and heavenly, except as He works it in us, that He means His very demands to become promises of what He will do, in watching over and leading us all the day. Not only in special difficulties and times of perplexity, but in the common course of everyday life, we may count upon Him to teach us *His* way, and show us *His* path.

And what is needed in us to receive this guidance? One thing: waiting for instructions, waiting on God. 'On Thee do I wait all the day.' We want in our times of prayer to give clear expression to our sense of need, and our faith in His help. We want definitely to become conscious of our ignorance as to what God's way may be, and the need of the Divine light shining within us, if our way is to be as of the sun, shining more and more unto the perfect day. And we want to wait quietly before God in prayer, until the deep, restful assurance fills us: It will be given—'the meek will He guide in the way.'

'On Thee do I wait all the day.' The special surrender to the Divine guidance in our seasons of prayer must cultivate, and be followed up by, the habitual looking upwards 'all the day.' As simple as it is, to one who has eyes, to walk all the day in the light of the sun, so simple and delightful can it become to a soul practiced in waiting on God, to walk all the day in the enjoyment of God's light and leading. What is needed to help us to such a life is just one thing: the real knowledge and faith of God as the one only source of wisdom and goodness, as ever ready, and longing much to be to us all that we can possibly require—yes! this is the one thing we need. If we but saw our God in His love, if we but believed that He waits to be gracious, that He waits to be our life and to work all in us,—how this waiting on God would become our highest joy, the natural and spontaneous response of our hearts to His great love and glory!

'My soul, wait thou only upon God!'

Day 6: For all Saints.

'Let none that wait on Thee be ashamed.'—Ps. 25:3

LET us now, in our meditation of today, each one forget himself, to think of the great company of God's saints throughout the world, who are all with us waiting on Him. And let us all join in the fervent prayer for each other, 'Let none that wait on Thee be ashamed.'

Just think for a moment of the multitude of waiting ones who need that prayer; how many there are, sick and weary and solitary, to whom it is as if their prayers are not answered, and who sometimes begin to fear that their hope will be put to shame. And then, how many servants of God, ministers or missionaries, teachers or workers, of various name, whose hopes in their work have been disappointed, and whose longing for power and blessing remains unsatisfied. And then, too, how many, who have heard of a life of rest and perfect peace, of abiding light and fellowship, of strength and victory, and who cannot find the path. With all these, it is nothing but that they have not yet learned the secret of full waiting upon God. They just need, what we all need, the living assurance that waiting on God can never be in vain. Let us remember all who are in danger of fainting or being weary, and all unite in the cry, 'Let none that wait on Thee be ashamed'!

If this intercession for all who wait on God becomes part of our waiting on Him for ourselves, we shall help to bear each other's burdens, and so fulfil the law of Christ.

There will be introduced into our waiting on God that element of unselfishness and love, which is the path to the highest blessing, and the fullest communion with God. Love to the brethren and love to God are inseparably linked. In God, the love to His Son *and to us* are one: 'That the love wherewith Thou hast loved Me, may be in them.' In Christ, the love of the Father to Him, and *His love to us,* are one: 'As the Father loved me, so have I loved you.' In us, He asks that His love to us shall be *ours* to the brethren: 'As I have loved you, that ye love one another.' All the love of God, and of Christ, are inseparably linked with love to the brethren. And how can we, day by day, prove and cultivate this love otherwise than by daily praying for each other? Christ did not seek to enjoy the Father's love for Himself; He passed it all on to us. All true seeking of God and His love for ourselves, will be inseparably linked with the thought and the love of our brethren in prayer for them.

'Let none that wait on Thee be ashamed.' Twice in the psalm David speaks of his waiting on God for himself; here he thinks of *all* who wait on Him. Let this page take the message to all God's tried and weary ones, that there are more praying for them than they know. Let it stir them and us in our waiting to make a point of at times forgetting ourselves, and to enlarge our hearts, and say to the Father, *'These all wait upon Thee,* and Thou givest them their meat in due season.' Let it inspire us all with new courage—for who is there who is not at times ready to faint and be weary? 'Let none that wait on Thee be ashamed' is a promise in a prayer, 'They that wait on Thee shall not be ashamed'! From many and many a witness the cry comes to everyone who needs the help, brother, sister, tried one, 'Wait on the Lord; be of good courage, and He shall strengthen your heart; wait, I say, on the Lord. Be of good courage, and He shall strengthen your heart, all ye that wait on the Lord.'

Blessed Father! we humbly beseech Thee, Let none that wait on Thee be ashamed; no, not one. Some are weary, and the time of waiting appears long. And some are feeble, and scarcely know how to wait. And some are so entangled in the effort of their prayers and their work, they think that they can find no time to wait continually. Father! teach us all how to wait. Teach us to think of each other, and pray for each other. Teach us to think of Thee, the God of all waiting ones. Father! let none that wait on Thee be ashamed. For Jesus' sake. Amen.

'My soul, wait thou only upon God!'

Day 7: A Plea in Prayer.

'Let integrity and uprightness preserve me; for I wait on Thee.'—Ps. 25:21

FOR the third time in this psalm we have the word wait. As before in ver. 5, 'On Thee do I wait all the day,' so here, too, the believing supplicant appeals to God to remember that he is waiting on Him, looking for an answer. It is a great thing for a soul not only to wait upon God, but to be filled with such a consciousness that its whole spirit and position is that of a waiting one, that it can, in childlike confidence, say, Lord! Thou knowest, I wait on Thee. It will prove a mighty plea in prayer, giving ever-increasing boldness of expectation to claim the promise, 'They that wait on Me shall not be ashamed'!

The prayer in connection with which the plea is put forth here is one of great importance in the spiritual life. If we draw near to God, it must be with a true heart. There must be perfect integrity, wholeheartedness, in our dealing with God. As we read in the next Psalm (26:1, 11), 'Judge me, O Lord, for I have walked in my integrity,' 'As for me, I will walk in my integrity,' there must be perfect uprightness or single-heartedness before God. As it is written, 'His righteousness is for the upright in heart.' The soul must know that it allows nothing sinful, nothing doubtful; if it is indeed to meet the Holy One, and receive His full blessing, it must be with a heart wholly and singly given up to His will. The whole spirit that animates us in the waiting must be, 'Let integrity and uprightness'—Thou seest that I desire to come so to Thee, You know I am looking to Thee to work them perfectly in me;—let them 'preserve me, for I wait on Thee.'

And if at our first attempt truly to live the life of fully and always waiting on God, we begin to discover how much that perfect integrity is wanting, this will just be one of the blessings which the waiting was meant to work. *A soul cannot seek close fellowship with God, or attain the abiding consciousness of waiting on Him all the day, without a very honest and entire surrender to all His will.*

'For I wait on Thee': it is not only in connection with the prayer of our text but with every prayer that this plea may be used. To use it often will be a great blessing to ourselves. Let us therefore study the words well until we know all their bearings. It must be clear to us *what we are waiting for*. There may be very different things. It may be waiting for God in our times of prayer to take his place as God, and to work in us the sense of His holy presence and nearness. It may be some special petition, to which we are expecting an answer. It may be our whole inner life, in which we are on the lookout for God's putting forth of His power. It may be the whole state of His Church and saints, or some part of His work, for which our eyes are ever toward Him. It is good that we sometimes count up to ourselves exactly what the things are we are waiting for, and as we say definitely of each of them, 'On Thee do I wait,' we shall be emboldened to claim the answer, '*For on Thee do I wait.*'

It must also be clear to us, *on Whom we are waiting*. Not an idol, a God of whom we have made an image by our conceptions of what He is. No, but the living God, such as He really is in His great glory, His infinite holiness, His power, wisdom, and goodness, in His love and nearness. It is the presence of a beloved or a dreaded master that wakens up the whole attention of the servant who waits on him. It is *the presence of God, as He can in Christ by His Holy Spirit make Himself known*, and keep the soul under its covering and shadow, that will awaken and strengthen the true waiting spirit. Let us be still and wait and worship until we know how near He is, and then say, '*On Thee do I wait.*'

And then, let it be very clear, too, that *we are waiting*. Let that become so much our consciousness that the utterance comes spontaneously, 'On Thee *I do wait* all the day; I *wait* on Thee.' This will indeed imply sacrifice and separation, a soul entirely given up to God as its all, its only joy. This waiting on God has hardly yet been acknowledged as the only true Christianity. And yet, if it be true that God alone is goodness and joy and love; if it be true that our highest blessedness is in having as much of God as we can; if it be true that Christ has redeemed us wholly for God, and made a life of continual abiding in His presence possible, nothing less ought to satisfy than to be ever breathing this blessed atmosphere, 'I wait on Thee.'

'My soul, wait thou only upon God!'

Day 8: Strong and of Good Courage.

'Wait on the Lord: be strong,
And let your heart take courage:
Yea, wait thou on the Lord.'—Ps. 27:14 (R.V.)

THE psalmist had just said, 'I had fainted, unless I had believed to see the goodness of the Lord in the land of the living.' If it had not been for his faith in God, his heart had fainted. But in the confident assurance in God which faith gives, he urges himself and us to remember one thing above all,—to wait upon God. 'Wait on the Lord: be strong, and let your heart take courage: yea, wait on the Lord.' One of the chief needs in our waiting upon God, one of the deepest secrets of its blessedness and blessing, is a quiet, confident persuasion that it is not in vain; courage to believe that God will hear and help; that we are waiting on a God who never could disappoint His people.

'Be strong and of good courage.' These words are frequently found in connection with some great and difficult enterprise, in prospect of the combat with the power of strong enemies, and the utter insufficiency of all human strength. Is waiting on God a work so difficult, that, for that too, such words are needed, 'Be strong, and let your heart take courage'? Yes, indeed. The deliverance, for which we often have to wait, is from enemies, in presence of whom we are impotent. The blessings for which we plead are spiritual and all unseen; things impossible with men; heavenly, supernatural, divine realities. Our souls are so little accustomed to hold fellowship with God, the God on whom we wait so often appears to hide Himself. We who have to wait are often tempted to fear that we do not wait aright, that our faith is too feeble, that our desire is not as upright or as earnest as it should be, that our surrender is not complete. Our heart may well faint and fail. Amid all these causes of fear or doubt, how blessed to hear the voice of God, 'Wait on the Lord! Be strong, and let your heart take courage! Yea, wait thou upon the Lord! Let nothing in heaven or earth or hell—let nothing keep you from waiting on your God in full assurance that it cannot be in vain.

The one lesson our text teaches us is thus, that when we set ourselves to wait on God, we ought beforehand to resolve that it shall be with the most confident expectation of God's meeting and blessing us. We ought to make up our minds to this, that nothing was ever so sure, as that waiting on God will bring us untold and unexpected blessing. We are so accustomed to judge of God and His work in us by *what we feel*, that the great probability is that when we begin more to cultivate the waiting on Him, we shall be discouraged, because we do not find any special blessing from it. The message comes to us, 'Above everything, when you wait on God, do so in the spirit of abounding hopefulness. It is God in His glory, in His power, in His love longing to bless you that you are waiting on.'

If you say that you are afraid of deceiving yourself with vain hope, because you do not see or feel any warrant in your present state for such special expectations, my answer is, it is God, who is the warrant for your expecting great things. Oh, do learn the lesson. You are not going to wait on yourself to see what you feel and what changes come to you. You are going to WAIT ON GOD, to know *first*, WHAT HE IS, and then, after that, what He will do. The whole duty and blessedness of waiting on God has its root in this, that He is such a blessed Being, full, to overflowing, of goodness and power and life and joy, that we, however wretched, cannot for any time come into contact with Him, without that life and power secretly, silently beginning to enter into us and blessing us. God is Love! That is the one only and all-sufficient warrant of your expectation. Love seeks not its own: God's love is just *His delight to impart Himself and His blessedness* to His children. Come, and however feeble you feel, just wait in His presence. As a feeble, sickly invalid is brought out into the sunshine to let its warmth go through him, come with all that is dark and cold in you *into the sunshine of God's holy, omnipotent love*, and sit and wait there, with the one thought: Here I am, in the sunshine of His love. As the sun does its work in the weak one who seeks its rays, *God will do His work in you.* Oh, do trust Him fully. 'Wait on the Lord! Be strong, and let your heart take courage! Yea, wait on the Lord'!

'My soul, wait thou only upon God!'

Day 9: With the Heart.

'Be strong, and let your heart take courage,
All ye that wait for the Lord.'—Ps. 31:24. (R.V.)

THE words are nearly the same as in our last meditation. But I gladly avail myself of them again to press home a much-needed lesson for all who desire to learn truly and fully what waiting on God is. The lesson is this: It is *with the heart* we must wait upon God. 'Let *your heart* take courage.' All our waiting depends upon the state of the heart. As a man's heart is, so is he before God. We can advance no further or deeper into the holy place of God's presence to wait on Him there, than our heart is prepared for it by the Holy Spirit. The message is, 'Let *your heart* take courage, all you that wait on the Lord.'

The truth appears so simple, that some may ask, Do not all admit this? where is the need of insisting on it so specially? Because very many Christians have no sense of the great difference between the religion of the mind and the religion of the heart, and the former is far more diligently cultivated than the latter. They know not how infinitely greater the heart is than the mind. It is in this that one of the chief causes must be sought of the feebleness of our Christian life, and it is only as this is understood that waiting on God will bring its full blessing.

Proverbs 3:5 may help to make my meaning plain. Speaking of a life in the fear and favor of God, it says, 'Trust in the Lord with all your heart, and lean not upon your own understanding.' In all religion we have to use these two powers. The mind has to gather knowledge from God's word, and prepare the food by which the heart with the inner life is to be nourished. But here comes in a terrible danger, of our leaning to our own understanding, and trusting in our understanding of divine things. People imagine that if they are occupied with the truth, the spiritual life will as a matter of course be strengthened. And this is by no means the case. The understanding deals with conceptions and images of divine things, but it cannot reach the real life of the soul. Hence the command, 'Trust in the Lord with all your heart, and lean not upon your own understanding.' It is with the heart man believes, and comes into touch with God. It is in the heart God has given His Spirit, to be there to us the presence and the power of God working in us. In all our religion it is the heart that must trust and love and worship and obey. My mind is utterly impotent in creating or maintaining the spiritual life within me: the heart must wait on God for Him to work it in me.

It is in this even as in the physical life. My reason may tell me what to eat and drink, and how the food nourishes me. But in the eating and feeding my reason can do nothing: the body has its organs for that special purpose. Just so, reason may tell me what God's word says, but it can do nothing to the feeding of the soul on the bread of life—this the heart alone can do by its faith and trust in God. A man may be studying the nature and effects of food or sleep; when he wants to eat or sleep he sets aside his thoughts and study, and uses the power of eating or sleeping. And so the Christian needs ever, when he has studied or heard God's word, to cease from his thoughts, to put no trust in them, and to awaken his heart to open itself before God, and seek the living fellowship with Him.

This is now the blessedness of waiting upon God, that I confess the impotence of all my thoughts and efforts, and set myself still to bow my heart before Him in holy silence, and to trust Him to renew and strengthen His own work in me. And this is just the lesson of our text, 'Let *your heart* take courage, all you that wait on the Lord.' Remember the difference between knowing with the mind and believing with the heart. Beware of the temptation of leaning upon your understanding, with its clear strong thoughts. They only help you to know what the heart must get from God: in themselves they are only images and shadows. 'Let *your heart* take courage, all ye that wait on the Lord.' Present it before Him as that wonderful part of your spiritual nature in which God reveals Himself, and by which you can know Him. Cultivate the greatest confidence that, though you cannot see into your heart, God is working there by His Holy Spirit. Let the heart wait at times in perfect silence and quiet; in its hidden depths God will work. Be sure of this, and just wait on Him. Give your whole heart, with its secret workings, into God's hands continually. He wants the heart, and takes it, and as God dwells in it. 'Be strong, and let your heart take courage, all ye that wait on the Lord.'

'My soul, wait thou only upon God!'

Day 10: In Humble Fear and Hope.

'Behold, the eye of the Lord is upon them that fear Him,
Upon them that hope in His mercy;
To deliver their soul from death,
And to keep them alive in famine.
Our soul hath waited for the Lord;
He is our help and our shield.
For our heart shall rejoice in Him,
Because we have trusted in His holy name.
Let thy mercy, O Lord, be upon us,
According as we wait for thee.'
—Ps. 33:18-22(R.V.).

GOD'S eye is upon His people: their eye is upon Him. In waiting upon God, our eye, looking up to Him, meets His looking down upon us. This is the blessedness of waiting upon God, that it takes our eyes and thoughts away from ourselves, even our needs and desires, and occupies us with our God. We worship Him in His glory and love, with His all-seeing eye watching over us, that He may supply our every need. Let us consider this wonderful meeting between God and His people, and mark well what we are taught here of those on whom God's eye rests, and of Him on whom our eye rests.

'The eye of the Lord is on them that fear Him, on them that hope in His mercy.' Fear and hope are generally thought to be in conflict with each other; in the presence and worship of God they are found side by side in perfect and beautiful harmony. And this because in God Himself all apparent contradictions are reconciled. Righteousness and peace, judgment and mercy, holiness and love, infinite power and infinite gentleness, a majesty that is exalted above all heaven, and a condescension that bows very low, meet and kiss each other. There is indeed a fear that has torment, that is cast out entirely by perfect love. But there is a fear that is found in the very heavens. In the song of Moses and the Lamb they sing, 'Who shall not fear Thee, O Lord, and glorify Thy name?' And out of the very throne the voice came, 'Praise our God, all His servants, and ye that fear Him.' Let us in our waiting ever seek 'to fear the glorious and fearful name, The Lord thy God.' The deeper we bow before His holiness in holy fear and adoring awe, in deep reverence and humble self-abasement, even as the angels veil their faces before the throne, the more will His holiness rest upon us, and the soul be fitted to have God reveal Himself; the deeper we enter into the truth 'that no flesh glory in His presence,' will it be given us to see His glory. 'The eye of the Lord is on them that fear Him.'

'On them that hope in His mercy.' So far will the true fear of God be from keeping us back from hope, it will stimulate and strengthen it. The lower we bow, the deeper we feel we have nothing to hope in but His mercy. The lower we bow, the nearer God will come, and make our hearts bold to trust Him. Let every exercise of waiting, let our whole habit of waiting on God, be pervaded by abounding hope—a hope as bright and boundless as God's mercy. The fatherly kindness of God is such that, in whatever state we come to Him, we may confidently hope in His mercy.

Such are God's waiting ones. And now, think of the God on whom we wait. 'The eye of the Lord is on them that fear Him, on them that hope in His mercy; to deliver their soul from death, and to keep them alive in famine.' Not to prevent the danger of death and famine—this is often needed to stir up to wait on Him—but to deliver and to keep alive. For the dangers are often very real and dark; the situation, whether in the temporal or spiritual life, may appear to be utterly hopeless; there is always one hope: *God's eye is on them.*

That eye sees the danger, and sees in tender love His trembling waiting child, and sees the moment when the heart is ripe for the blessing, and sees the way in which it is to come. This living, mighty God, oh, let us fear Him and hope in His mercy. And let us humbly but boldly say, 'Our soul waiteth for the Lord; He is our help and our shield. Let Thy mercy be upon us, O Lord, according as we wait for Thee.'

Oh, the blessedness of waiting on such a God! a very present help in every time of trouble; a shield and defense against every danger. Children of God! will you not learn to sink down in entire helplessness and impotence, and in stillness to wait and see the salvation of God? In the utmost spiritual famine, and when death appears to prevail, oh, wait on God. He does deliver, He does keep alive. Say it not only in solitude, but say it to each other—the psalm speaks not of one but of God's people—'Our soul waits on the Lord: He is our help and our shield.' Strengthen and encourage each other in the holy exercise of waiting, that each may not only say it of himself, but of his brethren, 'We have waited for Him; we will be glad and rejoice in His salvation.'

'My soul, wait thou only upon God!'

Day 11: Patiently.

'Rest in the Lord, and wait patiently for Him.
Those that wait upon the Lord, they shall inherit the land.'—Ps. 37:7, 9(R.V.).

'IN patience possess your souls.' 'Ye have need of patience.' 'Let patience have its perfect work, that ye may be perfect and entire.' Such words of the Holy Spirit show us what an important element in the Christian life and character patience is. And nowhere is there a better place for cultivating or displaying it than in waiting on God. There we discover how impatient we are, and what our impatience means. We confess at times that we are impatient with men and circumstances that hinder us, or with ourselves and our slow progress in the Christian life. If we truly set ourselves to wait upon God, we shall find that it is with Him we are impatient, because He does not at once, or as soon as we could wish, do our bidding. It is in waiting upon God that our eyes are opened to believe in His wise and sovereign will, and to see that the sooner and the more completely we yield absolutely to it, the more surely His blessing can come to us.

'It is not of him that wills, nor of him that runs, but of God that shows mercy.' We have as little power to increase or strengthen our spiritual life, as we had to originate it. We 'were born not of the will of the flesh, nor of the will of man, but of the will of God.' Even so, our willing and running, our desire and effort, avail nought; all is 'of God that showeth mercy.' All the exercises of the spiritual life, our reading and praying, our willing and doing, have their very great value. But they can go no farther than this, that they point the way and prepare us in humility to look to and to depend alone upon God Himself, and in patience to await His good time and mercy. The waiting is to teach us our absolute dependence upon God's mighty working, and to make us in perfect patience place ourselves at His disposal. They that wait on the Lord shall inherit the land; the promised land and its blessing. The heirs must wait; they can afford to wait.

'Rest in the lord, and wait patiently for Him.' The margin gives for 'Rest in the Lord,' 'Be silent to the Lord,' or R.V., 'Be still before the Lord.' It is resting in the Lord, in His will, His promise, His faithfulness, and His love, that makes patience easy. And the resting in Him is nothing but being silent unto Him, still before Him. Having our thoughts and wishes, our fears and hopes, hushed into calm and quiet in that great peace of God which passeth all understanding. That peace keeps the heart and mind when we are anxious for anything, because we have made our request known to Him. The rest, the silence, the stillness, and the patient waiting, all find their strength and joy in God Himself.

The needs be, and the reasonableness, and the blessedness of patience will be opened up to the waiting soul. Our patience will be seen to be the counterpart of God's patience. He longs far more to bless us fully than we can desire it. But, as the husbandman has long patience until the fruit be ripe, so God bows Himself to our slowness and bears long with us. Let us remember this, and wait patiently: of each promise and every answer to prayer the word is true: 'I the Lord will hasten it *in its time.*'

'Rest in the Lord, and wait patiently for Him.' Yes, for Him. Seek not only the help, the gift, you need; seek Himself; wait for Him. Give God His glory by resting in Him, by trusting him fully, by waiting patiently for Him. This patience honors Him greatly; it leaves Him, as God on the throne, to do His work; it yields self wholly into His hands. It lets God be God. If your waiting be for some special request, wait patiently. If your waiting be more the exercise of the spiritual life seeking to know and have more of God, wait patiently. Whether it be in the shorter specific periods of waiting, or as the continuous habit of the soul; rest in the Lord, be still before the Lord, and wait patiently. 'They that wait on the Lord shall inherit the land.'

'My soul, wait thou only upon God!'

Day 12: Keeping His Ways.

'Wait on the Lord, and keep His way,
And He shalt exalt thee to inherit the land.'—Ps. 37:34.

IF we desire to find a man whom we long to meet, we inquire where the places and the ways are where he is to be found. When waiting on God, we need to be very careful that we keep His ways; out of these we never can expect to find Him. 'Thou meetest him that rejoices and worketh righteousness; those that remember *Thee in Thy ways.*' We may be sure that God is never and nowhere to be found but in His ways. And that there, by the soul who seeks and patiently waits, He is always most surely to be found. 'Wait on the Lord, and keep His ways, and He shall exalt thee.'

How close the connection between the two parts of the injunction. 'Wait on the Lord,'—that has to do with worship and disposition; 'and keep His ways,'—that deals with walk and work. The outer life must be in harmony with the inner; the inner must be the inspiration and the strength for the outer. It is our God who has made known His ways in His Word for our conduct, and invites our confidence for His grace and help in our heart. If we do not keep His ways, our waiting on Him can bring no blessing. The surrender to a full obedience to all His will, is the secret of full access to all the blessings of His fellowship.

Notice how strongly this comes out in the psalm. It speaks of the evildoer who prospers in his way, and calls on the believer not to fret himself. When we see men around us prosperous and happy while they forsake God's ways, and ourselves left in difficulty or suffering, we are in danger of first fretting at what appears so strange, and then gradually yielding to seek our prosperity in their path. The psalm says, 'Fret not thyself; trust in the Lord, and do good. Rest in the Lord, and wait patiently for Him; cease from anger, and forsake wrath. Depart from evil, and do good; the Lord forsakes not His saints. The righteous shall inherit the land. The law of his God is in his heart; none of his steps shall slide.' And then follows—the word occurs for the third time in the psalm—'Wait on the Lord, and keep His ways.' Do what God asks you to do; God will do more than you can ask Him to do.

And let no one give way to the fear: I cannot keep His ways; it is this robs us of our confidence. It is true you have not the strength yet to keep all His ways. But keep carefully those for which you have received strength already. Surrender yourself willingly and trustingly to keep all God's ways, in the strength which will come in waiting on Him. Give up your whole being to God without reserve and without doubt; He will prove Himself God to you, and work in you that which is pleasing in His sight through Jesus Christ. Keep His ways, as you know them in the Word. Keep His ways, as nature teaches them, in always doing what appears right. Keep His ways, as Providence points them out. Keep His ways, as the Holy Spirit suggests. Do not think of waiting on God while you say you are not willing to walk in His path. However weak you feel, only be willing, and He who has worked to will, will work to do by His power.

'Wait on the Lord, and keep His ways.' It may be that the consciousness of shortcoming and sin makes our text look more like a hindrance than a help in waiting on God. Let it not be so. Have we not said more than once, the very starting-point and groundwork of this waiting is utter and absolute impotence? Why then not come with everything evil you feel in yourself, every memory of unwillingness, unwatchfulness, unfaithfulness, and all that causes such unceasing self-condemnation? Put your trust in God's omnipotence, and find in waiting on God your deliverance. Your failure has been owing to only one thing: you sought to conquer and obey in your own strength. Come and bow before God until you learn that He is the God who alone is good, and alone can work any good thing. Believe that in you, and all that nature can do, there is no true power. Be content to receive from God each moment the inworking of His mighty grace and life, and waiting on God will become the renewal of your strength to run in His ways and not be weary, to walk in His paths and never faint. 'Wait on the Lord, and keep His ways' will be command and promise in one.

'My soul, wait thou only upon God!'

Day 13: For More Than We Know.

'And now, Lord, what wait I for? My hope is in Thee. Deliver me from all my transgressions.'—Ps. 39:7, 8.

THERE may be times when we feel as if we knew not what we are waiting for. There may be other times when we think we do know, and when it would just be so good for us to realize that we do not know what to ask as we ought. God is able to do for us exceeding abundantly above what we ask or think, and we are in danger of limiting Him, when we confine our desires and prayers to our own thoughts of them. It is a great thing at times to say, as our psalm says: 'And now, Lord, what wait I for?' I scarce know or can tell; this only I can say—'My hope is in Thee.'

How we see this limiting of God in the case of Israel! When Moses promised them meat in the wilderness, they doubted, saying, 'Can God furnish a table in the wilderness? He smote the rock that the water gushed out; can He give bread also? Can He provide flesh for His people?' If they had been asked whether God could provide streams in the desert, they would have answered, Yes. God had done it: He could do it again. But when the thought came of God doing something new, they limited Him; their expectation could not rise beyond their past experience, or their own thoughts of what was possible. Even so we may be limiting God by our conceptions of what He has promised or is able to do. Do let us beware of limiting the Holy One of Israel in our very prayer. Let us believe that every promise of God we plead has a divine meaning, infinitely beyond our thoughts of them. Let us believe that His fulfilment of them can be, in a power and an abundance of grace, beyond our largest grasp of thought. And let us therefore cultivate the habit of waiting on God, not only for what we think we need, but for all His grace and power are ready to do for us.

In every true prayer there are two hearts in exercise. The one is your heart, with its little, dark, human thoughts of what you need and God can do. The other is God's great heart, with its infinite, its divine purposes of blessing. What think you? To which of these two ought the larger place to be given in your approach to Him? Undoubtedly, to the heart of God: everything depends upon knowing and being occupied with that. But how little this is done. This is what waiting on God is meant to teach you. Just think of God's wonderful love and redemption, in the meaning these words must have to Him. Confess how little you understand what God is willing to do for you, and say each time as you pray 'And now, what wait I for?' My heart cannot say. God's heart knows and waits to give. 'My hope is in Thee.' Wait on God to do for you more than you can ask or think.

Apply this to the prayer that follows: 'Deliver me from all my transgressions.' You have prayed to be delivered from temper, or pride, or self-will. It is as if it is in vain. May it not be that you have had your own thoughts about the way or the extent of God's doing it, and have never waited on the God of glory, according to the riches of His glory, to do for you what has not entered the heart of man to conceive? Learn to worship God as the God who does wonders, who wishes to prove in you that He can do something supernatural and divine. Bow before Him, wait upon Him, until your soul realizes that you are in the hands of a divine and almighty worker. Consent not to know what and how He will work; expect it to be something altogether godlike, something to be waited for in deep humility, and received only by His divine power. Let the, 'And now, Lord, what wait I for? My hope is in Thee' become the spirit of every longing and every prayer. He will in His time do His work.

Dear soul, in waiting on God you may often be ready to be weary, because you hardly know what you have to expect. I pray you, be of good courage—this ignorance is often one of the best signs. He is teaching you to leave all in His hands, and to wait on Him alone. 'Wait on the Lord! Be strong, and let your heart take courage. Yea, wait on the Lord.'

'My soul, wait thou only upon God!'

Day 14: The Way to the New Song.

'I waited patiently for the Lord, and He inclined unto me, and heard my cry... And
He hath put a new song in my mouth, even praise unto our God.'—Ps. 40:1-3.

COME and listen to the testimony of one who can speak from experience of the sure and blessed outcome of patient waiting upon God. True patience is so foreign to our self-confident nature, it is so indispensable in our waiting upon God, it is such an essential element of true faith, that we may well once again meditate on what the word has to teach us.

The word patience is derived from the Latin word for suffering. It suggests the thought of being under the constraint of some power from which we want to be free. At first we submit against our will; experience teaches us that when it is vain to resist, patient endurance is our wisest course. In waiting on God it is of infinite consequence that we not only submit, because we are compelled to, but because we lovingly and joyfully consent to be in the hands of our blessed Father. Patience then becomes our highest blessedness and our highest grace. It honors God, and gives Him time to have His way with us. It is the highest expression of our faith in His goodness and faithfulness. It brings the soul perfect rest in the assurance that God is carrying on His work. It is the token of our full consent that God should deal with us in such a way and time as He thinks best. True patience is the losing of our self-will in His perfect will.

Such patience is needed for the true and full waiting on God. Such patience is the growth and fruit of our first lessons in the school of waiting. To many a one it will appear strange how difficult it is truly to wait upon God. The great stillness of soul before God that sinks into its own helplessness and waits for Him to reveal Himself; the deep humility that is afraid to let its own will or its own strength work aught except as God works to will and to do; the meekness that is content to be and to know nothing except as God gives His light; the entire resignation of the will that only wants to be a vessel in which His holy will can move and mold: all these elements of perfect patience are not found at once. But they will come in measure as the soul maintains its position, and ever again says: 'Truly my soul waiteth upon God; from Him cometh my salvation: He only is my rock and my salvation.'

Have you ever noticed what proof we have that patience is a grace for which very special grace is given, in these words of Paul: 'Strengthened with all might, according to His glorious power, unto all'—what? 'patience and long-suffering with joyfulness.' Yes, we need to be strengthened with all God's might, and that according to the measure of His glorious power, if we are to wait on God in all patience. It is God revealing Himself in us as our life and strength, that will enable us with perfect patience to leave all in His hands. If any are inclined to despond, because they have not such patience, let them be of good courage; it is in the course of our feeble and very imperfect waiting that God Himself by His hidden power strengthens us and works out in us the patience of the saints, the patience of Christ Himself.

Listen to the voice of one who was deeply tried: 'I waited patiently for the Lord, and He inclined unto me, and heard my cry.' Hear what he passed through: 'He brought me up also out of an horrible pit, out of the miry clay, and set my feet upon a rock, and established my goings. And He has put a new song in my mouth, even praise unto our God.' Patient waiting upon God brings a rich reward; the deliverance is sure; God Himself will put a new song into your mouth. O soul! be not impatient, whether it be in the exercise of prayer and worship that you find it difficult to wait, or in the delay in respect of definite requests, or in the fulfilling of your heart's desire for the revelation of God Himself in a deeper spiritual life—fear not, but rest in the Lord, and wait patiently for Him. And if you sometimes feel as if patience is not your gift, then remember it is God's gift, and take that prayer (2 Thess. 3:5 R.V.): 'The Lord direct your hearts into the patience of Christ.' Into the patience with which you are to wait on God, He Himself will guide you.

'My soul, wait thou only upon God!'

Day 15: For His Counsel.

'They soon forgot His works: they waited not for His counsel.'—Ps. 106:13.

THIS is said of the sin of God's people in the wilderness. He had wonderfully redeemed them, and was prepared as wonderfully to supply their every need. But, when the time of need came, 'they waited not for His counsel.' They thought not that the Almighty God was their Leader and Provider; they asked not what His plans might be. They simply thought the thoughts of their own heart, and tempted and provoked God by their unbelief. 'They waited not for His counsel.'

How this has been the sin of God's people in all ages! In the land of Canaan, in the days of Joshua, the only three failures of which we read were owing to this one sin. In going up against Ai, in making a covenant with the Gibeonites, in settling down without going up to possess the whole land, they waited not for His counsel. And so even the advanced believer is in danger from this most subtle of temptations—taking God's word and thinking his own thoughts of them, and not waiting for His counsel. Let us take the warning and see what Israel teaches us. And let us very specially regard it not only as a danger to which the individual is exposed, but as one against which God's people, in their collective capacity, need to be on their guard.

Our whole relation to God is rooted in this, that His will is to be done in us and by us as it is in heaven. He has promised to make known His will to us by His Spirit, the Guide into all truth. And our position is to be that of waiting for His counsel, as the only guide of our thoughts and actions. In our church worship, in our prayer-meetings, in our conventions, in all our gatherings as managers, or directors, or committees, or helpers in any part of the work for God, our first object ought ever to be to ascertain the mind of God. God always works according to the counsel of His will; the more that counsel of His will is sought and found and honored, the more surely and mightily will God do His work for us and through us.

The great danger in all such assemblies is that in our consciousness of having our Bible, and our past experience of God's leading, and our sound creed, and our honest wish to do God's will, we trust in these, and do not realize that with every step we need and may have a heavenly guidance. There may be elements of God's will, applications of God's word, experiences of the close presence and leading of God, manifestations of the power of His Spirit, of which we know nothing as yet. God may be willing, no, God is willing to open up these to the souls who are intently set upon allowing Him to have His way entirely, and who are willing in patience to wait for His making it known. When we come together praising God for all He has done and taught and given, we may at the same time be limiting Him by not expecting greater things. It was when God had given the water out of the rock that they did not trust Him for bread. It was when God had given Jericho into his hands that Joshua thought the victory over Ai was sure; he now knew what God could do, and waited not for counsel from God. And so, while we think that we know and trust the power of God for what we may expect, we may be hindering Him by not giving time, and not definitely cultivating the habit of waiting for His counsel.

A minister has no more solemn duty than teaching people to wait upon God. Why was it that in the house of Cornelius, when 'Peter spoke these words, the Holy Ghost fell upon all that heard him'? They had said, 'We are here *before God* to hear all things that are commanded you *of God*.' We may come together to give and to listen to the most earnest exposition of God's truth with little spiritual profit if there be not the waiting for God's counsel. In all our gatherings we need to believe in the Holy Spirit as the Guide and Teacher of God's saints when they wait to be led by Him into the things which God has prepared, and which the heart cannot conceive.

More stillness of soul to realize God's presence; more consciousness of ignorance of what God's great plans may be; more faith in the certainty that God has greater things to show us; more longing that He Himself may be revealed in new glory: these must be the marks of the assemblies of God's saints, if they would avoid the reproach, 'They waited not for His counsel.'

'My soul, wait thou only upon God!'

Day 16: For His Light in the Heart.

'I wait for the Lord, my soul doth wait,
And in His word do I hope.
My soul waiteth for the Lord
more than they that watch for the morning:
More than they that watch for the morning.'—Ps. 130:5, 6.

WITH what intense longing the morning light is often waited for. By the mariners in a shipwrecked vessel; by a benighted traveler in a dangerous country; by an army that finds itself surrounded by an enemy. The morning light will show what hope of escape there may be. The morning may bring life and liberty. And so the saints of God in darkness have longed for the light of His countenance, more than watchmen for the morning. They have said, 'More than watchmen for the morning, my soul waiteth for the Lord.' Can we say that too? Our waiting on God can have no higher object than simply having His light shine on us, and in us, and through us, all the day.

God is Light. God is a Sun. Paul says: 'God has shined in our hearts to give the light.' What light? 'The light of the glory of God, in the face of Jesus Christ.' Just as the sun shines its beautiful, life-giving light on and into our earth, so God shines into our hearts the light of His glory, of His love, in Christ His Son. Our heart is meant to have that light filling and gladdening it all the day. It can have it, because God is our sun, and it is written, 'Your sun shall no more go down forever.' God's love shines on us without ceasing.

But can we indeed enjoy it all the day? We can. And how can we? Let nature give us the answer. Those beautiful trees and flowers, with all this green grass, what do they do to keep the sun shining on them? They do nothing; they simply bask in the sunshine, when it comes. The sun is millions of miles away, but over all that distance it sends its own light and joy; and the tiniest flower that lifts its little head upwards is met by the same exuberance of light and blessing as flood the widest landscape. We have not to care for the light we need for our day's work; the sun cares, and provides and shines the light around us all the day. We simply count upon it, and receive it, and enjoy it.

The only difference between nature and grace is this, that what the trees and the flowers do unconsciously, as they drink in the blessing of the light, is to be with us a voluntary and a loving acceptance. Faith, simple faith in God's word and love, is to be the opening of the eyes, the opening of the heart, to receive and enjoy the unspeakable glory of His grace. And even as the trees, day by day, and month by month, stand and grow into beauty and fruitfulness, just welcoming whatever sunshine the sun may give, so it is the very highest exercise of our Christian life just to abide in the light of God, and let it, and let Him, fill us with the life and the brightness it brings.

And if you ask, but can it really be, that even as naturally and heartily as I recognize and rejoice in the beauty of a bright sunny morning, I can rejoice in God's light all the day? It can, indeed. From my breakfast-table I look out on a beautiful valley, with trees and vineyards and mountains. In our spring and autumn months the light in the morning is exquisite, and almost involuntarily we say, How beautiful! And the question comes, Is it only the light of the sun that is to bring such continual beauty and joy? And is there no provision for the light of God being just as much an unceasing source of joy and gladness? There is, indeed, if the soul will but be still and wait on Him, will only let God shine.

Dear soul! learn to wait on the Lord, more than watchers for the morning. All within you may be very dark; is that not the very best reason for waiting for the light of God? The first beginnings of light may be just enough to discover the darkness, and painfully to humble you on account of sin. Can you not trust the light to expel the darkness? Do believe it will. Just bow, even now, in stillness before God, and wait on Him to shine into you. Say, in humble faith; God is light, infinitely brighter and more beautiful than that of the sun. God is light. The Father, the eternal, inaccessible, and incomprehensible light. The Son, the light concentrated, and embodied, and manifested. The Spirit, the light entering and dwelling and shining in our hearts. God is light, and is here shining on my heart. I have been so occupied with the rushlights of my thoughts and efforts, I have never opened the shutters to let His light in. Unbelief has kept it out. I bow in faith: God's light is shining into my heart. The God of whom Paul wrote, 'God hath shined into our heart,' is my God. What would I think of a sun that could not shine? what shall I think of a God that does not shine? No, God shines! God is light! I will take time, and just be still, and rest in the light of God. My eyes are feeble, and the windows are not clean, but I will wait on the Lord. The light does shine, the light will shine in me, and make me full of light. And I shall learn to walk all the day in the light and joy of God. My soul waits on the Lord, more than watchers for the morning.

'My soul, wait thou only upon God!'

Day 17: In Times of Darkness.

'I will wait upon the Lord, that hideth His face from the house of Jacob; and I will look for Him.'—Isa. 8:17.

HERE we have a servant of God, waiting upon Him, not on behalf of himself, but of his people, from whom God was hiding his face. It suggests to us how our waiting upon God, though it commences with our personal needs, with the desire for the revelation of Himself, or of the answer to personal petitions, need not, may not, stop there. We may be walking in the full light of God's countenance, and God yet be hiding His face from His people around us; far from our being content to think that this is nothing but the just punishment of their sin, or the consequence of their indifference, we are called with tender hearts to think of their sad estate, and to wait on God on their behalf. The privilege of waiting upon God is one that brings great responsibility. Even as Christ, when He entered God's presence, at once used His place of privilege and honor as intercessor, so we, no less, if we know what it is really to enter in and wait upon God, must use our access for our less favored brethren. 'I will wait upon the Lord, who hides His face from the house of Jacob.'

You worship with a certain congregation. Possibly there is not the spiritual life or joy either in the preaching or in the fellowship that you could desire. You belong to a Church, with its many congregations. There is so much of error or worldliness, of seeking after human wisdom and culture, of trust in ordinances and observances, that you do not wonder that God hides His face, in many cases, and that there is but little power for conversion or true edification. Then there are branches of Christian work with which you are connected—a Sunday school, a gospel hall, a young men's association, a mission work abroad—in which the feebleness of the Spirit's working appears to indicate that God is hiding His face. You think, too, you know the reason. There is too much trust in men and money; there is too much formality and self-indulgence; there is too little faith and prayer; too little love and humility; too little of the spirit of the crucified Jesus. At times you feel as if things are hopeless; nothing will help.

Do believe that God can help and will help. Let the spirit of the prophet come into you, as you take his words, and set yourself to wait on God, on behalf of His erring children. Instead of the tone of judgment or condemnation, of despondency or despair, realize your calling to wait upon God. If others fail in doing it, give yourself doubly to it. The deeper the darkness, the greater the need of appealing to the one only Deliverer. The greater the self-confidence around you, that knows not that it is poor and wretched and blind, the more urgent the call on you who profess to see the evil and to have access to Him who alone can help, to be at your post, waiting upon God. As often as you are tempted to complain, or to sigh and say ever afresh: 'I will wait on the Lord, who hides His face from the house of Jacob.'

There is a still larger circle—the Christian Church throughout the world. Think of Greek, Roman Catholic, and Protestant churches, and the state of the millions that belong to them. Or think only of the Protestant churches with their open Bible and orthodox creeds. How much nominal profession and formality! how much of the rule of the flesh and of man in the very temple of God! And what abundant proof that God does hide His face!

What are those to do who see and mourn this? The first thing to be done is this: 'I will wait on the Lord, who hides His face from the house of Jacob.' Let us wait on God, in the humble confession of the sins of His people. Let us take time and wait on Him in this exercise. Let us wait on God in tender, loving intercession for all saints, our beloved brethren, however wrong their lives or their teaching may appear. Let us wait on God in faith and expectation, until He shows us that He will hear. Let us wait on God, with the simple offering of ourselves to Himself, and the earnest prayer that He would send us to our brethren. Let us wait on God, and give Him no rest until He make Zion a joy in the earth. Yes, let us rest in the Lord, and wait patiently for Him who now hides His face from so many of His children. And let us say of the lifting up of the light of His countenance we desire for all His people, 'I wait for the Lord, my soul doth wait, and my hope is in His word. My soul waits for the Lord, more than the watchers for the morning, the watchers for the morning.'

'My soul, wait thou only upon God!'

Day 18: To Reveal Himself.

'And it shall be said in that day, Lo, this is our God; we have waited for Him, and
He will save us: THIS IS THE LORD; we have waited for Him, we will
rejoice and be glad in His salvation,'—Isa. 25:9.

IN this passage we have two precious thoughts.

The one, that it is the language of God's people who have been unitedly waiting on Him; the other, that the fruit of their waiting has been that God has so revealed Himself, that they could joyfully say, Lo, this is our God: this is the Lord. The power and the blessing of united waiting is what we need to learn.

Note the twice repeated, 'We have waited for Him.' In some time of trouble the hearts of the people had been drawn together, and they had, ceasing from all human hope or help, with one heart set themselves to wait for their God. Is not this just what we need in our churches and conventions and prayer-meetings? Is not the need of the Church and the world great enough to demand it? Are there not in the Church of Christ evils to which no human wisdom is equal? Have we not ritualism and rationalism, formalism and worldliness, robbing the Church of its power? Have we not culture and money and pleasure threatening its spiritual life? Are not the powers of the Church utterly inadequate to cope with the powers of infidelity and iniquity and wretchedness in Christian countries and in heathendom? And is there not in the promise of God, and in the power of the Holy Spirit, a provision made that can meet the need, and give the Church the restful assurance that she is doing all her God expects of her? And would not united waiting upon God for the supply of His Spirit most certainly seem the needed blessing? We cannot doubt it.

The object of a more definite waiting upon God in our gatherings would be very much the same as in personal worship. It would mean a deeper conviction that God must and will do all; a more humble and abiding entrance into our deep helplessness, and the need of entire and unceasing dependence upon Him; a more living consciousness that the essential thing is, giving God His place of honor and of power; a confident expectation that to those who wait on Him, God will, by His Spirit, give the secret of His acceptance and presence, and then, in due time, the revelation of His saving power. The great aim would be to bring every one in a praying and worshipping company under a deep sense of God's presence, so that when they part there will be the consciousness of having met God Himself, of having left every request with Him, and of now waiting in stillness while He works out His salvation.

It is this experience that is indicated in our text. The fulfilment of the words may, at times, be in such striking interpositions of God's power that all can join in the cry, 'Lo, this is our God; this is the Lord!' They may equally become true in spiritual experience, when God's people in their waiting times become so conscious of His presence that in holy awe souls feel, 'Lo, this is our God; this is the Lord!' It is this, alas, that is too much missed in our meetings for worship. The godly minister has no more difficult, no more solemn, no more blessed task, than to lead his people out to meet God, and, before ever he preaches, to bring each one into contact with Him. 'We are now here in the presence of God' —these words of Cornelius show the way in which Peter's audience was prepared for the coming of the Holy Spirit. Waiting before God, and waiting for God, and waiting on God, are the one condition of God showing His presence.

A company of believers gathered with the one purpose, helping each other by little intervals of silence, to wait on God alone, opening the heart for whatever God may have of new discoveries of evil, of His will, of new openings in work or methods of work, would soon have reason to say, 'Lo, this is our God; we have waited for Him, He shall save us: this is the Lord; we have waited for Him, we will be glad and rejoice in His salvation.'

'My soul, wait thou only upon God!'

Day 19: As a God of Judgment.

'Yea, in the way of Thy judgments, O Lord, have we waited for Thee:... for when
Thy judgments are on the earth, the inhabitants of the world learn
righteousness.'—Isa. 26:8, 9.

*'The Lord is a God of judgment: blessed are all they that wait for Him.'—Isa.
30:18.*

GOD is a God of mercy and a God of judgment. Mercy and judgment are ever together in His
dealings. In the flood, in the deliverance of Israel out of Egypt, in the overthrow of the Canaanites,
we ever see mercy in the midst of judgment. Within the inner circle of His own people, we see it
too: the judgment punishes the sin, while mercy saves the sinner. Or, rather, mercy saves the sinner,
not in spite of, but by means of, the very judgment that came upon his sin. In waiting on God, we
must beware of forgetting this: as we wait we must expect Him as a God of judgment.

'In the way of Thy judgments, have we waited for Thee.' That will prove true in our inner
experience. If we are honest in our longing for holiness, in our prayer to be wholly the Lord's, His
holy presence will stir up and discover hidden sin, and bring us very low in the bitter conviction of
the evil of our nature, its opposition to God's law, its impotence to fulfil that law. The words will
come true, 'Who may abide the day of His coming, for HE is like a refiner's fire.' 'O that Thou
would come down, as when the melting fire burns!' In great mercy God executes, within the soul,
His judgments upon sin, as He makes it feel its wickedness and guilt. Many a one tries to flee from
these judgments: the soul that longs for God, and for deliverance from sin, bows under them in
humility and in hope. In silence of soul it says, 'Arise, O Lord! and let Thine enemies be scattered.
In the way of Thy judgments we have waited for Thee.'

Let no one who seeks to learn the blessed art of waiting on God, wonder if at first the attempt
to wait on Him only discovers more of his sin and darkness. Let no one despair because
unconquered sins, or evil thoughts, or great darkness appear to hide God's face. Was not, in His
own Beloved Son, the gift and bearer of His mercy on Calvary, the mercy as if hidden and lost in
the judgment? Oh, submit, and sink down deep under the judgment of thine every sin: judgment
prepares the way, and breaks out in wonderful mercy. It is written, 'Thou shalt be redeemed with
judgment.' Wait on God, in the faith that His tender mercy is working out in you His redemption
in the midst of judgment: wait for Him, He will be gracious to thee.

There is another application still, one of unspeakable solemnity. We are expecting God, in the
way of His judgments, to visit this earth: we are waiting for Him. What a thought! We know of
these coming judgments; we know that there are tens of thousands of our professing Christians who
live on in carelessness, and who, if no change come, must perish under God's hand. Oh, shall we
not do our utmost to warn them, to plead with and for them, if God may have mercy on them. If we
feel our want of boldness, want of zeal, want of power, shall we not begin to wait on God more
definitely and persistently as a God of judgment, asking Him so to reveal Himself in the judgments
that are coming on our very friends, that we may be inspired with a new fear of Him and them, and
constrained to speak and pray as never yet. Verily, waiting on God is not meant to be a spiritual
self-indulgence. Its object is to let God and His holiness, Christ and the love that died on Calvary,
the Spirit and fire that burns in heaven and came to earth, get possession of us, to warn and rouse
men with the message that we are waiting for God in the way of His judgments. O Christian! prove
that you really believe in the God of judgment.

'My soul, wait thou only upon God!'

Day 20: Who Waits on Us.

*'And therefore will the Lord wait, that He may be gracious unto you; and therefore
will He be exalted, that He may have mercy upon you: for the Lord is a God
of judgment: blessed are all they that wait for Him.'—Isa. 30:18*

WE must not only think of our waiting upon God, but also of what is more wonderful still, of
God's waiting upon us. The vision of Him waiting on us, will give new impulse and inspiration to
our waiting upon Him. It will give an unspeakable confidence that our waiting cannot be in vain. If
He waits for us, then we may be sure that we are more than welcome; that He rejoices to find those
He has been seeking for. Let us seek even now, at this moment, in the spirit of lowly waiting on
God, to find out something of what it means: 'Therefore will the Lord wait, that He may be gracious
unto you.' We shall accept and echo back the message: 'Blessed are all they that wait for Him.'

Look up and see the great God upon His throne. He is Love—an unceasing and inexpressible
desire to communicate His own goodness and blessedness to all His creatures. He longs and delights

to bless. He has inconceivably glorious purposes concerning every one of His children, by the power of His Holy Spirit, to reveal in them His love and power. He waits with all the longings of a father's heart. He waits that He may be gracious unto you. And each time you come to wait upon Him, or seek to maintain in daily life the holy habit of waiting, you may look up and see Him ready to meet you, waiting that He may be gracious unto you. Yes, connect every exercise, every breath of the life of waiting, with faith's vision of your God waiting for you.

And if you ask, how is it, if He waits to be gracious, that even after I come and wait upon Him, He does not give the help I seek, but waits on longer and longer? There is a double answer. The one is this: God is a wise husbandman, 'who waits for the precious fruit of the earth, and has long patience for it.' He cannot gather the fruit until it is ripe. He knows when we are spiritually ready to receive the blessing to our profit and His glory. Waiting in the sunshine of His love is what will ripen the soul for His blessing. Waiting under the cloud of trial, that breaks in showers of blessing, is as needful. Be assured that if God waits longer than you could wish, it is only to make the blessing doubly precious. God waited four thousand years, until the fulness of time, before He sent His Son: our times are in His hands: He will avenge His elect speedily: He will make haste for our help, and not delay one hour too long.

The other answer points to what has been said before. The giver is more than the gift; God is more than the blessing; and our being kept waiting on Him is the only way for our learning to find our life and joy in Himself. Oh, if God's children only knew what a glorious God they have, and what a privilege it is to be linked in fellowship with Himself, then they would rejoice in Him, even when He keeps them waiting. They would learn to understand better than ever; 'Therefore will the Lord wait, that He may be gracious unto you.' His waiting will be the highest proof of His graciousness.

'Blessed are all they that wait for Him.' Our queen has her ladies-in-waiting. The position is one of subordination and service, and yet it is considered one of the highest dignity and privilege, because a wise and gracious sovereign makes them companions and friends. What a dignity and blessedness to be attendants-in-waiting on the Everlasting God, ever on the watch for every indication of His will or favor, ever conscious of His nearness, His goodness, and His grace! 'The Lord is good to them that wait for Him.' 'Blessed are all they that wait for Him.' Yes, it is blessed when a waiting soul and a waiting God meet each other. God cannot do His work without His and our waiting His time: let waiting be our work, as it is His. And if His waiting be nothing but goodness and graciousness, let ours be nothing but a rejoicing in that goodness, and a confident expectancy of that grace. And let every thought of waiting become to us simply the expression of unmingled and unutterable blessedness, because it brings us to a God who waits that He may make Himself known to us perfectly as the Gracious One.

'My soul, wait thou only upon God!'

Day 21: The Almighty One.

'They that wait on the Lord shall renew their strength; they shall mount up with
eagle wings; they shall run and not be weary; they shall walk and not
faint.'—Isa. 40:31.

WAITING always partakes of the character of our thoughts of the one on whom we wait. Our waiting on God will depend greatly on our faith of what He is. In our text we have the close of a passage in which God reveals Himself as the Everlasting and Almighty One. It is as that revelation enters our soul that the waiting will become the spontaneous expression of what we know Him to be—a God altogether most worthy to be waited upon.

Listen to the words: 'Why sayest thou, O Jacob, my way is hid from the Lord?' Why speakest thou as if God does not hear or help?

'Hast thou not known, hast thou not heard, that the Everlasting One, the Lord, the Creator of the ends of the earth, *fainteth not, neither is weary*?' So far from it, 'He giveth power to the faint, and to them that have no might He increaseth strength. Even the youths'—'the glory of young men is their strength'—'even the youths shall faint, and the young men shall utterly fall:' all that is accounted strong with man shall come to nought. *But* they that wait on the Lord,' on the Everlasting One, who does not faint, neither is weary, they 'shall renew their strength; they shall mount up with wings as eagles; they shall run and,'—listen now, they shall be strong with the strength of God, and, even as He, *'shall not be weary*; they shall walk and,' even as He, *'not faint.'*

Yes, 'they shall mount up with wings as eagles.' You know what eagles' wings mean. The eagle is the king of birds, it soars the highest into the heavens. Believers are to live a heavenly life, in the very Presence and Love and Joy of God. They are to live where God lives; they need God's strength to rise there. To them that wait on Him it shall be given.

You know how the eagles' wings are obtained. Only in one way—by the eagle birth. You are born of God. You have the eagles' wings. You may not have known it: you may not have used them; but God can and will teach you to use them.

You know how the eagles are taught the use of their wings. See yonder cliff rising a thousand feet out of the sea. See high up a ledge on the rock, where there is an eagle's nest with its treasure of two young eaglets. See the mother bird come and stir up her nest, and with her beak push the timid birds over the precipice. See how they flutter and fall and sink toward the depth. See now (Deut. 32:11) 'how she fluttereth over her young, spreadeth abroad her wings, taketh them, beareth them on her wings,' and so, as they ride upon her wings, brings them to a place of safety. And so she does once and again, each time casting them out over the precipice, and then again taking and carrying them. 'So the Lord alone did lead him.' Yes, the instinct of that eagle mother was God's gift, a single ray of that love in which the Almighty trains His people to mount as on eagles' wings.

He stirs up your nest. He disappoints your hopes. He brings down your confidence. He makes you fear and tremble, as all your strength fails, and you feel utterly weary and helpless. And all the while He is spreading His strong wings for you to rest your weakness on, and offering His everlasting Creator-strength to work in you. And all He asks is that you should sink down in your weariness and wait on Him; and allow Him in His Jehovah-strength to carry you as you ride upon the wings of His Omnipotence.

Dear child of God! I pray you, lift up your eyes, and *behold your God*! Listen to Him who says that He faints not, neither is weary, who promiseth that you too shall not faint or be weary, who asketh nought but this one thing, that you should *wait on Him*. And let your answer be, With such a God, so mighty, so faithful, so tender,

> *'My soul, wait thou only upon God!'*

Day 22: It Certainty of Blessing.

'Thou shalt know that I am the Lord; for they shall not be ashamed that wait for Me.' —Isa. 49:23.

'Blessed are all they that wait for Him.' —Isa. 30:18.

WHAT promises! How God seeks to draw us to waiting on Him by the most positive assurance that it never can be in vain: 'They shall not be ashamed that wait for Me.' How strange that, though we should so often have experienced it, we are yet so slow of learning that this blessed waiting must and can be as the very breath of our life, a continuous resting in God's presence and His love, an unceasing yielding of ourselves for Him to perfect His work in us. Let us once again listen and meditate, until our heart says with new conviction: 'Blessed are they that wait for Him!' In our sixth day's lesson we found in the prayer of Psalm 25: 'Let none that wait on Thee be ashamed.' The very prayer shows how we fear lest it might be. Let us listen to God's answer, until every fear is banished, and we send back to heaven the words God speaks, Yes, Lord, we believe what You say: *'All they* that wait for Me shall *not* be ashamed.' 'Blessed are *all they* that wait for Him.'

The context of each of these two passages points us to times when God's Church was in great straits, and to human eye there was no possibility of deliverance. But God interposes with His word of promise, and pledges His Almighty Power for the deliverance of His people. And it is as the God who has Himself undertaken the work of their redemption, that He invites them to wait on Him, and assures them that disappointment is impossible. We, too, are living in days in which there is much in the state of the Church, with its profession and its formalism, that is indescribably sad. Amid all we praise God for, there is, alas, much to mourn over! Were it not for God's promises we might well despair. But in His promises the Living God has given and bound Himself to us. He calls us to wait on Him. He assureth us we shall not be put to shame. Oh that our hearts might learn to wait before Him, until He Himself reveals to us what His promises mean, and in the promises reveals Himself in His hidden glory! We shall be irresistibly drawn to wait on Him alone. God increase the company of those who say, 'Our soul waiteth for the Lord: He is our Help and our Shield.'

This waiting upon God on behalf of His Church and people will depend greatly upon the place that waiting on Him has taken in our personal life. The mind may often have beautiful visions of what God has promised to do, and the lips may speak of them in stirring words, but these are not really the measure of our faith or power. No; it is what we really know of God in our personal experience, conquering the enemies within, reigning and ruling, revealing Himself in His Holiness and Power in our inmost being, —it is this will be the real measure of the spiritual blessing we expect from Him, and bring to our fellowmen. It is as we know how blessed the waiting on God has become to our own souls, that we shall confidently hope in the blessing to come on the Church around us, and the key-word of all our expectations will be; He hath said: 'All they that wait on Me shall not be ashamed.' From what He has done in us, we shall trust Him to do mighty things around us. 'Blessed are all they that wait for Him.' Yes, blessed even now in the waiting. The promised blessings, for ourselves, or for others, may tarry; the unutterable blessedness of knowing and having Him who has promised, the Divine Blesser, the Living Fountain of the coming blessings, is even now ours. Do let this truth get full possession of your souls, that waiting on God is itself the highest privilege of the creature, the highest blessedness of His redeemed child.

Even as the sunshine enters with its light and warmth, with its beauty and blessing, into every little blade of grass that rises upward out of the cold earth, so the Everlasting God meets, in the greatness and the tenderness of His love, each waiting child, to shine in his heart 'the light of the knowledge of the glory of God in the face of Jesus Christ.' Read these words again, until your heart learns to know what God waits to do to you. Who can measure the difference between the great sun and that little blade of grass? And yet the grass has all of the sun it can need or hold. Do believe that in waiting on God, His greatness and your littleness suit and meet each other most wonderfully. Just how in emptiness and poverty and utter impotence, in humility and meekness and surrender to His will, before His great glory, and be still. As you wait on Him, God draws near. He will reveal Himself as the God who will fulfil mightily His every promise. And let your heart ever again take up the song: 'Blessed are all they that wait for Him.'

'My soul, wait thou only upon God!'

Day 23: For Unlooked-for Things.

*'For since the beginning of the world men have not heard, nor perceived by the
ear, neither hath the eye seen, O God, beside Thee, what He hath prepared
for him that waiteth for Him.'—Isa. 64:4.*

THE R.V.[2] has: *'Neither hath the eye seen a God beside Thee, which worketh for him that waiteth for Him.'* In the A.V.[3] the thought is, that no eye hath seen *the thing* which God hath prepared. In the R.V. no eye hath seen a God, beside our God, who worketh for him that waiteth for Him. To both the two thoughts are common: that our place is to wait upon God, and that there will be revealed to us what the human heart cannot conceive. The difference is: in the R.V. it is *the God* who works, in the A.V. *the thing* He is to work. In 1 Cor. 2:9, the citation is in regard to the things which the Holy Spirit is to reveal, as in the A.V., and in this meditation we keep to that.

The previous verses, specially from chap. 63:15, refer to the low state of God's people. The prayer has been poured out, 'Look down from heaven.' (ver. 15.) 'Why hast Thou hardened my heart from Thy fear? Return for Thy servants' sake.' (ver. 19.) And 64:1, still more urgent, 'Oh that Thou wouldest rend[4] the heavens, that thou wouldest come down,... as when the melting fire burneth, to make Thy name known to Thy adversaries!' Then follows the plea from the past, 'When Thou didst terrible things we looked not for, Thou camest down, the mountains flowed down at Thy presence.' 'For'—this is now the faith that has been awakened by the thought of things we looked not for, He is still the same God—'eye hath not seen beside Thee, O God, what He hath

---

[2] RV: Revised Version. 1885 British revision of the King James Bible
[3] AV: Authorized Version. 1611 King James Version Bible
[4] 'Rend' is to 'tear.'

prepared for him that waiteth for Him.' God alone knows what He can do for His waiting people. As Paul expounds and applies it: 'The things of God knoweth no man, save the Spirit of God.' 'But God hath revealed them to us by His Spirit.'

The need of God's people, and the call for God's interposition, is as urgent in our days as it was in the time of Isaiah. There is now, as there was then, as there has been at all times, a remnant that seek after God with their whole heart. But if we look at Christendom as a whole, at the state of the Church of Christ, there is infinite cause for beseeching God to rend the heavens and come down. Nothing but a special interposition of Almighty Power will avail. I fear we have no right conception of what the so-called Christian world is in the sight of God. Unless God comes down 'as the melting fire burneth, to make known His name to His adversaries,' our labors are comparatively fruitless. Look at the ministry—how much it is in the wisdom of man and of literary culture —how little in demonstration of the Spirit and of power. Think of the unity of the body—how little there is of the manifestation of the power of a heavenly love binding God's children into one. Think of holiness— the holiness of Christ-like humility and crucifixion to the world—how little the world sees that they have men among them who live in Christ in heaven, in whom Christ and heaven live.

What is to be done? There is but one thing. We must wait upon God. And what for? We must cry, with a cry that never rests, 'Oh that Thou wouldest rend the heavens and come down, that the mountains might flow down at Thy presence.' We must desire and believe, we must ask and expect, that God will do unlooked-for things. We must set our faith on a God of whom men do not know what He has prepared for them that wait for Him. The wonder-doing God, who can surpass all our expectations, must be the God of our confidence.

Yes, let God's people enlarge their hearts to wait on a God able to do exceeding abundantly above what we can ask or think. Let us band ourselves together as His elect who cry day and night to Him for things men have not seen. He is able to arise and to make His people a name, and a praise in the earth. 'He will wait, that He may be gracious unto you; blessed are all they that wait for Him.'

'My soul, wait thou only upon God!'

Day 24: To Know His Goodness.

'The Lord is good unto them that wait for Him.' —Lam. 3:25

'THERE is none good but God.' 'His goodness is in the heavens.' 'Oh how great is Thy goodness, which Thou hast laid up for them that fear Thee!' 'Oh, taste and see that the Lord is good!' And here is now the true way of entering into and rejoicing in this goodness of God— waiting upon Him. The Lord is good—even His children often do not know it, for they wait not in quietness for Him to reveal it. But to those who persevere in waiting, whose souls do wait, it will come true. One might think that it is just those who have to wait who might doubt it. But this is only when they do not wait, but grow impatient. The truly waiting ones will all have to say, 'The Lord is good to them that wait for Him.' Wouldst thou fully know the goodness of God, give thyself more than ever to a life of waiting on Him.

At our first entrance into the school of waiting upon God, the heart is chiefly set upon the blessings which we wait for. God graciously uses our need and desire for help to educate us for something higher than we were thinking of. We were seeking gifts; He, the Giver, longs to give Himself and to satisfy the soul with His goodness. It is just for this reason that He often withholds the gifts, and that the time of waiting is made so long. He is all the time seeking to win the heart of His child for Himself. He wishes that we should not only say, when He bestows the gift, How good is God! but that long ere it comes, and even if it never comes, we should all the time be experiencing: *'It is good* that a man should quietly wait': 'The Lord *is good* to them that wait for Him.'

What a blessed life the life of waiting then becomes, the continual worship of faith, adoring and trusting His goodness. As the soul learns its secret, every act or exercise of waiting just becomes a quiet entering into the goodness of God, to let it do its blessed work and satisfy our every need. And every experience of God's goodness gives the work of waiting new attractiveness, and instead of only taking refuge in time of need, there comes a great longing to wait continually and all the day. And however duties and engagements occupy the time and the mind, the soul gets more familiar with the secret art of always waiting. Waiting becomes the habit and disposition, the very second nature and breath of the soul.

Dear Christian! do you not begin to see that waiting is not one among a number of Christian virtues, to be thought of from time to time, but that it expresses that disposition which lies at the very root of the Christian life? It gives a higher value and a new power to our prayer and worship, to our faith and surrender, because it links us, in unalterable dependence, to God Himself. And it gives us the unbroken enjoyment of the goodness of God: 'The Lord is good to them that wait for Him.'

Let me press upon you once again to take time and trouble to cultivate this so much needed element of the Christian life. We get too much of religion at second hand from the teaching of men. That teaching has great value if, even as the preaching of John the Baptist sent his disciples away from himself to the Living Christ, it leads us to God Himself. What our religion needs is—*more of God.* Many of us are too much occupied with our work. As with Martha, the very service we want to render the Master separates from Him; it is neither pleasing to Him nor profitable to ourselves. The more work, the more need of waiting upon God; the doing of God's will would then, instead of exhausting, be our meat and drink, nourishment and refreshment and strength. 'The Lord is good to them that wait for Him.' How good none can tell but those who prove it in waiting on Him. How good none can fully tell but those who have proved Him to the utmost.

'*My soul, wait thou only upon God!*'

Day 25: Quietly.

'*It is good that a man should both hope and quietly wait for the salvation of the Lord.*'—*Lam. 3:26*

'TAKE heed, and be quiet: fear not, neither be faint-hearted.' 'In quietness and in confidence shall be your strength.' Such words reveal to us the close connection between quietness and faith, and show us what a deep need there is of quietness, as an element of true waiting upon God. If we are to have our whole heart turned towards God, we must have it turned away from the creature, from all that occupies and interests, whether of joy or sorrow.

God is a being of such infinite greatness and glory, and our nature has become so estranged from Him, that it needs our whole heart and desires set upon Him, even in some little measure to know and receive Him. Everything that is not God, that excites our fears, or stirs our efforts, or awakens our hopes, or makes us glad, hinders us in our perfect waiting on Him. The message is one of deep meaning: 'Take heed and be quiet;' 'In quietness shall be your strength;' 'It is good that a man should quietly wait.'

How the very thought of God in His majesty and holiness should silence us, Scripture abundantly testifies.

'The Lord is in His holy temple; let all the earth keep silence before Him' (Hab. 2:20).

'Hold thy peace at the presence of the Lord God.' (Zeph. 1:7).

'Be silent, O all flesh, before the Lord; for He is raised up out of His holy habitation' (Zech. 2:13).

As long as the waiting on God is chiefly regarded as an end towards more effectual prayer, and the obtaining of our petitions, this spirit of perfect quietness will not be obtained. But when it is seen that the waiting on God is itself an unspeakable blessedness, one of the highest forms of fellowship with the Holy One, the adoration of Him in His glory will of necessity humble the soul into a holy stillness, making way for God to speak and reveal Himself. Then it comes to the fulfilment of the precious promise, that all of self and self-effort shall be humbled: 'The haughtiness of man shall be brought down, and the Lord alone shall be exalted in that day.'

Let everyone who would learn the art of waiting on God remember the lesson: 'Take heed, and be quiet;' 'It is good that a man quietly wait.' Take time to be separate from all friends and all duties, all cares and all joys; time to be still and quiet before God. Take time not only to secure stillness from man and the world, but from self and its energy. Let the Word and prayer be very precious; but remember, even these may hinder the quiet waiting. The activity of the mind in studying the Word, or giving expression to its thoughts in prayer, the activities of the heart, with its desires and hopes and fears, may so engage us that we do not come to the still waiting on the All-Glorious One;

our whole being is not prostrate in silence before Him. Though at first it may appear difficult to know how thus quietly to wait, with the activities of mind and heart for a time subdued, every effort after it will be rewarded; we shall find that it grows upon us, and the little season of silent worship will bring a peace and a rest that give a blessing not only in prayer, but all the day.

'*It is good* that a man should quietly wait for the salvation of the Lord.' Yes, it is good. The quietness is the confession of our impotence, that with all our willing and running, with all our thinking and praying, it will not be done: we must receive it from God. It is the confession of our trust that our God will in His time come to our help—the quiet resting in Him alone. It is the confession of our desire to sink into our nothingness, and to let Him work and reveal Himself. Do let us wait quietly. In daily life let there be in the soul that is waiting for the great God to do His wondrous work, a quiet reverence, an abiding watching against too deep engrossment with the world, and the whole character will come to bear the beautiful stamp: Quietly waiting for the salvation of God.

'*My soul, wait thou only upon God!*'

Day 26: In Holy Expectancy.

'*Therefore will I look to the Lord; I will wait for the God of my salvation; my God will hear me.*'—Micah 7:7.

HAVE you ever read a beautiful little book, *Expectation Corner*? If not, get it; you will find in it one of the best sermons on our text. It tells of a king who prepared a city for some of his poor subjects. Not far from them were large storehouses, where everything they could need was supplied if they but sent in their requests. But on one condition—that they should be on the outlook for the answer, so that when the king's messengers came with the gifts they had desired, they should always be found waiting and ready to receive them. The sad story is told of one desponding one who never expected to get what he asked, because he was too unworthy. One day he was taken to the king's storehouses, and there, to his amazement, he saw, with his address on them, all the packages that had been made up for him, and sent. There was the garment of praise, and the oil of joy, and the eye salve, and so much more; they had been to his door, but found it closed; he was not on the outlook. From that time on he understood the lesson Micah would teach us today; 'I will look to the Lord; I will wait for the God of my salvation; my God will hear me.'

We have more than once said: Waiting for the answer to prayer is not the whole of waiting, but only a part. Today we want to take in the blessed truth: It is a part, and a very important one. When we have special petitions, in connection with which we are waiting on God, our waiting must be very definitely in the confident assurance: 'My God will hear me.' A holy, joyful expectancy is of the very essence of true waiting. And this not only in reference to the many varied requests every believer has to make, but most especially to the one great petition which ought to be the chief thing every heart seeks for itself —that The Life of God in the soul may have full sway; that Christ may be fully formed within; and that we may be filled to all the fullness of God. This is what God has promised. This is what God's people too little seek, very often because they do not believe it possible. This is what we ought to seek and dare to expect, because God is able and waiting to work it in us.

But God Himself must work it. And for this end our working must cease. We must see how entirely it is to be the faith of the operation of God who raised Jesus from the dead—just as much as the resurrection, the perfecting of God's life in our souls is to be directly His work. And waiting has to become more than ever a tarrying before God in stillness of soul, counting upon Him who raises the dead, and calls the things that are not as though they were.

Just notice how the threefold use of the name of God in our text points us to Himself as the one from whom alone is our expectation. 'I will look to The Lord; I will wait for The God of my Salvation; My God will hear me.' Everything that is salvation, everything that is good and holy, must be the direct mighty work of God Himself within us. For every moment of a life in the will of God, there must be the immediate operation of God. And the one thing I have to do is this: to look to the Lord; to wait for the God of my salvation; to hold fast the confident assurance, 'My God will hear me.'

God says: 'Be still, and know that I am God.'

There is no stillness like that of the grave. In the grave of Jesus, in the fellowship of His death, in death to self with its own will and wisdom, its own strength and energy, there is rest. As we cease from self, and our soul becomes still to God, God will arise and show Himself. 'Be still, and know,' then you shall know 'that I am God.' There is no stillness like the stillness Jesus gives when He speaks, 'Peace, be still.' In Christ, in His death, and *in His life*, in His perfected redemption, the soul may be still, and God will come in, and take possession, and do His perfect work.

'My soul, wait thou only upon God!'

Day 27: For Redemption.

'Simeon was just and devout, waiting for the consolation of Israel, and the Holy Ghost was upon him. Anna, a prophetess,... spake of Him to all then that looked for redemption in Jerusalem.'—Luke 2:25, 38.

HERE we have the mark of a waiting believer. *Just*, righteous in all his conduct; *devout*, devoted to God, ever walking as in His presence; *waiting for the consolation* of Israel, looking for the fulfilment of God's promises: *and the Holy Ghost was on him*. In the devout waiting he had been prepared for the blessing. And Simeon was not the only one. Anna spoke to all that looked for redemption in Jerusalem. This was the one mark, amid surrounding formalism and worldliness, of a godly band of men and women in Jerusalem. They were waiting on God; looking for His promised redemption.

And now that the Consolation of Israel has come, and the redemption has been accomplished, do we still need to wait? We do indeed. But will not our waiting, who look back to it as come, differ greatly from those who looked forward to it as coming? It will, especially in two aspects. We now wait on God in the full power of the redemption: and we wait for its full revelation.

Our waiting is now in the full power of the redemption. Christ spoke, 'In that day you shall know that you are in Me. Abide in Me.' The Epistles teach us to present ourselves to God 'as indeed dead to sin, and alive to God in Christ Jesus,' 'blessed with all spiritual blessings in heavenly places in Christ Jesus.' Our waiting on God may now be in the wonderful consciousness, wrought and maintained by the Holy Spirit within us, that we are accepted in the Beloved, that the love that rests on Him rests on us, that we are living in that love, in the very nearness and presence and sight of God. The old saints took their stand on the word of God, and waited, hoping on that word; we rest on the word too —but, oh! under what exceeding greater privileges, as one with Christ Jesus. In our waiting on God, let this be our confidence: in Christ we have access to the Father; how sure, therefore, may we be that our waiting cannot be vain.

Our waiting differs also in this, that while they waited for a redemption to come, we see it accomplished, and now wait for its revelation *in us*. Christ not only said, Abide in Me, but also *I in you*. The Epistles not only speak of us *in Christ*, but of Christ *in us*, as the highest mystery of redeeming love. As we maintain our place in Christ day by day, God waits to reveal Christ in us, in such a way that He is formed in us, that His mind and disposition and likeness acquire form and substance in us, so that by each it can in truth be said, 'Christ liveth in me.'

My life in Christ up there in heaven and Christ's life in me down here on earth —these two are the complement of each other. And the more my waiting on God is marked by the living faith *I in Christ*, the more the heart thirsts for and claims the CHRIST IN ME. And the waiting on God, which began with special needs and prayer, will increasingly be concentrated, as far as our personal life is concerned, on this one thing, Lord, reveal Your redemption fully in me; let Christ live in me.

Our waiting differs from that of the old saints in the place we take, and the expectations we entertain. But at root it is the same: waiting on God, from whom alone is our expectation.

Learn from Simeon and Anna one lesson. How utterly impossible it was for them to do anything towards the great redemption —towards the birth of Christ or His death. It was God's work. They could do nothing but wait. Are we as absolutely helpless as regards the revelation of Christ in us? We are indeed. God did not work out the great redemption in Christ as a whole, and leave its application in detail to us.

The secret thought that it is so lies at the root of all our feebleness. The revelation of Christ in every individual believer, and in each one the daily revelation, step by step and moment by moment, is as much the work of God's omnipotence as the birth or resurrection of Christ. Until this truth enters and fills us, and we feel that we are just as dependent upon God for each moment of our life in the enjoyment of redemption as they were in their waiting for it, our waiting upon God will not bring its full blessing. The sense of utter and absolute helplessness, the confidence that God can and will do all, —these must be the marks of our waiting as of theirs. As gloriously as God proved Himself to them the faithful and wonder-working God, He will to us also.

'My soul, wait thou only upon God!'

Day 28: For the Coming of His Son.

'Be ye yourselves like unto men that wait for their Lord.'—Luke 12:36.

'Until the appearing of our Lord Jesus Christ, which, in His own time, He shall shew, who is the blessed and only Potentate, the King of kings, and Lord of lords.'—1 Tim. 6:14, 15(R.V.).

'Turned to God from idols to serve the living and true God, and to wait for His Son from heaven.'—1 Thess. 1:9, 10.

WAITING on God in heaven, and waiting for His Son from heaven, these two God has joined together, and no man may put them asunder. The waiting on God for His presence and power in daily life will be the only true preparation for waiting for Christ in humility and true holiness. The waiting for Christ coming from heaven to take us to heaven will give the waiting on God its true tone of hopefulness and joy. The Father who in His own time will reveal His Son from heaven, is the God who, as we wait on Him, prepares us for the revelation of His Son. The present life and the coming glory are inseparably connected in God and in us.

There is sometimes a danger of separating them. It is always easier to be engaged with the religion of the past or the future than to be faithful in the religion of today. As we look to what God has done in the past, or will do in time to come, the personal claim of present duty and present submission to His working may be escaped. Waiting on God must ever lead to waiting for Christ as the glorious consummation of His work; and waiting for Christ must ever remind us of the duty of waiting upon God, as our only proof that the waiting for Christ is in spirit and in truth. There is such a danger of our being so occupied with the things that are coming more than with Him who is to come; there is such scope in the study of coming events for imagination and reason and human ingenuity, that nothing but deeply humble waiting on God can save us from mistaking the interest and pleasure of intellectual study for the true love of Him and His appearing. All ye that say ye wait for Christ's coming, be sure that you wait on God now. All ye that seek to wait on God now to reveal His Son in you, see to it that ye do so as men waiting for the revelation of His Son from heaven. The hope of that glorious appearing will strengthen you in waiting upon God for what He is to do in you now: the same omnipotent love that is to reveal that glory is working in you even now to fit you for it.

'The blessed hope and the appearing of the glory of our great God and Savior Jesus Christ,' is one of the great bonds of union given to God's Church throughout the ages. 'He shall come to be glorified in His saints, and to be marveled at in all them that believe.' Then we shall all meet, and the unity of the body of Christ be seen in its divine glory. It will be the meeting-place and the triumph of divine love. Jesus receiving His own and presenting them to the Father. His own meeting Him and worshiping in speechless love that blessed face. His own meeting each other in the ecstasy of God's own love. Let us wait, long for, and love the appearing of our Lord and Heavenly Bridegroom. Tender love to Him and tender love to each other is the true and only bridal spirit.

I fear greatly that this is sometimes forgotten. A beloved brother in Holland was speaking about the expectancy of faith being the true sign of the bride. I ventured to express a doubt. An unworthy bride, about to be married to a prince, might only be thinking of the position and the riches that she was to receive. The expectancy of faith might be strong, and true love utterly wanting. It is love in the bridal spirit. It is not when we are most occupied with prophetic subjects, but when in humility and love we are clinging close to our Lord and His brethren, that we are in the bride's place. Jesus refuses to accept our love except as it is love to His disciples. Waiting for His coming means waiting for the glorious coming manifestation of the unity of the body, while we seek here to maintain that unity in humility and love. Those who love most are the most ready for His coming. Love to each other is the life and beauty of His bride, the Church.

And how is this to be brought about? Beloved child of God! if you would learn aright to wait for His Son from heaven, live even now waiting on God in heaven. Remember how Jesus lived ever waiting on God. He could do nothing of Himself. It was God who perfected His Son through suffering and then exalted Him. It is God alone who can give you the deep spiritual life of one who is really waiting for His Son: wait on God for it. Waiting for Christ Himself is, oh, so different from waiting for things that may come to pass! The latter any Christian can do; the former, God must work in you every day by His Holy Spirit. Therefore all you who wait on God, look to Him for grace to wait for His Son from heaven in the Spirit which is from heaven. And you who would wait for His Son, wait on God continually to reveal Christ in you.

The revelation of Christ in us as it is given to them who wait upon God is the true preparation for the full revelation of Christ in glory.

'My soul, wait thou only upon God!'

Day 29: For the Promise of the Father.

'He charged them not to depart from Jerusalem, but to wait for the promise of the Father.'—Acts 1:4.

IN speaking of the saints in Jerusalem at Christ's birth, with Simeon and Anna, we saw how, though the redemption they waited for is come, the call to waiting is no less urgent now than it was then. We wait for the full revelation in us of what came to them, but what they scarce could comprehend. Even so it is with waiting for the promise of the Father. In one sense, the fulfillment can never come again as it came at Pentecost. In another sense, and that in as deep reality as with the first disciples, we daily need to wait for the Father to fulfil His promise in us.

The Holy Spirit is not a person distinct from the Father in the way two persons on earth are distinct. The Father and the Spirit are never without or separate from each other: the Father is always in the Spirit; the Spirit works nothing but as the Father works in Him. Each moment the same Spirit that is in us, is in God too, and he who is most full of the Spirit will be the first to wait on God most earnestly, further to fulfil His promise, and still strengthen him mightily by His Spirit in the inner man. The Spirit in us is not a power at our disposal. Nor is the Spirit an independent power, acting apart from the Father and the Son. The Spirit is the real living presence and the power of the Father working in us, and therefore it is just he who knows that the Spirit is in him, who will wait on the Father for the full revelation and experience of what the Spirit's indwelling is, for His increase and abounding more and more.

See this in the apostles. They were filled with the Spirit at Pentecost. When they, not long after, on returning from the Council, where they had been forbidden to preach, prayed afresh for boldness to speak in His name—a fresh coming down of the Holy Spirit was the Father's fresh fulfillment of His promise.

At Samaria, by the word and the Spirit, many had been converted, and the whole city filled with joy. At the apostles' prayer the Father once again fulfilled the promise. Even so to the waiting company—'We are all here before God'—in Cornelius' house. And so, too, in Acts 13. It was when men, filled with the Spirit, prayed and fasted, that the promise of the Father was afresh fulfilled, and the leading of the Spirit was given from heaven: 'Separate Me Barnabas and Saul.'

So also we find Paul in Ephesians, praying for those who have been sealed with the Spirit, that God would grant them the spirit of illumination. And later on, that He would grant them, according to the riches of His glory, to be strengthened with might by the Spirit in the inner man.

The Spirit given at Pentecost was not a something that God parted with in heaven, and sent away out of heaven to earth. God does not, cannot, give away anything in that way. When He gives grace, or strength, or life, He gives it by giving Himself to work it —it is all inseparable from Himself. (See note on Law, *The Power of the Spirit*, at the end of this volume.) Much more so is the Holy Spirit. He is God, present and working in us: the true position in which we can count upon that working with an unceasing power is as we, praising for what we have, still unceasingly wait for the Father's promise to be still more mightily fulfilled.

What new meaning and promise does this give to our life of waiting! It teaches us ever to keep the place where the disciples tarried at the footstool of the Throne. It reminds us that, as helpless as they were to meet their enemies, or to preach to Christ's enemies, until they were endued with power, we, too, can only be strong in the life of faith, or the work of love, as we are in direct communication with God and Christ, and they maintain the life of the Spirit in us. It assures us that the Omnipotent God will, through the glorified Christ, work in us a power that can bring to pass things unexpected, things impossible. Oh! what will not the Church be able to do when her individual members learn to live their lives waiting on God, and when together, with all of self and the world sacrificed in the fire of love, they unite in waiting with one accord for the promise of the Father, once so gloriously fulfilled, but still unexhausted.

Come and let each of us be still in presence of the inconceivable grandeur of this prospect: the Father waiting to fill the Church with the Holy Ghost. And willing to fill me, let each one say.

With this faith let there come over the soul a hush and a holy fear, as it waits in stillness to take it all in. And let life increasingly become a deep joy in the hope of the ever fuller fulfilment of the Father's promise.

'My soul, wait thou only upon God!'

Day 30: Continually.

'Therefore turn thou to thy God: keep mercy and judgment, and wait on thy God continually.'—Hos. 12:6.

CONTINUITY is one of the essential elements of life. Interrupt it for a single hour in a man, and it is lost, he is dead. Continuity, unbroken and ceaseless, is essential to a healthy Christian life. God wants me to be, and God waits to make me, I want to be, and I wait on Him to make me, every moment, what He expects of me, and what is well-pleasing in His sight. If waiting on God be of the essence of true religion, the maintenance of the spirit of entire dependence must be continuous. The call of God, 'Wait on your God continually,' must be accepted and obeyed. There may be times of special waiting: the disposition and habit of soul must be there unchangeably and uninterrupted.

This waiting continually is indeed a necessity. To those who are content with a feeble Christian life, it appears a luxury something beyond what is essential to being a good Christian. But all who are praying the prayer, 'Lord! make me as holy as a pardoned sinner can be made! Keep me as near to Thee as it is possible for me to be! Fill me as full of Thy love as You are willing to do!' feel at once that it is something that must be had. They feel that there can be no unbroken fellowship with God, no full abiding in Christ, no maintaining of victory over sin and readiness for service, without waiting continually on the Lord.

The waiting continually is a possibility. Many think that with the duties of life it is out of the question. They cannot be always thinking of it. Even when they wish to, they forget.

They do not understand that it is a matter of the heart, and that what the heart is full of, occupies it, even when the thoughts are otherwise engaged. A father's heart may be filled continuously with intense love and longing for a sick wife or child at a distance, even though pressing business requires all his thoughts. When the heart has learned how entirely powerless it is for one moment to keep itself or bring forth any good, when it has understood how surely and truly God will keep it, when it has, in despair of itself, accepted God's promise to do for it the impossible, it learns to rest in God, and in the midst of occupations and temptations it can wait continually.

This waiting is a promise. God's commands are enablings: gospel precepts are all promises, a revelation of what our God will do for us. When first you begin waiting on God, it is with frequent intermission and frequent failure. But do believe God is watching over you in love and secretly strengthening you in it. There are times when waiting appears to be just losing time, but it is not so. Waiting, even in darkness, is unconscious advance, because it is God you have to do with, and He is working in you. God who calls you to wait on Him, sees your feeble efforts, and works it in you. Your spiritual life is in no respect your own work: as little as you began it, can you continue it; it is God's Spirit who has begun the work in you of waiting upon God; He will enable you to wait continually.

Waiting continually will be met and rewarded by God Himself working continually. We are coming to the end of our meditations. Would that you and I might learn one lesson: God must, God will work continually. He ever does work continually, but the experience of it is hindered by unbelief. But He who by His Spirit teaches you to wait continually, will bring you to experience also how, as the Everlasting One, His work is never-ceasing. In the love and the life and the work of God there can be no break, no interruption.

Do not limit God in this by your thoughts of what may be expected. Do fix your eyes upon this one truth: in His very nature, God, as the only Giver of life, *cannot do otherwise than every moment work in His child.* Do not look only at the one side: 'If I wait continually, God will work continually.' No, look at the other side. Place God first and say, '*God works continually, every moment I may wait on Him continually.*' Take time until the vision of your God working continually, without one moment's intermission, fill your being. Your waiting continually will then come of itself. Full of trust and joy, the holy habit of the soul will be, 'On Thee do I wait *all the day.*' The Holy Spirit will keep you ever waiting.

'My soul, wait thou only upon God!'

Moment by Moment[5]

'I the Lord do keep it: I will water it every moment.'
Dying with Jesus, by death reckoned mine,
Living with Jesus a new life divine;
Looking to Jesus till glory doth shine,
Moment by moment, O Lord, I am Thine.

Chorus—Moment by moment I'm kept in His love,
Moment by moment I've life from above;
Looking to Jesus till glory doth shine;
Moment by moment, O Lord, I am Thine.

Never a battle with wrong for the right,
Never a contest that He doth not fight;
Lifting above us His banner so white,
Moment by moment I'm kept in His sight.
Chorus.

Never a trial that He is not there,
Never a burden that He doth not bear,
Never a sorrow that He does not share,
Moment by moment I'm under His care.
Chorus

Never a heartache, and never a groan,
Never a teardrop, and never a moan;
Never a danger but there on the throne
Moment by moment He thinks of His own.
Chorus.

Never a weakness that He doth not feel,
Never a sickness that He cannot heal;
Moment by moment, in woo or in weal,
Jesus, my Savior, abides with me still.
Chorus.

---

[5] (Music in *Christian Endeavor Hymns* by I. D. Sankey). Or on leaflet by Morgan & Scott

Day 31: Only.

'My soul, wait thou only upon God;
For my expectation is from Him.
He only is my rock and my salvation.'—Isa. 62:5, 6.

It is possible to be waiting continually on God, but not only upon Him; there may be other secret confidences intervening and preventing the blessing that was expected. And so the word *only* must come to throw its light on the path to the fulness and certainty of blessing. 'My soul, wait thou *only* upon God. He only is my Rock.'

Yes, 'My soul, wait thou only upon God.' There is but one God, but one source of life and happiness for the heart; He *only* is my Rock; my soul, wait thou *only* upon Him. Thou desirest to be good. 'There is none good but God,' and there is no possible goodness but what is received directly from Him. Thou hast sought to be holy: 'There is none holy but the Lord,' and there is no holiness but what He by His Spirit of holiness every moment breathes in thee. Thou wouldest live and work for God and His kingdom, for men and their salvation. Hear how He says, 'The Everlasting God, the Creator of the ends of the earth. He "alone" fainteth not, neither is weary. He giveth power to the faint, and to them that have no might He increaseth strength. They that wait upon the Lord shall renew their strength.' He only is God; He only is thy Rock: 'My soul, wait thou only upon God.'

'My soul, wait thou only upon God.' Thou will not find many who can help you in this. Enough there will be of thy brethren to draw thee to put trust in churches and doctrines, in schemes and plans and human appliances, in means of grace and divine appointments. But, 'My soul, wait thou only upon God Himself.' His most sacred appointments become a snare when trusted in. The brazen serpent becomes Nehushtan;[6] the ark and the temple a vain confidence. Let the Living God alone, none and nothing but He, be thy hope.

'My soul, wait thou only upon God.' Eyes and hands and feet, mind and thought, may have to be intently engaged in the duties of this life; 'My soul, wait thou only upon God.' Thou art an immortal spirit, created not for this world but for eternity and for God. O, my soul! Realize thy destiny. Know thy privilege, and 'wait thou only upon God.' Let not the interest of religious thoughts and exercises deceive you; they very often take the place of waiting upon God. My soul, wait *thou*, thy very self, your inmost being, with all its power, 'wait thou only upon God.' God is for thee, thou art for God; wait only upon Him.

Yes, 'my soul, wait thou only upon God.' Beware of your two great enemies —the World and Self. Beware lest any earthly satisfaction or enjoyment, however innocent it appears, keep you back from saying, 'I will go to God, my exceeding joy.' Remember and study what Jesus says about denying self, 'Let a man deny himself.' Tersteegen[7] says: 'The saints deny themselves in everything.' Pleasing self in little things may be strengthening it to assert itself in greater things. 'My soul, wait thou only upon God;' let Him be all your salvation and all your desire. Say continually and with an undivided heart, 'From Him comes my expectation; He only is my Rock; I shall not be moved.' Whatever be thy spiritual or temporal need, whatever the desire or prayer of thy heart, whatever thy interest in connection with God's work in the Church or the world—in solitude or in the rush of the world, in public worship or other gatherings of the saints, 'My soul, wait thou *only* upon God.' Let your expectations be from Him alone. He only is your Rock.

'My soul, wait thou only upon God.' Never forget the two foundation-truths on which this blessed waiting rests. If ever you are inclined to think this 'waiting only' is too hard or too high, they will recall thee at once. They are: your absolute helplessness; and, the absolute sufficiency of thy God. Oh! enter deep into the entire sinfulness of all that is of self, and think not of letting self have anything to say one single moment. Enter deep into thy utter and unceasing impotence ever to change what is evil in thee, or to bring forth anything that is spiritually good. Enter deep into thy relation of dependence as creature on God, to receive from Him every moment what He gives. Enter

---

[6] 2 Kings 18:4, "He removed the high places, and brake the images, and cut down the groves, and brake in pieces the brazen serpent that Moses had made: for unto those days the children of Israel did burn incense to it: and he called it Nehushtan."

[7] Gerhard Tersteegen

deeper still into His covenant of redemption, with His promise to restore more gloriously than ever what thou hadst lost, and by His Son and Spirit to give within you unceasingly, His actual divine Presence and Power. And thus wait upon your God continually and only.

'My soul, wait thou only upon God.' No words can tell, no heart conceive, the riches of the glory of this mystery of the Father and of Christ. Our God, in the infinite tenderness and omnipotence of His love, waits to be our Life and Joy. Oh, my soul! let it be no longer needed that I repeat the words, 'Wait upon God,' but let all that is in me rise and sing: 'Truly my soul waits upon God. On Thee do I wait all the day.'

'My soul, wait thou only upon God!'

Note.

My publishers have just issued a work of William Law on the Holy Spirit.[8] In the Introduction I have said how much I owe to the book. I cannot but think that anyone who will take the trouble to read it thoughtfully will find rich spiritual profit in connection with a life of Waiting upon God.

What he puts more clearly than I have anywhere else found are these cardinal truths:—

1. That the very Nature and Being of a God, as the only Possessor and Dispenser of any life there is in the universe, imply that He must every moment communicate to every creature the power by which it exists, and therefore also much more the power by which it can do that which is good.

2. That the very Nature and Being of a creature, as owing its existence to God alone, and equally owing to Him each moment the continuation of that existence, imply that its happiness can only be found in absolute unceasing momentary dependence upon God.

3. That the great value and blessing of the gift of the Spirit at Pentecost, as the fruit of Christ's Redemption, is that it is now possible for God to take possession of His redeemed children and work in them as He did before the fall in Adam. We need to know the Holy Spirit as the Presence and Power of God in us restored to their true place.

4. That in the spiritual life our great need is the knowledge of two great lessons. The one, our entire sinfulness and helplessness, our utter impotence by any effort of our own to do anything towards the maintenance and increase of our inner spiritual life. The other, the infinite willingness of God's love, which is nothing but a desire to communicate Himself and His blessedness to us to meet our every need, and every moment to work us in by His Son and Spirit what we need.

5. That, therefore, the very essence of true religion, whether in heaven or upon earth, consists in an unalterable dependence upon God, because we can give God no other glory, than yielding ourselves to His love, which created us to show forth in us its glory, that it may now perfect its work in us.

I need not point out how deep down these truths go to the very root of the spiritual life, and specially the life of waiting upon God. I am confident that those who are willing to take the trouble of studying this thoughtful writer will thank me for the introduction in his book. The book referred to is The Power of the Spirit, by William Law, An Humble, Earnest and Affectionate Address to the Clergy.

---

[8] The Power of the Holy Spirit: An humble earnest, and affectionate Address to the Clergy. With Additional Extracts and Introduction, by Rev. Andrew Murray. (Fleming H. Revell Company. $1.00)